THE ULTIMATE GIFT

A Unique True Story of Perseverance & Love

George Uche Oriahi

www.georgeoriahibook.com

First published in the United States of America in 2023
by Amazon Marketing Hub

First published in the United Kingdom in 2023
by Amazon Marketing Hub

1

British Library Cataloguing-in-Publication Data
A catalogue record for this book is available from the British Library.

Hardback ISBN 978-1-916798-18-2
Paperback ISBN 978-1-916798-16-8
eBook ISBN 978-1-916798-17-5

Amazon Marketing Hub
82 King St,
Manchester
M2 4WQ
United Kingdom

www.amzmarketinghub.co.uk

Printed in Great Britain by Bell and Bain Ltd, Glasgow

MIX
Paper | Supporting
responsible forestry
FSC
www.fsc.org
FSC® C007785

Table of Contents

Author's Note

I have written this book to the best of my abilities in recounting the true events as narrated to me by my parents and the recollection of my own experiences. My parents have revealed their life experiences with me in detail so that I could one day share them with my children and the rest of the world. I want to bring excitement to the story; hence I have dramatised some scenes to give life to the event and make it impactful. I have chosen not to include certain events that may be known to the public for personal reasons. I also may have misrepresented some facts, which is completely accidental. All the names, apart from mine and my parents, and some identifying details have been changed to protect the privacy of individuals mentioned in this book. Writing this book was challenging as it was difficult to recount the life my parents had lived and had to endure. There were chapters and scenes that reduced me to tears as I wrote them and led me to question why I was putting myself through this painful process. The most excruciating to write were the final three chapters.

Dedication

To my father, late Chief Jacob Okwueze Oriahi, the memory of your smile keeps me going. To my late mother, Cecilia Oriahi, you are the gift that keeps on giving. My promise is to pass on the love you both showed me to my children and everyone that I touch.

Acknowledgements

It was when I was in my thirties that I realised that I must write a book about my father's life and our relationship. I never had a time frame when I would start to write the book and did not imagine how long it would take. I also did not think of any support I may need. So, although I liked the idea of being an author, I actually had no serious plans on when I would start writing. Every time I have told my father's story to close friends, I get comments that remind me that I should write a book as if I did not already know that!

Eventually, I did get my act together and started to write. To my surprise, this book took me only five months to write. So, I want to thank everyone that has supported me throughout the journey of writing this book, especially my friends and family.

About the Author

George Uche Oriahi was born in Nigeria and was the youngest of seven children. After his teenage years, he lived in London, where he attended university to achieve a bachelor's and master's degree. He has lived amongst different cultures, which enriched his multicultural experience. George now lives in Scotland, where he works as a Business Consultant, and enjoys walking in the beautiful landscape and climbing mountains.

The Ultimate Gift is his first book. George was inspired by the unique life of his father, a Nigerian Chief. He narrates this true and incredible story of his father's challenging life journey and their relationship.

CHAPTER ONE

The Word of a King

JOHN AND MARGARET had celebrated their marriage and had moved into a small two-bedroom house in the first quarter of their village. John had liked Margaret for a long while but only had the courage to speak to her on her birthday when she turned seventeen. John was twenty years old at that time. He was not a tall man, standing at five feet six inches. He had a medium build and was considered a quiet and shy man in the village. John was a farmer and a hard worker, just like his father, who unfortunately lost his life in an accident to a fallen tree. He was only thirty-six years old. John was thirteen years old when he lost his father. His mother had remained single until her death at the age of fifty-two. John was their only child and was adored by his mother.

Margaret worked in the only village mill, which was owned by her parents. She was not interested in going to school and started following her parents to the mill when she was just five years old. She had two brothers who were her seniors and were farmers. Margaret's parents had been looking for a suitor for her since she turned sixteen. Margaret was from the fourth quarter of the village. She was a beautiful woman, fair in complexion, about five feet and five inches tall, with a slim built body.

John's mother had watched Margaret grow and blossom into a young woman. She frequented the mill sometimes with John to grind her casava, which she then dried and fried to make garri that she then sold. Although John had noticed Margaret and liked her, he was never able to find the courage to speak to her. John's mother had been producing garri for sales since she was sixteen and had made her living doing so.

Garri is a staple food in Nigeria, which is a product of casava root. Casava is easily cultivated in the beginning of the rainy season and can be harvested after ten months to up to two years. The cassava roots are peeled after being uprooted, washed, and then milled into granulate. This is then compressed with weights to gently squeeze out the moisture. It is then mixed with palm oil if preferred to get a yellow garri colour after being dry fried over a fire. Garri is then consumed by adding water or milk to it in a bowl and eaten with a spoon. Garri can also be made into a starchy paste to be eaten with several types of Nigerian soups.

John's mother knew Margaret's parents well due to her regular visits and knew that a suitor for their daughter was being sought. At first, John was too shy to discuss meeting Margaret with his mother, let alone talk about marriage. However, with time, she was able to encourage John, and he was able to visit Margaret at her home on her seventeenth birthday gathering. John and Margaret fell in love several weeks later, and they were married a few months after. John's mother had helped in the building of their two-bedroom home from the money she had saved from her garri business.

Their village, called Alihagwu, consisted of a large community that seemed to be segregated into four quarters. The population of the entire village was about one thousand two hundred people at the beginning of the twentieth century. Alihagwu is situated in the southern region of Nigeria. The village and the neighbouring areas are rich in fertile lands and grow green vegetation mostly in the rainy season, which is from April to October. The village's main agricultural produce includes garri and okra. The village is completely cut off from any civilisation. However, the people and their communities continued to achieve self-sustenance in isolation. There were no roads other than walking and bicycle tracks that connected the village to the next vibrant town called Agbor. Farmers would carry their produce by head and walk to neighbouring villages and Agbor town to sell and buy what they needed.

Alihagwu, just like many other villages in the area, falls under the district of the Agbor Kingdom. The Kingdom is ruled by a King with his palace located about two miles from Alihagwu village. It was the rightful honour of the King to decide and rule on the affairs of the citizens of his Kingdom. In addition to no roads, there was no fresh running water or electricity. For water, the village relied on rainwater that is channelled into excavated round holes that form wells. The well diameter can range from four to eight feet with a depth of around ten to fifteen feet. The well walls would be plastered with mud to give it a smooth finish and help to reduce water leakage. The top of the well is covered with tree trunks and other available materials. This helps prevent dirt and other unwanted objects from getting inside the well.

Alihagwu is only about four to five miles in distance to Agbor town. However, the civilisation enjoyed by the communities of Agbor town and other areas did not cascade to Alihagwu. As Nigeria developed with time, Alihagwu did not benefit from any advancement to their civilisation, and their quality of life remained stagnant with the past. Although the people were hardworking and good at agriculture, they were too shy in nature to collaborate with their neighbouring villages due to the lack of trust in anyone and anything not original to their community. John and Margaret had not left the village since they were born. They were accustomed to the ways of life in the village and were expecting to make a home and grow their family just like any household in their community. They knew that there would be support from their families if they ran into any difficulties.

Unfortunately, a few months into their marriage, Margaret's father had died in his sleep. It was also unbearable for the couple that exactly two months later, Margaret's mother died after a short illness.

Living in Alihagwu in the early nineteen hundreds presented significant challenges. John and Margaret were already thinking of having children, and they were aware that it was almost certain that like anybody else, any birth would take place at home as the nearest maternity hospital was several miles away. The villagers were not used to going out of their communities in search of help.

Margaret was delighted when she became pregnant in 1925. Unfortunately, John's mother had died a few months into Margaret's pregnancy. She complained of stomach pains for over four weeks before she became seriously ill and died. It was not possible to actually learn the cause of her death as also in the case of Margaret's parents. It was a sad moment for John and the communities as his mother was loved by all for her kindness and generosity. However, the progression of Margaret's pregnancy had kept the couple emotionally occupied.

Although they were delighted about the pregnancy, what Margaret and John did not realise was that they were in for a life-changing experience. An experience that would have a significant impact on the village and the neighbouring towns and cities. There was a village midwife that went around checking the health of expectant mothers. She would measure the stomach to determine the age and the due date of the pregnancy. Surprisingly, this pregnancy carried on into the twelfth month. All native and traditional means and processes to induce the pregnancy failed. There was concern, and the whole village and their neighbours waited in anticipation. However, the baby was showing strong signs of good health and continued to kick in the womb. Finally, on the thirteenth month into the pregnancy, Margaret went into labour. After many hours of agony, a larger than normal size baby was delivered without any complications at birth.

Although the villagers were glad that the long-awaited baby had arrived safely and without complications, the mother and child were healthy and doing alright, they were not ready to accept yet another dreadful surprise. The baby had a tooth! This news was initially concealed but had soon become known to all. It was concealed because John and Margaret were not sure how the communities would react, but they surely felt it was not going to be favourable. John and Margaret quickly named their baby Jacob in line with their religious beliefs, and expected to carry on living their normal life, perhaps in a low-profile way. Unfortunately, no religious belief and neither was the low-profile way of living going to protect them from the trauma they were about to experience. It was as if the birth of their child had unleashed an all-out war with the entire village communities, far and beyond. There was no one to help, and all prayers seemed unanswered.

It was around four o'clock in the morning, before the first light of the day, that a group of villagers approached the home of John and Margaret. They were carrying with them fire torches and machetes in addition to other handheld weapons such as sticks and so on. They cited death to the new baby because he was born with a tooth and chanted that the child must be taken into the forest and be killed. The head of the village tried to reason with John and Margaret to give up their baby as he was a curse and a danger to the village and their livelihood. He added that the people of the village were aware that their baby was born with a tooth and that it was an abomination to the land and society. He also went on to say that the communities believed that a child born with a tooth was the work of the devil that would bring bad luck and devastation to the entire village and beyond. Therefore, to prevent the curse and bad luck, the evil baby must be destroyed.

However, with some courage and determination, John and Margaret refused to hand over the child. They disregarded the demands of the village and refused to believe that their child was evil, regardless of the length of the pregnancy and the baby being born with a tooth. Although John and Margaret were aware that they were not in a position to win the battle to keep their newborn baby, they agreed to let the King decide the fate of their child.

John and Margaret knew very well that the village head answers to the King. Therefore, refusing to allow the King to decide the case before a life is taken would be going against the laws of the Kingdom. Although the villagers were confident that the King would side with them and agree for the baby to be killed, they accepted John and Margaret's request and receded temporarily. They had witnessed a few instances where the King had agreed to similar demands when babies were born with rare birth defects and abnormalities. The petition to the King was later made, and John and Margaret, together with their new baby, Jacob, and the village's head chief, were summoned to the King's palace to hear the case.

The night before the hearing, John and Margaret made a special prayer asking for Jacob's life to be spared. However, they also had to say goodbye to Jacob. As much as they did not want to lose their child, they understood the plight of the village. They so much wished the dreadful situation had not besieged them. All the same, they were ready for whatever came next. Margaret recalled feeling numb and had said she felt devastated being alive the morning of the hearing. The King's palace was just two miles away from the village. John and Margaret, with Jacob, were escorted as they walked the two miles to the King's palace.

All customary procedures were followed upon arrival at the palace. The case was then heard, and Jacob was presented to the King. After much deliberation, the King reached a decision. Jacob was to be saved and unharmed, the King decreed. The King added that he felt something special about Jacob. He then decided to name Jacob, Okwueze – meaning "words of the king" as a marker that he is the one the King favours and to be regarded. John and Margaret were delighted and could not control their joy. They believed that the world they knew was about to change forever. The King no longer favoured the condemnation of babies deformed from birth.

CHAPTER TWO

The Boy in a Ring of Fire

WATCHING JACOB GROW into a boy was not as easy as John and Margaret had expected. Although they were aware that the village allowed Jacob to live, they were not prepared for the constant abuse and terrorisation they continued to receive from their own people, the villagers. They would have stones thrown on the roof of their home, verbal attacks on the streets, and refusal to allow the family to participate in village events. As much as these challenges were completely devastating, Jacob's parents could not consider leaving the village. They did not have the confidence to believe that life outside the village would be any better. They actually believed that life would be harder if they left. They felt that the attacks they would receive from strangers in another village or town would be greater than what they were being subjected to by their own people.

Life for Jacob's parents continued to be difficult, but the attacks on the family did reduce after Margaret gave birth to a baby girl five years after Jacob was born. The pregnancy was normal; delivery happened in the ninth month, there were no complications, and the baby was completely normal. She was called Anna. This brought a sense of relief to John and Margaret as it was the chance to demonstrate to the village that they were not evil or some sorcerers of any kind. However, the overall hate towards Jacob's parents continued to impact their finances. John would normally help other farmers for a wage in addition to his own farming. Unfortunately, due to their situation, farm owners were reluctant to offer John any job.

John also struggled to rent farmland, which meant that they could not really grow enough produce to sell to maintain a good standard of living. Where they were able to secure farmland, they had to pay above the normal rent. Jacob was not yet five years old when he started helping at the farm. Although Jacob had started schooling when he turned six, unfortunately, his parents were unable to pay his school fees, and he had to stop his education. To his father's distress, Jacob had to become a fulltime farmer by the time he was just seven years old. His father wanted him to go to school and achieve his best potential. Knowing that this was not going to be the case for Jacob, John promised to educate his daughter and every other child he would raise.

Although the family attacks had reduced, unfortunately, it was only because the village had hatched a plan to kill Jacob outside his family home. The village had never accepted that Jacob should live in accordance with the King's ruling. The plan to eliminate Jacob remained the case even after the ruling of the King to spare his life. It was only because the village hardly saw an opportunity where the killing could be seen as an accident rather than an execution or a direct killing, was the reason the plan lingered. However, now that Jacob had grown into a boy and could move about alone, the villagers believed they had a better chance to succeed in their quest.

As a farmer, Jacob mostly went to the farm with his father and sometimes alone. It was only because Jacob's parents noticed a reduction in attacks in relation to them bringing a curse to the communities by giving birth to a child with no tooth that they felt it was safe to allow Jacob to roam with less precaution. They believed the threat no longer existed for their son. Unfortunately, they were to realise they were wrong.

IT WAS ON A SUNNY day during the dry season that Jacob, not yet ten years old, was asked by his father to walk the half a mile bush path journey alone to their farm. Jacob's task was to set fire to the newly weeded farmland – a process called slash-and-burn agriculture. The process requires the cutting down of the natural vegetation of the land; this would then be allowed to dry over a few days before they would be set on fire to burn, thereby making space for agricultural crops. The farmers believed that the remnants of the burnt vegetation added nutrients to the soil, as fertilizer was extremely hard to come by and unaffordable to John and Margaret. As Jacob hurried down the narrow, lonely path leading to the farmland, he was noticed by a few villagers. Unfortunately for Jacob, these were the group assigned to monitor, abduct, and kill him. They had been watching Jacob for a long time, and they felt that they may now have the opportunity to carry out the killing. However, the killing must look like an accident. So, they decided to follow Jacob, trailing behind.

Jacob reached his farmland, and he did not notice the village men trailing him. So, he began to prepare the cut-down vegetation in a way that the burning is contained within their own perimeters. This process is necessary to prevent the fire from spreading into neighbouring farmland, as this could cause serious disputes. To achieve this, the fire must burn from the perimeters and spread inwards. Jacob was skilful at this as he had carried out the slash-and-burn process with his father several times successfully over the years. At this moment, the trailers understood what Jacob was preparing to do, and they saw a perfect opportunity to execute their plan. Jacob proceeded to light the fire, managing and controlling the spread to follow the perimeters until a burning circumference was achieved. The fire would be encouraged to burn inwards due to the perfectly arranged dead and dried-out vegetation. Jacob was delighted with his solo act of the burning process in preparing their farmland for crop cultivation. However, just as Jacob decided to head home, he was grabbed and thrown inside the perimeters of the burning vegetation.

Jacob knew that he was in great danger as the fire raged inwards towards him. He was surrounded, and he could not see a way out. The heat and the smoke of the fire started to overwhelm Jacob as he moved further toward the middle of the farmland. The fire was burning faster than he ever imagined. Normally, he would be outside the ring of the fire to appreciate the disappearance of the vegetation and leaving behind nutritious ashes for a rich cultivating soil that would enrich the crop yields. Just as Jacob realised that he had only a moment to save himself, the instinct to survive took over his thoughts.

The first thought was to scream for help, but he knew that the location of their farmland was outside the range where anyone, either someone walking by or other farmers, could hear him. Jacob was aware that due to his family's taboo, which was a result of his birth, they could only rent farmland that nobody wanted because of the distance and lack of walking tracks. Jacob clearly remembered the challenges he and his father faced as they cut down vegetation through the bushes to create a walking path to their farmland. The annoying thing, he thought, was that they knew they must maintain the tracks every now and again to prevent the vegetation from growing back mainly because hardly anyone from the village used the path, as it led nowhere other than Jacob's parents' farmland.

As Jacob regained his focus to deal with his situation, he realised that although he knew he was carried and thrown inside the ring of the fire, he could no longer see anyone around, and neither could he tell of the faces of those responsible. His second thought of survival was a daring one, as he knew he might not live to tell the tale. Jacob knew the time to execute that thought was right at that moment. So, he looked up into the skies, but all he could see were smoke clouds, and as he lowered his head to gaze at the blaze of the burning fire, his right foot was at the height of his left knee. Before his brain could catch up with his intentions, both of his legs were in high motion. Jacob ran out through the burning fires. He ran into the bushes as his instincts guided him away from the tracks. He could still smell the burning, but this time he was feeling intense pain, so he thought he should stop to examine himself. It was then he realised he was on fire. Jacob threw himself on the ground instantly and managed to extinguish the fire by continuously rolling his body against the soil. He had suffered severe burns to his arm, back, and legs. Jacob decided to endure his pain and wait in the bushes to prevent being seen by those who wanted to cause him harm. It was after sunset by the time Jacob decided to set out in search for the track home.

John and Margaret became anxious as Jacob was taking longer than necessary to execute the task of setting fire to their farmland vegetation and returning home. So, his father decided to set out in search of Jacob. He was halfway to their farmland when he heard a call from the bushes. Jacob had noticed the presence of someone and decided to hide in the bushes. He was not sure who would be walking on the path to their farmland, so he tried to look without being seen. "Father!" he shouted and ran out to embrace his dad, ignoring his burning pains. He was delighted to see his father.

John and Margaret's experience of life in the village after Jacob's birth was a challenge. There were many questions to be answered, they felt. However, they had no clue who to ask, so they continued to pray for God's guidance. Margaret had become pregnant for the third time, and the family became gripped with anxiety, wondering if history would repeat itself. The attempt to kill Jacob in the farmland was a reality check for the family. They realised that the danger never went away and that they needed to protect themselves and especially Jacob becoming their main priority.

CHAPTER THREE

A Boy in the Water Well

JACOB'S MOTHER HAD given birth to a baby boy. There was no complication, the baby was normal, and the mother was fine. The baby was called Noah. It was a good relief for the family, although they felt they were not out of danger. Jacob had recovered from his wounds but still suffered the psychological effects of the incident. He would wake in the middle of the night having nightmares, and the scars on his right hand near his wrist were a constant reminder of the incident. At first, it was an impossible task to visit the farmland, and Jacob's father had to do extra labour to attend to the growing crops. Jacob had to stay indoors with his mother and his younger siblings.

It was several months after the incident before Jacob regained the confidence to return to his farming chores alongside his father. It was the same farmland, and Jacob had to make an extra effort to prevent himself from the thoughts of the incident. On one occasion, Jacob decided to speak to his father about carrying his own machete with him whenever he needed to be alone. He had turned twelve years old and felt he should, to some extent, take responsibility for protecting himself and perhaps his family where necessary. John was not sure he would want Jacob to be alone at any time, never mind carrying a machete for self-protection. He informed Jacob that God was looking out for him and would protect him a lot better than the machete would. So, the answer to the idea was a "no," and they never discussed the matter again.

IT WAS ON A SUNDAY AFTERNOON in the middle of the rainy season. Jacob and his sister were playing outside as it rained. Sunday remained a rest day, and there was never a need to attend to the crops. Hardly anyone visited their farmland on Sundays. So, Jacob's parents sat under the covered porch and watched Jacob and his sister as they continued to play in the rain. "Jacob is still a child," Jacob's mother spoke out, and Jacob's father nodded his head in agreement. Only if they could afford for him to go to school, they discussed. Jacob's parents had believed that education was the only way out of poverty, and denying Jacob such a privilege was a conviction that Jacob would remain poor like them.

They thought of the death wish on Jacob by the village but reached no understanding of how to stop it. The only option available to them was to stay close to Jacob and keep him safe by all means possible. It was getting dark, and it was time to get Jacob and his sister inside the house. Jacob's father decided to check their water well and was delighted that they now had almost a full well with water to last a long time during the dry season. The family then retired indoors for dinner and went to their respective spaces to sleep. John and Margaret shared their room with the two younger children while Jacob slept in the living room.

It was just a few hours after the family settled into their respective sleeping areas, and Jacob was struggling to fall asleep. His mind wondered why he was born with a tooth. He thought about the attempt on his life and realised that running out through the burning vegetation was never his intention, yet it was what he had done to save his life. He imagined if he had died, what would become of his family. It was then that Jacob realised he had left his wooden whale outside. Jacob had carved a piece of wood into the shape of a fish and had carried it with him always since the attempt to burn him. Jacob had heard the story of Jonah and the Whale from his father and had believed if he always carried the whale, God would protect him and take him to safety. Jacob had slept with the wooden whale and could not imagine being without it. So, he decided he must go out to look for it by first light.

Jacob did not sleep well with the thought of his wooden whale not beside him. It was just first light as he heard the rooster's crow. He decided to go outside quietly without waking his family. So, Jacob opened the door by removing the two horizontal wooden bars that secured the door slab from being opened from the outside. It was a daunting task, but with many trials, Jacob had mastered the skill of opening their main doors. There were two main doors, the front that is mostly reinforced and the back door that leads into the backyard. It appeared that the majority of the confrontation came through the front door. Hence it made sense for it to be more reinforced than the back door. The family had taken the initiative to reinforce their doors and windows because of the ongoing threat from the village. Jacob had just removed the final bolt that secured the door to the frame, and before he pulled the door that swung inward into the house open, he listened for any sign of movement in the house. With confirmation that everyone was still fast asleep, Jacob pulled the door open.

The fresh morning mist of the atmosphere hit his face, and Jacob remembered when he used to wake up early to get ready for school. He remembered the early morning walks with his father to school. He imagined for the first time the knowledge he would have gained if he had stayed at school. Jacob's peers in the village hardly spoke with him because of his circumstances. He felt he was marked as evil, and he would never be accepted by anyone. The thought of not having friends made him upset, but then he remembered that his mother had said he was a special child, and that the village was not aware of the positivity of his uniqueness. Jacob trusted his family and knew he was not a devil as the village made him out to be. It was at that moment that Jacob felt something special inside him, although he did not know what that meant, or how if at all, he would be able to change the opinion of his village people.

As Jacob stepped outside into the early morning of the day, he realised there was a possibility he might not find his wooden whale. It was still dark, and he could not see much, so he went back inside the house to take the lantern. He started to search for his wooden whale but could not find it. Just as he was going to give up, he realised that the rainwater may have carried it into their water well. So, Jacob proceeded to investigate. He removed the wood log that secured the covering of the water well. The water well covering prevents debris and other unwanted objects from entering the well. However, the excavated channels that direct the rainwater through the side wall of the well had no covering hence allowing smaller debris and objects to enter it. Upon the examination of the water well, Jacob could see his wooden whale floating on top of the water. With excitement, he tried to reach it but was not able.

Drawing water from the well was a skilful task that anyone from five years old in the village had to master. It was a means of survival to fetch water from the well. Although during rainy seasons, the villagers would use containers, including cooking pots, to collect rainwater. The containers were left outside as it rains to collect the water. Drinking water would be stored in special clay pots and would be placed in the most dark and cool area of the house. This would ensure that the water was cool to drink anytime of the day as the temperature can rise to thirty-seven degrees centigrade. In the dry seasons, the water in the well is collected, filtered, and then stored in the clay pot. However, the water in the well must be drawn at first light and first thing in the morning. This will ensure that the residues in the well have not been disturbed and remain settled at the bottom of the well. Therefore, the water at the topmost level of the well is the cleanest, which is then fetched for additional filtering before storing for drinking and cooking.

Jacob had decided to use the fetching bucket meant for drawing water from the well to scoop up his wooden whale. The fetching bucket consisted of a rubber material shaped like a half vessel and stitched with a long string that could stand the weight of the water when pulled up and out of the well. As Jacob extended the fetch bucket into the well, he decided to lower his full body by lying on the ground to allow his upper body the freedom to manoeuvre the fetch bucket to the wooden whale.

Just as he had succeeded in securing the wooden whale in the fetch bucket, Jacob felt someone holding his two ankles, and before he realised what was happening, he was in the water well. Jacob was sinking to the bottom of the well with his head down quicker than he could have imagined. He realised he could not breathe, and his first instinct was to turn his body to the upright position so he could pull himself up towards the top of the well to reach for air. As Jacob propelled himself upwards, reaching the surface of the water, he noticed a protruding tree root from the side of the well, which he grabbed on to.

CHAPTER FOUR

Finding Jacob

JACOB'S MOTHER THOUGHT she heard some noise outside and decided to check. She opened the window and looked outside, but all seemed calm. She was able to sight the water well, and all seemed normal as the cover remained intact. It was still early in the morning, and she was reluctant to leave the room to start the chores of the day. So, she decided to go back to sleep for a little longer while Jacob's father continued snoring as usual.

It was almost two hours later, and the new baby, called Noah, woke up and started to cry, waking up Margaret. She had to breastfeed Noah and then lay him down while she checked on her other children. It was then she noticed that Jacob's father had left the room, and she wondered if he had gone to the farm. John preferred attending to his farm as early in the morning as possible. This meant that he was able to work on the farm during cooler temperatures before the heat of the sun became unbearable. Apparently, on that Monday morning, Jacob's father had left for the farm and would not be returning until just after noon.

Margaret had just noticed that Jacob was not in the house. Her instinct was that Jacob had followed his father to the farm. Although, she had some reservations about her instinct as Jacob normally did not go to the farm on Mondays. Jacob's Monday task was to weed and tidy the backyard of their home. So, she decided to have a look; perhaps Jacob was up early weeding the backyard. As she approached the door that led into the back garden, she noticed that the wooden barricades had been removed and placed in the secured position. She thought that would have been her husband as he usually would leave for the farmland through the back door.

There was no obvious sign of Jacob. She then called out Jacob's name, but there was no answer. As she investigated the backyard for signs of Jacob, she noticed a single footprint that headed towards the direction of their farmland. She examined further, looking for a smaller size footprint, a sign that Jacob had walked ahead or behind his father along the narrow footpath, but there was nothing.

The thought that Jacob could have been abducted shot a lightning ray of anxiety down Margaret's spine that she was partially paralysed and fell to the ground. However, she quickly regained control of her body and decided to check the front door. To her grief, the front door was not secured. She noticed that the wooden barricades had been removed and placed at their secured positions. This reassured her that the door had been unlocked by someone inside the house. Who could have opened the door, she asked herself? She pulled the door, and it swung open without any resistance. She stepped outside and examined the area for footprints.

What she noticed made no sense to her. The yard in front of the house was bare ground without grass or any vegetation, and she would sweep it every morning. Jacob would then remove any weeds as they emerged. Just like the backyard, the bare ground made it possible to see footprints. Jacob's mother was able to see multiple footprints, which included a small foot and an adult-sized print. There were the small footprints that headed towards the water well and back, and back again to the well. The large print proceeded from the road into the front yard, heading towards the well and back again to the road. The water well was situated about fourteen feet away from the house and aligned with the right window of the house. This was Jacob's parents' bedroom window.

Margaret remembered the noise she had heard earlier in the morning but noticed nothing when she looked out through the window. As she thought of the footprints, she felt something was wrong. She investigated further and walked closer to the water well. She was shocked when she noticed a lantern laid beside the water well. She examined the lantern and noticed that it was theirs. She grabbed hold of it and looked further around the area but found nothing. She then returned inside the house. Speaking to Jacob's little sister, Anna, revealed no lead she could act upon. She wished she could call a neighbour to help look for Jacob or send someone to reach out to her husband in the farmland, but she was aware that no one would help them because of their stigma. So, she planned to get herself and the children ready and head to the farm to alert her husband. She had noticed that the sky was getting darker, indicating that it may rain shortly. However, she must hurry up and needed to get some fresh water from the well. She settled the baby in his handmade wooden cot and asked his toddler sister to keep an eye on him.

Jacob had been in the water well for nearly five hours. Surely his chances of being alive after this time would be low, if not impossible. The prospect of rain would affect Jacob's survival as the well would be flooded with more rainwater. Margaret remained distraught about not knowing where Jacob was. She started to hope that Jacob was with his father and that they were both alright working at the farm. However, the thought of the lantern being outside near the water well and the footprints gave her another fright that she decided to sit on the floor to think for a while. She focused on the prints. She imagined the small footprints to be that of Jacob as it was similar to his size. Then she asked herself if that was Jacob's footprint, where could he be? She tried to imagine where Jacob could be. Jacob was aware of the challenges he faced and knew the risk of being out alone, Margaret reasoned. As she continued to repeatedly run through her mind the danger surrounding Jacob, she suddenly realised that she had to try and trace his footprints until she understood where he could be.

Margaret stood behind the front door. She examined the process of opening the door and thought whether Jacob was able to remove the wooden barricades and store them in their location when not in use. She then realised that she had taught Jacob how to open the door and recollected that Jacob had once or twice unsecured the front door in her presence. She then proceeded to open the door, which she pulled inwards and then stood by the threshold without stepping outside. She immediately stared at the footprints in front of her. She realised that she needed to identify her own footprints and excluded them from her analysis. She focused on the small footprints she had presumed to be those of Jacob. As she traced the footprints, she suspected that Jacob had made three journeys. She noticed that he had stepped outside and walked the length of the front garden a few times before returning to the house and then stepped outside again and headed towards the water well. So, she headed straight to the water well, and at the same time, she noticed a larger footprint which was obviously larger than hers and those of Jacob.

Standing by the water well, Jacob's mother thought the impossible. Just as she started to imagine the possibility of Jacob being in the water well, the thought of the larger footprint sent a cold feeling to her heart. She realised that the larger footprint had come from the road and then headed back the same way. She thought of the villager's desire to kill Jacob by any means that made it look like an accident, that made her realise that Jacob was likely going to be in the water well. She felt shivers in her spine as she realised he must have drowned and died, given the length of time he had been in the water well. With all her strength, she called out Jacob's name and, at the same time pulling off the wooden logs that restrained the water well cover.

"Mama, Mama," Jacob cried out. The sound of his voice echoed, and Margaret could feel the fear that had distorted the rhythm of Jacob's pronunciation of "Mama." The thought that Jacob was alive gave Margaret the extra strength and determination that she removed the entire covering of the water well more quickly than she ever imagined. She looked down in the well and saw Jacob's head resting just above the water level. Jacob gazed at his mother with tears in his eyes and cried out, "Mama, I am alive."

Jacob's mothers' emotions had taken control of her body. She felt as though she was fainting but at the same time realised that she had to be strong to pull Jacob out. So, she recomposed herself and tried to stay focused. She wasn't sure how Jacob had managed to stay above the water level for the long time he had been in there. She started to cry louder for help but at the same time knew that no one would come. Without thinking and knowing she couldn't reach Jacob, she extended her hand into the water well. Jacob cried out, "Pull me out, Mama, Mama, pull me out."

CHAPTER FIVE

The Rescue

RESCUING JACOB FROM the water well ended up becoming a challenging task. There was no one to call that would be inclined to help, and Margaret could not reach Jacob. Nevertheless, she decided to shout for help, but at the same time did not want to lose sight of Jacob. Jacob was exhausted and was too weak to attempt any manoeuvres. So as Margaret shouted out for help, she continued to try and reach Jacob with her outstretched arm, which was unfortunately not long enough to reach him. As Margaret waited for help, the thought of losing her son flooded her mind. However, at the same time, she realised that Jacob had come such a long way already and believed that this should not be his end.

There was no one answering her distressed call, but she was not surprised. She realised that she must do something different and perhaps drastic to try and save her son. She took off her clothing, a wrap-around cloth that was tied to her waist. She rolled and twisted the wrapper to form a rope and extended it into the well. At this stage, Jacob was completely exhausted and could barely hold on to the tree root in the water well. Jacob's head was at this stage, only half above the water level, and he was losing consciousness. "Jacob, Jacob," his mother called out. Jacob managed to raise his head only slightly, and he noticed the twisted cloth and attempted to grab hold of it. It was only after a few attempts that he was able to reach and grab the twisted cloth. "Hold on tight to the cloth," shouted Jacob's mother.

The sky looked rough and was threatening to rain. The lightning struck, and the sound of the thunder was so loud that Jacob's baby brother, Noah, was woken, and his younger sister, Anna, ran outside and cried for her mother. However, their mother was too focused on trying to pull Jacob out of the water well. Unfortunately, she was not making any good progress because she was not strong enough to pull Jacob out. She then started encouraging Jacob to climb up the twisted cloth, but sadly, he was too weak to pull himself up. It had started to rain, and the thought that the rainwater would flood the well, further raising the water level, was a serious worry for Jacob's mother. However, she was also delighted that the rain would force her husband to return home. So, she thought that all she must do now would be to keep Jacob conscious and holding on to the twisted cloth and the support of the tree root.

"Papa! Papa!" Jacob's younger sister called out. This was a relief to Margaret as she thought that the ordeal would soon be over. "What is going on there? Why are you not indoors?" Jacob's father shouted. He had returned home from the farm through the back garden of the house and had no knowledge of the situation with Jacob. He was shocked when he reached the front yard of the house and noticed Jacob's mother leaning into the water well. "Help me, quick!" she shouted. "Jacob is inside the well." Shocked and confused, Jacob's father proceeded to take charge of the situation. After a quick evaluation, he came to the realisation that he needed a good strategy for getting Jacob out of the well. Otherwise, the rescuer may end up falling into the well.

Unfortunately, there was no time to formulate a well-thought-out plan before the rescue could begin. Jacob was feeling weak and unable to hold on to the tree root. His eyes were heavy and almost closed. "Jacob! Jacob!" Jacob's father called out. Although Jacob could feel some excitement about his father's presence, he felt he might not have the energy to hold on for long. Jacob tried to raise his head to look at his father in response to the call. "Father, I am cold, and I cannot hold on any longer." John was not sure how Jacob ended up in the well and for how long he had been in there, but he felt it was pointless asking and wanted to focus on rescuing his son. After a quick assessment of the situation, and knowing his hands could not reach Jacob, and that the twisted cloth would not work, he ran for his farm bag, which was lying on the ground in the backyard.

The rain had stopped suddenly. Jacob's father, armed with his machete, ran into the bush through his back garden in search of a tree branch. Knowing that he had no time to spare, he quickly scanned for the right tree branch with precision and did it as fast as he could. With hardly any time wasted, from his assessment, he found and cut down the right tree branch and was heading back home. However, it had been thirty minutes at least since he had left. Jacob was now at the point of losing consciousness, and he was no longer able to raise his head or answer calls to his name. Jacob's mother was not sure if her husband knew what he was doing to get Jacob out. She tried to shout for help, but no one was coming. "Jacob, Jacob," John called out. He could see Jacob was becoming lifeless, but he needed him to be alert to help his rescue out of the well. Using the tree branch, Jacob's father supported Jacob's upper body, and he was able to wedge the end of the tree branch on the opposite side of the well. A few more wooden supports were put in place, and he was able to guide himself toward Jacob and pulled him out.

Jacob was carried indoors, stripped of his wet clothing, and he was wrapped in blankets. He was later taken to the outdoor kitchen where the fire was burning slightly above normal to radiate intense heat to quickly normalise Jacobs's body temperature. His mother was able to quickly prepare fish pepper soup with extra chilli, which was forced down Jacob's throat. Jacob was responding but continued to shiver. His younger sister, Anna, looked on with fear and concern for her family. Jacob continued to fall asleep, but each time was deliberately disrupted by his mother. "Jacob, you cannot fall asleep, please. Stay awake, and you can sleep after you are fully conscious." Perhaps they failed to realise that Jacob had been in the water well for over eight hours and could be suffering from hypothermia and needed proper medical assessment and treatment. Unfortunately, this was not available to Jacob's parents and family. Besides, the nearest medical facility was over six miles away, and it would be impossible to carry Jacob on a long trek. Therefore, they must attend to Jacob as well as they could in-house and hope for the best.

It was about three hours since Jacob was rescued from the well. He had been laying by the fire in the outdoor kitchen, and every attempt had been made to keep him awake. Luckily, Jacob's temperature began to normalise. He was able to sit up with his back supported by the kitchen wall. Jacob tried to call out to his mother but struggled initially. His parents sitting around him knew there was progress, and they were hopeful. Jacob was then given the leftover rice and stew from the previous day, which was mixed and stir-fried with fresh vegetables, including extra chilli. Jacob was able to feed himself but slowly. This was encouraging to his parents, and even his sister, Anna, felt some relief and smiled at Jacob. "How are you?" Anna asked. "I am not feeling good, but I am glad I am out of the water well," Jacob answered. This was the first proper and meaningful statement Jacob had uttered since being rescued. Jacob's parents were delighted that the worse was behind them.

It was the following morning after Jacob was rescued from the water well, and after checking Jacob was awake and speaking fluently, Jacob's father decided to visit the head chief and elders of the village to report the incident. As usual, it was dismissed as an attempt on Jacob's life and instead accepted their own hypotheses that Jacob accidentally fell into the well while he was playing or fetching water. However, Jacob's parents knew there was no point in challenging their views as there was no explanation as to how the water well was completely covered after Jacob had supposedly fallen in accidentally. However, Jacob's parents did receive a visit from a handful of sympathisers, and they promised that they would have come to help if they had heard the call. Reassurance was then given in case help was needed in the future.

This group of well-wishers became close friends with Jacob's parents and family. For the first time since Jacob was born, they felt that they could go to someone for help and protection if needed. However, over the course of the day, John managed to visit the King's palace and report the incident. As there was no evidence, the case was not taken further. In all, Jacob's parents knew that although they had a handful of allies in the village who they could call for help and support, they realised that they still must be extra careful and increase their own protection for Jacob.

CHAPTER SIX

The Exit

IT WAS MARCH OF 1940, and Jacob had turned fourteen years of age. He was no longer a child and was seen in the village as a young man that could perhaps manage farmland in his own capacity and even able to get married. Jacob could make enough of a living wage by selling seventy percent of his farmland harvest and the remainder for him and his wife's consumption. However, Jacob was aware of his stigma and was afraid that no one would want to buy what he produced and did not bother to exploit that opportunity. Instead, his parents would prefer that he left the village for another region where he would be unknown and, therefore, could be treated properly and have the same opportunity to strive like everyone else.

The question they could not answer was where could Jacob go? The family did not have any relatives outside of the village and did not know any towns or cities that Jacob could go. The family was also concerned that although Jacob was fourteen, he was still young and could struggle to provide for himself, let alone protect himself. In addition, there was a World War going on, and the family had no knowledge of its implication to their area, not to mention other regions that were closer to urban civilisation.

The thought of leaving the village excited Jacob. Margaret was not sure if letting Jacob leave her sight was a good decision. She did feel, though, that it was impossible for Jacob to reach his potential if he stayed in the village. Several months had passed since the family initially came up with the idea. Still, there was no progress in developing the plan any further. The main obstacle was where Jacob could go, how he would get there, and who would look after him? However, with time they reached a consensus that Jacob should leave the village. They believed that was good progress, and they just must work out where and how.

Since the water well incident, Jacob was hardly allowed to leave his father's sight. His whereabouts were never more than a stone's throw from his father. They would trek to their family farmland and return together. This tactic worked, as there were hardly any attempts to attack Jacob in any way. It could also be as a result that the villagers had given up on their belief that Jacob remained a curse to the progress of the village. Although, there was no knowledge of any significant improvement to the village other than the fact that some farmers were able to produce good crops that fetched enough money to build homes.

It was on a Sunday afternoon, and Jacob and his family were hanging out in the front yard of their house. Surprisingly, one of their few new friends decided to drop in for a visit. This was a pleasant surprise for the family as they hardly got the opportunity to entertain any visitors. It was also the opportunity to ask questions about the villager's views on them, given it had been over fourteen years since Jacob was born. Jacob's mother was keen to show off her good cooking skills and rushed into the kitchen to prepare some food for their visitor. She made fish pepper soup with yam, and it was delicious. This was the first time that Jacob's mother had cooked for someone not a member of her family. So, she wanted to impress the guest and therefore went the extra mile to ensure the quality of the food was right, and the presentation was good. There was also the belief that the guest would speak of the good hospitality received and hopefully would help change the hostile minds of the village towards them. After the meal was consumed and the acknowledgement by their guest that the food was delicious, their visitor spoke about some of the village residents that travelled to the neighbouring towns to work. Some of them are carpenters, bricklayers and labourers working for the local councils and authorities, and others also worked in factories owned by the private sector.

The guest who worked in the nearest town also spoke about the new road being completed that connects the west of the country to the east, which was only about two miles from the village. Jacob's parents had no knowledge of the type of civilisation their guests had discussed. They felt some level of privilege with the detailed information about life outside the village. Their guest had stayed longer than anticipated and was glad he was also able to provide new and exciting information about neighbouring towns and cities. He left just before dinner time, but not without giving Jacob's mother a commendation about her fish pepper soup.

Jacob was in his bedroom and could hear all the conversation. He had never ventured outside the village and could only imagine some of the infrastructure their guest had described. He thought about going to town one day to see the reality for himself. It was the following morning, on the way to the farm, that Jacob asked his father for his opinion on the conversation they had with their guest the previous day. Jacob thought he could see an exciting opportunity for him to leave the village but was not sure if his father shared that vision. "Yes, Jacob, I have been thinking a lot about the things we discussed, and I am curious about the possibility of you going to town to experience it all," said Jacob's father. So, they spent their time trekking to the farm, on the farm, and on their way back, discussing a plan of how they could visit the neighbouring towns to experience some of the things their friend had mentioned.

It was nearly two weeks to the day that their friend visited that Jacob and his father decided to take the long walk to the neighbouring town called Boji-Boji, Agbor. First, they wanted to see the newly constructed road that connects the east to the west of the country. It was true, as they could see for themselves after walking about two miles from their village. Jacob's father realised that the King's palace was just a few yards from the newly constructed road, although it had been a few years since the last time he had visited. They arrived at the centre of the town after walking another three miles towards the east.

They saw different types of buildings, such as the newly constructed telecommunication centre and the post office. They also saw the British soldiers and civilians and wondered why they were white skinned. This was the closest that they had come to seeing the British that had colonised the country since eighteen eighty-four. Although they were aware of the slave trading started by the white men hundreds of years ago, they were not sure if the village had existed then. Overall, the trip to the town was a real eye-opener for both of them; they were excited and could not wait to share their experience with Margaret and the family as they headed home.

A few days after the trip to town, Jacob decided he had drawn up an exit plan for leaving the village. He planned to leave for Boji-Boji, Agbor town, alone and spend a whole day, if not a few days, exploring work opportunities. Jacob's parents agreed to the plan, and Jacob was given their blessing but not until after they had prayed. Although Jacob's father was concerned about some rumours he had heard from one of his friends in the village. The British were recruiting civilians into their military and were transporting them overseas to help fight in World War II. Although they were aware that the slave trade had ended, this seemed like an extension of it, forcing Nigerians out of their homes without the guarantee of returning again.

Jacob's parents were worried that he might be captured and forced to join the military and shipped out of the country. This could well be the case, as it was not a rumour; Jacob was not of the recruitment age of eighteen. Based on this new information, Jacob was allowed to travel to town to seek job opportunities, but not before a final trip to the farm with his father. The trip to the farm was a counselling session. Jacob was reminded of his limitations. This included his inability to read and write as he was not educated. He really could not speak the English language either. Jacob realised his limited ability to communicate but was willing to quickly learn in any way possible. He was also brought up to respect people and to always remain honest no matter the circumstances.

Jacob left for the town the following morning, all by himself. He had packed some fruits and food, and water with him. It was hard to say goodbye to his mother, but his sister, Anna, was hopeful that Jacob would accomplish something useful from the trip but did not know what. Noah, his brother, really did not understand why Jacob had to leave. He would miss him even though Jacob would be away for only two days at the maximum.

Jacob was excited to face a new world on his own at nearly the age of fifteen and was leaving his parents, that had protected him since birth, for the first time. He thought about the tooth he was born with and the stigma that surrounds it. He also remembered the name given to him by the king, Okwueze, meaning the 'King's words.' Jacob felt he was special because he was able to survive all the attempts to kill him. However, although he believed he would achieve something great for himself, he really was unable to know how to go about it. He could only assume that leaving home and the village that did not want him alive was the first step to self-actualisation.

CHAPTER SEVEN

The Lorry Boy

THE WALK TO THE new road from the village took Jacob less time compared to when he did it with his father. He was motivated and had high expectations, but he had no knowledge of how to do anything that could lead to any type of achievement or success. After a self-consultation, as he walked nearly two miles to the new road, he realised that the first thing to achieve was to get a job promise from an employer. The type of job that he could do was not easy for him to comprehend. He knew, though, that he could labour in factories or work in plantations, but he did not know how to seek those opportunities. The final thought that came to his mind was accommodation for a night or two. He was not sure what he could afford with the money he had. All the same, he was hopeful that some good would materialise from the self-exploration trip.

Jacob was impressed by the new road layout. He started to admire the construction techniques but could not even imagine how a road that smooth could be built. He decided to turn right and walk alongside the road for a while as he appreciated the quality of the construction. Jacob knew that the direction he was following would lead him to Boji-Boji, Agbor town, which was his destination, so he was happy to stay on the road. A mile into his walk, he came across a broken-down lorry, and the driver was in distress. "Are you alright?" Jacob asked in his native language, but the driver was not indigenous to the area and was unable to understand him. The driver, who was alone, then spoke the Nigerian Pidgin English language, which Jacob did not understand. The Pidgin is a mixture of English and different Nigerian languages. The Pidgin language is spoken widely across the country. However, Jacob's village was isolated and could not really benefit from such language development.

The lorry driver and Jacob immediately realised that they could not communicate verbally and decided to use hand gestures to express themselves. Jacob thought he could help the driver if he knew what he could do. So, with hand gestures, he was able to ask what the problem with the vehicle was. Jacob instantly became aware of the pungent smell coming from the carriage area of the vehicle. Before the driver could try to explain what the problem with the lorry was, Jacob had covered his nose with his hand, expressing that he could smell something bad. The lorry driver, who was suffering from olfactory fatigue due to the prolonged exposure to the smell, nodded his head and took Jacob to the back of the vehicle to show his cargo. It was rubber latex – sap from rubber trees.

The driver tried to explain that the sap was harvested from rubber trees on plantation farms. He continued to say that it takes the rubber tappers several weeks to collect enough sap to fill his lorry. However, during storage, the sap combines with natural air, which activates the coagulation and expansion process. It also starts to decompose after a few days, hence the smell. Jacob could not really understand the driver about the smell of his cargo. However, he proceeded to ask the driver what the problem with the vehicle was. A walk on the other side of the vehicle revealed a flat tyre. "Is that it?" Jacob asked with a hand gesture. "Yes, that is the problem," acknowledged the driver.

Jacob was able to help the driver to replace the flat tyre with the spare he was carrying underneath the vehicle chassis. "Do you need a lift?" asked the driver. Jacob, not sure what to say as he had never been in a vehicle, stared at the driver. "Get in," said the driver, using his hand to gesture to Jacob to get inside the vehicle. Jacob decided to climb into the vehicle with the driver, and they started the journey on the new road layout to town. It was only about two miles to Agbor town, and Jacob was impressed with how quickly the vehicle was going and reached the centre of town in no time. However, during that few minutes' drive into town, the lorry driver had encouraged Jacob to stay and accompany him to his discharge location, a rubber processing plant, which was about eighty miles east from Agbor town.

Jacob thought it would be a good experience to travel in a vehicle to a different region of the country, and he had become interested and curious to see what the rubber processing factory was like. The journey took them over seven hours, including a few stops for food and to allow the vehicle engine to cool. It was late in the evening of that day, which was a Friday, when they arrived at their destination. Unfortunately, they had missed their discharge slot and would have to wait until Monday when the plant reopened. Jacob and the lorry diver had no choice but to stay with the vehicle. Jacob slept underneath the vehicle while the driver slept inside the cab.

Over the weekend, Jacob had started to express himself by communicating using the Pidgin English language. He was not yet fluent with the language but certainly able to communicate effectively with the driver. It was on Monday morning when the plant opened, and they were able to discharge their cargo. Jacob was surprised at the large scale of the processing plant infrastructure and wondered if they may have a job for someone like him. The lorry driver did not think Jacob had what was required to gain a job at the processing plant due to his limited language skills and lack of education. "You can stay with me as my lorry buddy for a while and see how it goes," stated the lorry driver. The lorry driver agreed to pay Jacob a portion of his wage. In return, he would get help in the maintenance of the vehicle. He had also enjoyed the company of Jacob and wanted to help in any way he could after hearing the story of his life.

Agreeing to stay on with the driver, Jacob contemplated how he would reach out to his parents and inform them that he would not be returning home soon, at least not in two days. Nevertheless, Jacob was determined to see this new opportunity through to the end. He felt that it might lead to something new and believed that, with time, he would find out. The lorry driver announced his next assignment to collect another rubber latex consignment and deliver it to the processing plant. The overall journey distance would be in excess of three hundred miles. Jacob was excited that he could see the whole sap extraction process. Travelling to the rubber plantation took most of the day and another day for loading before embarking on the one hundred and fifty miles journey the following day to the processing plant. This presented Jacob with the opportunity to see how the sap was extracted from the rubber trees.

On the day the lorry was being loaded with rubber latex, Jacob was free, and he was privileged to join the tappers on their sap extraction trip. After several hours of watching and learning how the trees were prepared in order to harvest the sap, Jacob felt that, as a farmer, he might have found his career. He enjoyed the process as it was similar to the discipline of getting to the farm early, just after sunrise and working until the midday sun. Jacob spoke to the crew about a possible job, and he was told that they are always looking for rubber tappers.

It was the following day morning and time to start heading east, a one hundred and fifty-mile journey to the rubber processing plant. The lorry driver could sense Jacob's excitement and asked why he felt accomplished and happy. Jacob started by expressing his thanks to the driver for the exposure and for teaching him the Pidgin English language. He continued to explain to the driver that he may have found a career as a rubber tapper. "I have only just found you, and you are already leaving?" asked the lorry driver. Although the driver did not want to prevent Jacob from achieving his ambition, he knew that he would miss him as he felt that he was determined, honest, hardworking, and a good companion. The lorry driver was delighted to see the hunger for success in Jacob's eyes and decided to tell him all he knew about the rubber enterprise. Jacob was surprised to learn that the tyres of the vehicle were made from the sap of the rubber tree.

It was later agreed that on their return trip to a rubber plantation farm, Jacob would seek employment as a rubber tapper apprentice.

The offloading of Jacob's last consignment at the rubber processing plant took a few more days than expected. There were also vehicle issues that added extra days to their journey time. Jacob had been away from home for nearly three weeks and had no means of contacting his parents to let them know that he was alright. His mood suddenly changed as he started to miss home and wanted to hug his mother and younger siblings and let them know that he was doing well. He could not wait to tell his father about the vehicle journeys on the new road and to express the scale of the infrastructures he had seen. He thought about his new language and pondered if his family would be proud of him. He also wondered if the village was a much better place for his family, given that he was no longer living there with his alleged curse. However, the thought of becoming a rubber tapper brought him some relief and excitement as he knew that would keep him away from the village and make a life for himself too.

The time had just struck five o'clock in the morning. Jacob was still asleep, but the lorry driver was awake and pondering about something. "Jacob, Jacob, wake up!" Shouted the lorry driver. Used to waking up earlier than this, Jacob opened his eyes and asked what it was. The lorry driver continued, "It's five o'clock, and if we leave now heading west for my next consignment pickup, we would be able to stop at Agbor town to find someone that could relate a message to your parents." This was a great idea to wake up to, Jacob thought. After several hours of driving and a few stops, they arrived at Agbor. Jacob remembered the family friend that had visited his family home. He had a job in Boji-Boji, Agbor. After asking around, they discovered where the family friend worked, and they headed to the site.

"Jacob! Is that you?" shouted the family friend from afar. He ran towards Jacob and hugged him. "Your parents are worried sick about you," he added. Jacob expressed his thanks and asked him to pass on a message to his parents, including his destination and his potential career. However, Jacob felt their family friend may be withholding some information about his parent's situation. All the same, Jacob had the assurance that his family were all well and doing fine. He knew that the news that he was well and achieving something good would bring great comfort and excitement to his family.

CHAPTER EIGHT

The News

IT WAS ALMOST TIME to clock out from work for the day, and John and Margaret's family friend was eager to head home to the village. He knew that delivering the news about Jacob was important as it would bring relief to his family, especially his mother. Jacob's mother could not imagine the possibility of him being away from home beyond the agreed two days. For nearly four weeks, she had felt the pain and disappointment in herself for letting Jacob leave in the first place. Her concern about the welfare of Jacob became increasingly disheartening for her. Jacob's father, on the contrary, felt Jacob was sensible to always do the right thing. He believed that Jacob was capable of looking after himself in challenging circumstances and trusted that he was fine and would find a way to send a message.

There was a knock on the door, and Jacob's mother jumped to her feet, although answering the door remained the last thing on her mind. She was lost in thoughts, trying to find a way to console herself about the mistake she had made by letting Jacob leave. She continued to feel that she had let him down, unable to face up to what she had done, and therefore would not answer the door. She had become worn out pondering the question of Jacob's whereabouts. She acknowledged that since Jacob's absence, more of the villagers had started to speak to her. Jacob's father was not expected home that day, and she thought most of the villagers were aware of this, and she, therefore, wondered who could be knocking with the intent to see her.

Seeing their friend standing there as she opened the door was not a pleasant feeling for Margaret. She thought that their friend would by now know where her husband was. "Sorry, my husband is not here, and I thought you knew where to find him," uttered Jacob's mother. "Yes, I am aware he would not be here today, but I wanted to bring the news first to you," said their friend. Surprised that he thought she could be important to be the first person to be told of new information, she took a deep breath and refocused her attention. "What news do you have for me, Mr Johnston?" said Jacob's mother. This was a shocking moment for their friend as this was the first time anyone in Jacob's parents' household had referred to him by his name. He had always been referred to as "our friend."

The reason being that the family did not want anyone in the village to know that they had a friend, and if they somehow found out, they may not know who the friend was. So, Mr Johnston had agreed to be referred to as "Our friend." However, in the last few weeks after Jacob's departure, the family situation had changed, and it seemed as though the villagers had embraced them back into the community. The people of the village only had issues with Jacob and not the rest of the family. Therefore, the departure of Jacob from the village meant John and Margaret and their other two children were free from isolation and able to associate with everyone in the community.

"I have seen Jacob, and he is alright," Mr Johnston whispered with excitement. Jacob's confused mother could only utter, "How? where?" Mr Johnston was asked to come inside the house and was offered a seat. He then went on to tell Margaret the message from Jacob. Mr Johnston added that Jacob looked well and happy. Jacob's mother could not believe what she had heard, but she had always trusted Mr Johnston. He remained one of their only true few friends in the village, and therefore she had no reason to distrust him. This news changed everything for Jacob's mother. She was previously depressed and disappointed in herself, and now she felt relieved and comforted by the news that her son was fine and progressing well outside the confines of the village. She realised that although she would have wanted to see Jacob, this progress was what she had always wished for him. She was proud that Jacob had not let them down. Mr Johnston was then offered a lovely meal, which he enjoyed, and just before he left, he said, "I will let you share the news with your husband when next he is here."

A few days after Jacob left the village, it became clear to the community that Jacob was no longer around and, indeed, may never return. This news spread across the village, and this resulted in accepting Jacob's parents back into the community. They became friends of everyone again, just as it was before Jacob was born. Some sections of the community were even appeasing their gods for the exit of Jacob. The acceptance back into the community provided Jacob's father with the opportunity to be persuaded into joining the 'elite men' association. You are required to have achieved the age of forty, have a home, and own relatively decent farmland. This elite association consisted only of men, and their primary objective was to support each other in every way possible. However, being married to one wife is a sign of weakness and poverty. Members with one wife were teased as not being man enough.

John was married to a second wife in no time. Margaret had no choice but to accept the new situation. Her husband would be sharing his time with the two wives, and this was seen by most people in the community as strength. The community also believed that because of their isolation, their grown daughters were left unmarried since men outside the village were not seeking marriage with their women. The more wives a man has, the greater the chance of gaining respect and influence within the community. John went on to have two more daughters within the following three years. However, his fortune never improved as a result, and being a member of the elite association did not change the outcome. Mr Johnston had not informed Jacob of this change to his family's situation when he had seen him. This was mainly because he felt that it was not his place to provide this information, and he was also concerned it may trouble Jacob. However, during the meeting with Jacob's mother, Mr Johnston was asked to pass on the information to Jacob if he were to see him again.

A couple of days after Mr Johnston had visited with the news from Jacob, John had returned home to share his time with Margaret. The loving relationship between them had changed, as she had never thought that she would be sharing her husband with another woman. Although she was aware that this could happen, she was consumed with the task of protecting Jacob and never really had the chance to envisage the possibility. One thing was apparent, her husband preferred and enjoyed her food to that of the second wife. "You seem a little happier today than the last time I saw you," said John. Margaret had remained silent and only wanted to give him the news when she was ready. "Is this what you really want?" asked Margaret. Before John could answer, she proceeded, "Can you really cope with this lifestyle?" John did not respond to any of the questions.

"Our friend was here earlier today bearing news," uttered Margaret. "You mean Mr Johnston?" asked John. He asked because he now had a lot more friends that he openly related with since Jacob left the village. "Yes, he was here to say that he saw and spoke with our son, Jacob." With excitement, he reached out to Margaret and hugged her. He was delighted to hear all the news and reassured himself of his belief that Jacob would be fine. "I told you he will be fine and not to worry," stated John. He thought about Jacob's future, and he somehow had faith that he would be fine. He remembered the moment that the King pronounced that Jacob would not be killed, and he remained puzzled as to what the King was feeling or thinking to have reached that conclusion and saved Jacob's life. We will keep the whereabouts and progress of Jacob to ourselves and only to close friends and well-wishers. "You mean close friends like the elite association?" asked Margaret sarcastically. "I mean someone like Mr Johnston," John responded.

"You drove me into this," uttered John. He went on to explain that three days after Jacob left and did not return, Margaret's behaviour had become erratic, the meals were no longer as tasty as they used to be, and she became cold towards him. Therefore, it did not take much convincing to join the elite association and marry his second wife. "You did not have to take on a second wife within a blink of an eye," said Margaret, and added, "You could have waited for Jacob to return and discuss your plan."

John knew that she was right. He had acted too hastily, but only because he had been carried away with the affection which he received from the community and especially the elite association just after Jacob had left. He wondered how Jacob would react to the news that he had taken a second wife. All the same, he remained glad that Jacob had sent news and that he was doing well.

CHAPTER NINE

The Apprentice

IT WAS LATE IN THE EVENING when Jacob and the lorry driver arrived at their destination. Jacob and the driver were silent for the final one-hour journey. It was awkward for both to suddenly became quiet as they normally always had something to talk about. Jacob was deep in thought during the last hour of their journey. He knew that he would have to say goodbye to the driver and step into the newly chosen chapter of his life that was not quite familiar to him. He knew also he had learnt a lot from the driver. He had gone to places and seen things beyond his imagination. He had also learnt a new language that would help him to navigate his way through the new life he has to embrace. So, he really was not sure if walking out of his present job was the best thing to do. He thought about being in the farm tapping rubber trees, and there would be nothing else to see, and no new destinations to visit weekly. Then he thought of the new skills he would acquire that would stay with him for life, and he would be able to provide for himself and his family.

As the driver pulled to a halt in a designated area, he thought it was the right time to fully introduce himself to Jacob. "By the way, my name is Peter Omon" uttered the driver. He continued, "I am from Ogun State, the west, not far from Lagos State." Jacob, not knowing where that was, nodded, thanked him, and said, "I am Jacob Oriahi…" The driver interrupted him saying, "I know a lot about you, Jacob; you have told me enough." Jacob knew he owed him a huge gratitude for the exposure and knowledge that he had gained from him. He decided that there would be a time to express the appreciation, but it was not then. He needed to ensure that he could gain an apprentice position to train to become a professional rubber tapper before he could say goodbye.

"My family lives in Lagos, who knows, one day you may come and visit me," uttered Peter. Peter was about twenty-six years old and looked slightly old for his age. He was above average height, about five feet eleven inches tall, and skinny in size, looking underweight. Although he was a native of Ogun State, he lived in Lagos mainland area with his parents and siblings. Peter loved deep-fried squirrel meat and had complained of the lack of it in the western region of the country. "How can you eat such a small and innocent creature?" Jacob had asked him. "Do not judge me until you taste it," replied Peter. "You may never want to eat anything else once you had your first bite," he continued. "Is that why you are so skinny, because you cannot find a squirrel to eat here?" asked Jacob with a smile. Peter gave Jacob a bad look and decided to change the topic of conversation.

The plantation that they had arrived at was different from the farm where they had collected their previous consignment, and Jacob wondered if the people would be as welcoming and patient enough to teach him the technique of tapping just as the others had done. He was not even certain that this plantation was seeking more tappers and if they would hire him as an apprentice. It was late, and he thought he would get to speak to the plantation manager in the morning. So, he proceeded to secure the vehicle as he normally did for an overnight stay. As always, he had to sleep underneath the vehicle and went on to prepare his sleeping mat, but the driver called him into the cabin of the lorry. "I need to speak to you, Jacob," said the driver. He continued, "First, remember, you can call me Peter from now on. Is that clear?" Jacob nodded with a smile. The driver was twelve years older than Jacob and told him that he had a brother of a similar age to him. "I am the firstborn of my parents, and after I had completed my primary education, I decided I wanted to become a lorry driver because I wanted to see the country." He continued, "I enjoy driving to different locations and seeing new things." The driver carried on talking and shared his own challenging upbringing and his desire to achieve something great. Finally, he said, "Jacob, I think there is something special about you, and it is only you that can determine your destiny; you have to think big and do not let anything or anyone stop you from achieving your dreams." Jacob thanked him for the advice and proceeded to sleep underneath the vehicle.

The following morning was not so pleasant as it had started to rain. Jacob was already awake and managed to clean and tidy himself. He was planning and preparing how he would approach the farm manager to ask him for a job as an apprentice. He was arranging the words into the right sentences in his mind that he would use to persuade the manager for a position. He was hoping for the rain to stop to allow the manager and the tappers to come outside so he could approach them. "Jacob, meet Mr Dickson, the plantation manager," said the lorry driver, Peter. Jacob stood up and was shocked as he was not ready yet to meet the manager.

"Jacob, I heard that you are seeking an apprentice position for rubber tapping," said Mr Dickson, and continued before Jacob could say a word, "I can help you with that if you are ready to follow me, and I will introduce you to your new team leader." Jacob was introduced to the team leader, and almost immediately, he was employed as a rubber tapper apprentice. He did not have to speak much to persuade or influence the outcome. The plantation manager had known Peter for several years, and he was able to provide a reference for Jacob, which helped him to secure employment.

By the end of the day, Jacob had exceeded the expectations of the team leader, that is, training him on how to prime the rubber tree for the extraction of the sap. As a farmer, Jacob was able to learn fast and able to offer some advice on how to ensure that the trees were properly cared for so that they would continue to produce more sap for a longer period. Jacob was introduced to his accommodation and was asked to settle in. He felt some sense of belonging there and knew he could make a successful living out of being a rubber tapper. Jacob got acquainted with his accommodation and later decided to find Peter as he knew his lorry was fully loaded with the latex consignment and that he would be leaving as early as possible the following day. Jacob felt that meeting Peter was a miracle, and he wanted to let him know that he had changed his life for the better.

That evening Peter and Jacob had a meal together as they normally did, and a few exciting stories were shared. Peter had been teaching Jacob basic arithmetic and especially how to count and manage money. Jacob could now identify numbers and the letters of the alphabet and comprehend their meanings. He was able to add and subtract and understood units, tens, and hundreds. Jacob was learning fast but recognised that he would no longer get the opportunity provided to him by Peter. Jacob remembered reciting the alphabet during driving from one location to the next. He knew he had come a long way, and it was surely showing in his confidence.

Before they finished for the evening, Peter took out an envelope and offered it to Jacob, saying, "This is all the money that you have earned as my lorry boy." He asked Jacob to open the envelope, which he did, and he was surprised. "Count them, Jacob. Let's see if you are able to tell how much you have earned." Peter instructed. Jacob then proceeded to count the money, but the feeling of holding so much money in his hands that belonged to him overwhelmed him. He started to cry and then managed to say, "I wish I could give them to my Mama; I wish they could see what I am able to achieve." Peter, also an emotional person, could not hold back his tears and commented, "You need to keep learning, Jacob, and I have told Mr Dickson about your challenges, and he has agreed to help you."

It was the day to formally say goodbye to Peter. Jacob had woken up early and left his accommodation to find him. Unfortunately, Peter had already left. Jacob was saddened that he had gone without saying a final goodbye. "Jacob," called out Mr Dickson. "I know that you wanted to see Peter before he left, but he preferred it this way as he was too emotional and did not want to see you upset either." Mr Dickson went on to inform Jacob that Peter had left him a message. He had promised to find his family friend, Mr Johnston, so that he could pass on Jacob's whereabouts and situation to his parents. Jacob was also informed that Peter intended to advance some money to his mother through Mr Johnston. "Don't worry, Jacob; Peter will come back here again to collect a consignment, and we will know if he succeeded in reaching your family friend at Agbor," reassured Mr Dickson.

Jacob remained with Mr Dickson at his rubber plantation for over five years. He was now one of the most high-ranking experienced rubber tappers in the estate. Peter kept to his promise and, on two occasions, brought Jacob's mother to the plantation to visit. Margaret was able to update Jacob on her matrimonial situation with his father. She also informed Jacob that it would be better if he never visited the village again. The village had moved on from Jacob's situation, and visiting could revert the progress achieved in involving his family back into the community.

Jacob started to feel bad that he could never return to his home village and felt as though the curse was now on him. However, he quickly remembered all he had achieved and felt the village was too blind to see he was the blessed one. Jacob recollected his mother's last visit. She was able to give Jacob a detailed explanation of why the community wanted him killed or exiled. She said, "Jacob, many societies, if not all in Nigeria, would see your birth circumstances – 'A baby born with tooth' as an abomination." She continued, "Normally, to rectify the situation, the baby must be abandoned in the forest to die or be killed." This thought reassured Jacob once again that he was lucky to have been saved by the King.

CHAPTER TEN

You will be a Successful Man

JACOB HAD NOW TURNED twenty-one years of age and had yet to visit his birth village since he left. The constant thought that he was not wanted continued to affect him in many ways, including his self-esteem. His mother's last visit made it clear to him that he must stay away from his village. Jacob felt there was not much he could do but to stay on course with his personal development and see what type of man he could become. He knew that his belief in God was strong enough to keep him going. However, he started to feel bored tapping the rubber trees. Jacob felt that the routine remained the same, and he realised that he had missed the road trips with Peter. The thought of remaining on the plantation for most of his adult life was not what he wanted anymore. He had thought about starting his own family and wanted to provide the best education he could afford for his children. However, he was beginning to realise that such dreams could not materialise based on his current circumstances. He knew he had to change his career.

Jacob was in the plantation field priming the rubber trees when a message came to him that Mr Dickson had asked for him. He wondered why Mr Dickson would see the need to interrupt his task as they had been asked to increase production. Jacob felt that he was already tapping the trees as quickly as he possibly could, and he also knew that the apprentices he had trained were equally picking up the pace. So, he wondered what Mr Dickson would be needing him for. "Can he not wait till I finish for the day," asked Jacob. "He said you had to come right away," stated the messenger. Jacob informed his working group that he had to attend to Mr Dickson's call and asked them to carry on with their tasks.

"Jacob, I have received a message from the head office to build a new storage facility due to our expansion," uttered Mr Dickson. Jacob was not sure how he could help as he was not a builder, and neither did he know anything about construction techniques that could be useful to the cause. "How do you see me being of help?" said Jacob. "I promised Peter that I would provide you with every possible opportunity to acquire new skills, and this is something that is different, so I want you to learn and support the project," stated Mr Dickson.

Jacob spent the rest of his working shift with Mr Dickson, trying to understand the construction plan and what was required of him. "Mr Dickson, how could you imagine that I, who have no basic education of any type, could understand such a construction plan?" asked Jacob. He continued, "I cannot even read or write." Staring into Jacob's eyes, Mr Dickson said, "That is the entire point, Jacob; you will learn." For the first time in his life, Jacob had doubts about Mr Dickson's expectations of him. However, he trusted Mr Dickson's views.

He had become close to Mr Dickson from the moment they were introduced by Peter, and Jacob had benefited a lot from the friendship. Amongst the benefits included managing Jacob's finances and writing letters to Mr Johnston, their family friend. Mr Johnston then related the content of the letters to Jacob's family, and a reply would be written by him, which was sent back to Mr Dickson on Jacob's behalf. This means of communication had enabled Jacob to remain at the plantation with ease of mind knowing his family was doing fine. So, Jacob felt he had to trust Mr Dickson regarding the construction help he would be providing.

Laying on his bed that night, Jacob was struggling to fall asleep. His mind was full of thoughts he did not have the wisdom to understand. One of these thoughts was about Mr Dickson, a white man from the United Kingdom. Jacob wondered why he did not visit his country and also why he seemed to have no family. However, he was aware that the World War had prevented many British citizens from visiting home. Jacob knew that the war had ended over a year ago, but Mr Dickson had no intention of visiting home. Perhaps he had no one to visit back home, Jacob thought. He also wondered why Mr Dickson was so helpful to him. Jacob will never forget the comments from Mr Dickson saying, "You will be a successful man, Jacob." What was the meaning of 'successful'? Jacob continued to ponder since that day. As he thought he would have to wait and find out, he fell asleep.

Several weeks had passed, and Jacob had been busy with Mr Dickson learning the new storage construction plans. Jacob had started to understand the logic of the drawings as well as knowing why a set of construction plans for building the storage was an effective tool to have. Jacob did not stop thinking of Mr Dickson's comments about the plans, "It is like walking in the dark if you do not have a construction plan." Jacob could only wonder why Mr Dickson was so passionate about the construction. One morning, when Jacob and Mr Dickson were mapping out the area to site the new storage building, Mr Dickson told Jacob that initially, he had a career in Civil Engineering and was a Construction Manager of a few structures built in Nigeria by the British. Jacob was learning fast and was asking questions to aid his understanding of the construction project. To him, it was all about common sense. He had applied a common-sense approach to understanding the construction science, and Mr Dickson was impressed by his swift progress.

A week later, the construction started, and Jacob had immersed himself completely in the project. He was enjoying it as he realised that it was not just about the strength and determination one possesses but also by the application of systematic principles of construction for this particular structure, as designed and specified by the building plans. Jacob also learnt that the construction of the building was designed in different segments and really paid attention to the foundation of the building.

He learnt that the foundation was vital in guaranteeing that the building load could be absorbed and ensure the stability of the structure. Jacob was also able to see the importance of the beams and how they were supported by the pillars, which were dependent on the foundation footings. Jacob could also see that there were different types of construction skills required to build a structure. On site, there were carpenters, masons, and other specialists. There were also various machinery and equipment that were aiding the build. After six months, the structure was near completion, and it was time for the painters to do their job. Jacob had noticed that the mason had the most work to do and had stayed on the project longer than other specialists, apart from Mr Dickson, who was the construction manager.

Mr Dickson was on site from the beginning and translated the specifications from the construction plans onto the build. Jacob knew that without Mr Dickson's expertise and direction, no one would know exactly what to do. He was also aware that the construction manager must remain on the project till the end to ensure that all the final details, as specified by the plans, have been implemented. This experience gave Jacob the inquisitive mind to analyse and judge the structural integrity of every building and structure he had seen. He thought about his home in the village and the mega rubber processing plant structures he had seen. He then concluded that they all had to follow the basic construction principle. Otherwise, they would collapse.

A few days after the storage building was completed, Jacob was determined that he wanted a change of career. He had decided that he wanted to become a mason and work on building construction projects. He needed to speak to Mr Dickson. Similarly, Mr Dickson thought that Jacob needed to broaden his potential and that switching to the building construction sector may be right for him. So, before Jacob could leave his accommodation to approach Mr Dickson, he noticed that there was someone at his door. "Jacob, Jacob, are you in?" asked Mr Dickson. Without delay, Jacob had opened the door, and Mr Dickson was inside his living quarters. "This is actually small and basic," said Mr Dickson. Jacob realised he was referring to his accommodation, which Mr Dickson hardly ever entered.

Mr Dickson presented his thoughts and a plan to see Jacob trained as a mason and be transferred to one of the regional housing and commercial development units handling several building projects not too far away. Jacob realised that if he had not liked the proposition, he still would have accepted it mainly because he believed and trusted the ambition portrayed for him by Mr Dickson. Jacob was excited and was eager to take on the next journey to fulfilling his destiny of being a 'successful man.'

CHAPTER ELEVEN

Mr Simon Fisher

T RAINING TO BECOMING A MASON was Jacob's newly acquired mission. He had enjoyed observing the role that Mr Dickson played in the construction of the plantation storage building, and he wanted to be the one in charge. However, Jacob was aware that he lacked the education needed to be able to deliver the detailed construction management that Mr Dickson had provided. Perhaps he should go back to school, Jacob thought briefly but quickly dismissed the idea as he felt it was too late. He knew it would be impossible to allow a twenty-two-year-old man to study at the same level as primary two pupils. Jacob felt that the time for him to achieve a formal education at school had passed him by. So, he must focus on achieving the best he could with the knowledge that he had. He reviewed his abilities and strengths and recounted his achievements to date, and he thought that he had not done too badly for a cursed child.

Jacob had now left the rubber plantation and headed to the southern region called Warri. He had started his mason training and could not wait to qualify. He had to go through a formal apprentice programme being led by a man, Mr John Oken, from Boji-Boji, Agbor. Mr Oken was aware of Jacob's issues with his community. Although the majority of people in the region believed that Jacob was cursed and should have been put to death, they also did not mind associating with him because they felt that the curse would only affect him and his village community. However, as Mr Oken continued to train Jacob, he could see that there was something special about him.

Jacob's speed of learning and his determination to want to be better continued to drive him in excelling in everything that he did. Mr Oken also knew that Jacob had achieved some advanced skills in construction. He could see that Jacob had a natural ability to understand a building plan.

As part of Jacob's training, he must work on construction projects and his ability to qualify as a mason depended on the good feedback received from the project manager. Jacob was assigned to a construction project within the township of Warri. The project was managed by a British white man called Simon Fisher. Mr Fisher was a strong man with little empathy for anyone. He was tall, of stocky build, with greying hair. He must be in his mid or late fifties, pondered Jacob. Mr Fisher would wear a grey or brown safari suit with a fedora hat to the site, and his shoes somehow managed to avoid all dust and dirt by the end of the day. Jacob soon found out that Mr Fisher was not like the other white men he had dealt with in the past. Mr Simon Fisher was indeed feared by all the workers on his site. He demanded quality work and directed every skilled labourer on site to get their task done right the first time. Jacob noticed that he despised anyone that took too much time to complete their task and would not tolerate incompetence or laziness. Overall, Mr Fisher disliked his time being wasted regardless of the reason.

Jacob knew he might well be out of his depth with Mr Fisher as he felt he was a closed-up kind of man. He never wanted to be your friend or listen to your concerns or reasons. He just wanted the job done precisely as he had specified and instructed. After a week of hearing Mr Fisher's shouting demands, Jacob started to take a different look at his behaviour. Mr Dickson also got the job done on time and on scope, but he was friendly and compassionate. So, what is Mr Fisher trying to achieve by being aggressive, Jacob asked himself. It was during lunchtime on a Friday afternoon that Jacob was able to speak with the qualified masons that had worked for Mr Fisher for a few years that he realised the type of man he was. From Jacob's assessment, he thought that Mr Fisher feared failure and had no faith in the worker's ability to deliver. Therefore, he had to micromanage and used ruthlessness to control workers and their quality of work. However, Jacob knew that he had to persuade Mr Fisher to get to know him and his work quality if he had any chance of getting decent feedback.

It was just over two weeks since Jacob started working on Mr Fisher's project. Jacob had not had the opportunity to meet Mr Fisher on a one-to-one level but continued to work on it. It was nearly lunchtime when the site bell started to ring. Jacob was not sure what that meant. He knew that it was only usually at the 8 am start of shift and at 4 pm end of the shift that the bell was rung. He wondered what was expected from them now that the bell had rung at midday. Jacob asked a colleague, "Is this a new lunchtime ring?" The worker looked at Jacob and then at his watch and said, "No, we don't have lunchtime rings, but obviously, it looks like we have to stop working and hear what Mr Fisher wants."

The site supervisor that rang the bell knew that the workers would be confused regarding the bell ringing at midday and hence would not know what was expected from them. So, he decided to walk amongst the workers to inform them that Mr Fisher wanted them to stop working and assemble for an announcement. "I must ask you all to stop working now because I am leaving the country for the United Kingdom to attend to an urgent family matter," uttered Mr Fisher. He continued, "I will return in a week's time, but until then, you are not allowed to do any work."

Jacob lived on-site and had no home to return to during the absence of Mr Fisher. The majority of the workers left for their homes and returned to the site a week later. However, Mr Fisher had not returned, and there was no information regarding when he would be back. Another week passed, and there was still no sign of Mr Fisher. Jacob was bored one morning and decided to take a proper tour of the site. His tour took him near Mr Fisher's office, and Jacob was surprised when he caught a glimpse of the construction plans through the glass louvre windows. They were pinned to the wall, and Jacob decided to approach the windows where he was able to see the plans more clearly. Jacob spent a few days studying the plan, just as he did with Mr Dickson, and was able to determine how the construction could progress.

Jacob was driven by the fact that he was not being paid after two weeks of being on-site and believed they might receive their salaries if they continued to work. "Not without Mr Fisher's authority and supervision," stated most of the workers on site. However, Jacob was able to convince and encourage a few of the masons to work under his supervision. "We have all the necessary materials on site, and I can translate the construction plan into building work," said Jacob. After a few discussions and further reassurances, about twenty masons started work under Jacob's supervision. These masons, just like Jacob, were not too afraid of Mr Fisher's ruthless response to their actions. They were driven by the hope that they would be paid for a job well done.

A week into Jacob's supervision, the masons had completed a section of the building to the roofing level. Although Jacob was confident that they had properly replicated the requirement from the plans onto the build, a few of the workers that did not join him were not so convinced. However, as Jacob decided to raise another section of the building to the roofing stage, a few of the doubtful workers reluctantly joined in the construction work. The majority of the workers were qualified masons with enough experience to build a complete structure. Their motivation to join Jacob in the following building phase was reliant on the fact that they approved the initial construction work supervised by Jacob. The qualified masons had their reservations because Jacob did not have the formal education required to read and interpret a construction plan. Nevertheless, they carried on for another one week before Mr Fisher arrived back on site.

With utter furiousness, Mr Fisher demanded why the workers had disobeyed his direct instructions to stop work. "It was Jacob, Mr Fisher," said the workers that refused to work with Jacob. "Who is Jacob?" shouted Mr Fisher. Jacob, unaware that Mr Fisher had returned was busy directing the construction of the build. He was then informed that Mr Fisher had returned and wanted him immediately. However, before Jacob could reach the office, Mr Fisher inspected the initial section of work done by Jacob and his crew. Jacob obviously thought that Mr Fisher was in his office and headed there and had to wait for him when he could not find him. A few moments later, Jacob could hear Mr Fisher walking back to his office. Although Jacob was confident that the work he had done met the requirements and the expected quality, he was, to some extent, concerned that he may have made some mistakes. After all, he was not even a qualified mason nor a civil engineer. "Where are my plans?" demanded Mr Fisher as he entered his office. He reached for his desktop drawers and took out a set of keys, which he used to open the doors of a cabinet. He shortly produced the rolled-up blueprints, which he spread out on his desk.

Jacob felt as though his heart was going to pop out of his chest when he realised that Mr Fisher had ignored the plans on the wall. "Are you Jacob?" asked Mr Fisher. Unable to utter a word, Jacob nodded. "Why did you disobey my direct instructions?" asked Mr Fisher. Jacob remained silent. Upon reviewing the construction plans on his desk, Mr Fisher demanded that Jacob accompany him to inspect his work. Jacob was reluctant as he knew he had used a completely different plan for the work he had done. Nevertheless, he must walk with Mr Fisher to do the inspection. After a few measurements, the walls were inspected with a spirit level, and angles were checked.

Mr Fisher still appeared angry and asked Jacob back to his office. "You must have used a plan for the work you have done. Where did you get your plan?" asked Mr Fisher. Jacob pointed at the plans on the wall. Before Mr Fisher could ask how he got into his office, Jacob explained that he could see them from the glass windows. "Well, yes, they are the replica of the construction plans," uttered Mr Fisher.

Instantaneously, Jacob uttered a sigh of relief. Jacob went on to explain how he had learnt the skills for understanding construction plans and project management from Mr Dickson. "Well done, I am proud of your courage and determination," said Mr Fisher, stretching out his hand to shake Jacob's.

CHAPTER TWELVE

A Trip to the Village

JACOB HAD REACHED THE age of twenty-five and had been working closely with Mr Fisher on various projects. He was given good feedback that led to him becoming a qualified mason. He later became a master mason and was subsequently promoted to site foreman. Jacob felt that he was getting somewhere in life with his advancement. He was beginning to realise that his future was going to be bright like he had imagined. He also thought that he had so far done well for a cursed child that had no education. However, thinking ahead, Jacob felt he was surrounded by a mixture of a positive and negative outlooks. He was not sure if this was as far as he could go without a formal education. On the other hand, he felt that there were greater opportunities ahead, and he just needed to be brave enough to do what would be required.

UNFORTUNATELY, BACK IN THE VILLAGE, Jacob's father had died. He had not reached his fiftieth birthday and had died of an unknown medical condition. Although Jacob had again secured a means of communication with his family after he had relocated to Warri, it still did take several weeks to deliver a message to Jacob. This was mainly because his family needed to wait until their friend, Mr Johnston, was able to visit them to hear the verbal message, which he then translated into a letter and posted to Jacob's construction site address. Jacob, upon receiving the message had to wait till he was able to find a trusted friend that could read the letter to him. Mr Fisher had become that trusted friend to Jacob. The relationship with Mr Fisher had grown out of necessity. He knew he could rely on Jacob to deliver the quality of work needed, and hence he was able to leave the site to attend to other matters, including travelling overseas to be with his family. Through the friendship, Jacob was able to learn to understand the spoken English language. He was also able to speak, although not as fluently and would often overlap his sentences with the Pidgin English language. Jacob had a letter that was delivered to him a few weeks back, but he had to wait on Mr Fisher to return from his trip to learn the content.

"I am so sorry, Jacob, but your father has died," said Mr Fisher after reading the letter. Jacob was surprised and saddened to hear the news of his father passing away. He then thought his father would have been buried already, as it had been over four weeks since the letter was written. "What are you going to do, Jacob?" asked Mr Fisher. He continued, "Please take as much time as you need to travel home and grieve for your father." The look on Jacob's face brought a realisation to Mr Fisher that Jacob would not be welcomed to his village because of the circumstances surrounding his birth. "Jacob, you and I will drive to Agbor, and we will find a way to your village from there," stated Mr Fisher.

Jacob could not believe what he was hearing. Arriving at his village with a British white man is something he could never imagine. The thought of that eased Jacob's pain about losing his father. However, he was unable to sleep that night as he thought about his father and continued to question his mind about the cause of his death. The main thought that came to Jacob's mind to answer that question was that his father was unable to handle the complexity and stress of marrying two wives. This was something that he felt he would never do.

It was on a Saturday morning, and Jacob was travelling with Mr Fisher in his official vehicle. They were being chauffeured by Mr Fisher's driver heading to Agbor. Jacob knew that there was no road that would allow vehicles to reach his village. He wondered if Mr

Fisher was going to walk the nearly two miles from the road to his village. They arrived at Agbor, and Mr Fisher needed to visit the British regional administrative office. After a brief meeting, they were ready to visit Jacob's village and see his mother and siblings. "Drive us as close as you can, and we will walk the rest of the way to the village," instructed Mr Fisher. "Let's go, Jacob, lead the way," he continued. They arrived at Jacob's family house after trekking for just under an hour. Jacob could not believe that he had brought a white man to his remote village.

A knock on the door on the family house attracted Jacob's sister, Anna, to the door. Jacob had not seen her for several years and was delighted to hug her and lifted her up in his arms. "You are grown and heavy; how are you, and where is Mother?" asked Jacob. Then his sister noticed the presence of Mr Fisher and ran back into the house. "Mama, Mama, come and see Jacob and a white man," she yelled. Jacob and Mr Fisher had now entered inside the house. "Please sit down," Jacob offered, pointing to the best seat he could find. This was the first time Jacob had visited his home for more than ten years, and he was surprised that nothing much had changed. "Jacob! Jacob!" His mother shouted with excitement as she ran towards the living room. Jacob embraced his mother and introduced her to Mr Fisher. "Good afternoon, Madam, and it is a pleasure to meet you," uttered Mr Fisher. Jacob had to translate Mr Fisher's pleasantry to his mother.

Jacob was taken to his father's grave, where he was left alone for some time. He later met with his younger brother and, after a few hours, was on his way back to Mr Fisher's vehicle. Mr Fisher was treated to Jacob's mother's fish pepper soup, which he thought was delicious. On their way back to Warri, Mr Fisher needed to pick up some supplies, and they had to stop at one of the markets in Boji-Boji, Agbor town. Jacob had stayed back with the chauffeur as Mr Fisher entered the market to buy his supplies. Jacob decided to get out of the vehicle and take a brief walk before Mr Fisher returned. Then he came across a girl, but he did not know where she came from. Unaware that

Jacob was staring at her, she walked up to a woman that seemed to be her mother. "Cecilia, come on, let's head home," instructed the woman. The girl, Cecilia, could not be older than fourteen years of age, Jacob thought. This was the first time that Jacob had noticed any girl that he had liked and was inclined to get to know her. Just as Cecilia and her mother were leaving, they waved at the butcher whose shop they had visited. "We will see you in a week's time," said Cecilia's mother.

It was a few weeks after Jacob had visited his village. He wondered if some people around and within his village may have seen him and Mr Fisher. He thought that he might not be recognised easily as he must have aged over the last ten years he had been away. Jacob never stopped thinking about Cecilia and was hoping he could visit the butcher's shop to gather any useful information about where to find her. However, he felt he needed to have a place of his own and stop living on construction sites. A few months later, Jacob was able to secure rented accommodation in the township of Warri. The commute to work was not much of a problem as it was only two miles from the current project site, and he had always walked.

"Jacob, I think it is time you handled a project by yourself from start to finish," expressed Mr Fisher. Jacob was surprised that Mr Fisher thought he was ready to handle a project by himself. Although he was not sure if that would be too much of a responsibility given that he could not read and write. "Are you sure I am ready to take on projects by myself?" Jacob asked Mr Fisher. "Oh yes, you are ready, Jacob," reassured Mr Fisher. They discussed the challenges posed by Jacob's lack of education. Mr Fisher then spent a few hours explaining to Jacob how education is not only about the ability to read and write. He told him that although being able to read and write remains a necessary element of education, he went on to say that the most important of all is the knowledge one possesses and the ability to express it in a meaningful way to make a difference.

As part of Mr Fisher's wider portfolio of construction in the area, Jacob was assigned a building project. He was provided with the funds to procure the materials and equipment required for the project. Jacob selected his crew from the workforce he had known and trusted, and he was able to start the project as scheduled. He expected Mr Fisher to visit for inspections, but he never came. Although he continued to see Mr Fisher but only as a friend, and they never discussed the project.

Jacob completed the project and commissioned the handover a couple of weeks earlier than scheduled. The building was accepted by the authorities as satisfactory. This was Jacob's first of many projects as a subcontractor to Mr Fisher. He had also made some profit which he thought would come into good use soon. With Mr Fisher's advice, Jacob was registered as a builder with the regional authorities.

CHAPTER THIRTEEN

Cecilia

IT WAS ON A SUNDAY MORNING, and Jacob was free all day, and he decided to rest and take the time to think about his life so far, as well as try to plan for the future. He was in his one-bedroom rented accommodation when he heard a knock on the door. He wondered who it could be. Reluctantly, he walked to the door and opened it. Two women holding leaflets and bibles greeted Jacob with a smile. "We are from the God's Kingdom Society, GKS." After an hour of lecturing Jacob with the words of God through the views of the GKS doctrine, he was asked to attend church the following Sunday. The God's Kingdom Society 'GKS' was a breakaway church from the Watchtower Society, a branch of Jehovah's Witnesses. However, after a while, Jacob had to switch to the Watchtower Society, where he became a member of the Jehovah's Witnesses. Jacob found a renewed faith in God through Jehovah's Witnesses and was able to learn the content of the Bible, which also helped in improving his general knowledge and wisdom.

"My name is Jacob, and I wanted to ask you if you know where I can find Cecilia," Jacob asked the butcher. "I have seen you before, you visited the market with a white man a few months back, and you were staring at Cecilia" uttered the butcher. He continued, "My name is Martin the Butcher, I sell the best quality beef in this town, and I know everyone that eats meat." Jacob thought Martin was friendly and he could get somewhere if he was lucky. Before Jacob could utter another word, Martin asked, "What do you do, and who are your parents?" Jacob explained he was a builder based in Warri. He then expressed his intention to find Cecilia and wanted to know if she would marry him.

Martin could not help himself but to laugh at Jacob. "Cecilia is only fourteen, and she is the backbone of her family," stated Martin. Jacob did not understand what he meant but was not going to ask the butcher to explain why he would refer to a woman as a bone. "Where can I find her?" Jacob asked. "You don't find her; you find me; I am her relative," stated Martin. He continued by telling Jacob that Cecilia was the first child of her parents' five children and worked to help provide for her family. In summary, Martin was telling Jacob that it was impossible to marry Cecilia because her family needed her. "If you wait long enough, Cecilia will be here, she works for me a few hours every day, and you can say hello to her," offered Martin.

A few hours later, Jacob sighted Cecilia entering Matin's shop. He watched from a distance and noticed that she was listening to what Martin was saying. A few moments later, she was carrying a tray on her head and walking away from Martin's shop. Jacob was not sure what to do and decided to follow Cecilia without her knowing. Cecilia helped Martin to sell beef in the Market by taking the products to those that may not have the chance to visit the butcher's shop. This tactic ensured that Martin was able to sell as much beef as possible in a day.

Cecilia returned after a couple of hours, and she was paid by Martin. She received some beef and cash and she left. Martin noticed Jacob's intent to follow Cecilia and he called him into his shop. "You, young man, you stay here and wait for me. I need to have a word with you," stated Martin. It was after Martin had finished serving his last customer for the day that he spoke with Jacob. He had asked Jacob to return the following Sunday with a friend. Why come with a friend, Jacob thought in silence. Jacob departed for Warri but not after seeing Mr Johnston to get feedback on how his family was doing. He also told Mr Johnston about Cecilia.

Jacob was attending his bible study class at the Watchtower Society when he spoke of his intentions of marrying Cecilia. "You will have to marry from the church," said one of the elders. "Surely she could convert to be a Jehovah's Witness?" interrupted another elder. Jacob explained that he wanted to know if she would be welcomed to the church if they were married. Unfortunately, Cecilia would have to become a member of the Jehovah's Witnesses before he could marry her. Jacob decided to speak to Mr Fisher, who advised that it would be wise to wait until Cecilia agreed to marry him before involving the church. "She has not even met you yet, Jacob," uttered Mr Fisher. As instructed, the following Sunday, Jacob was on his way to Boji-Boji, Agbor with a close friend, Jonathan. Jonathan had been a friend of Jacob since he arrived in Warri as a mason's apprentice. They were to meet Martin at his home after church. Jacob had no knowledge of the church where Martin worshipped. He was sure of one thing, though; he would win the heart of Cecilia at all costs.

Although Martin had not made it obvious, he did have a warm feeling towards Jacob. As a result, he had spoken to Cecilia's parents on his behalf and informed them that Jacob would be visiting Sunday afternoon. He had also informed Cecilia of Jacob's intentions, to which she expressed her utter refusal from the onset. "Cecilia, you must wait to meet the young man first before you can refuse his intentions," stated Cecilia's father. Although Cecilia was aware that the decision to marry Jacob rested with her parents. Overall, Cecilia was not interested in getting married and had no inclination of living with a stranger. She would be turning fifteen in a few months' time, yet she had not thought of marriage even though she was aware that most girls marry at the age of fifteen and sixteen. Cecilia had discussed Jacob's intention with her close friends, and none of them seemed to support the proposal.

Jacob was heading back to Warri with his friend, Jonathan after Cecilia had categorically refused his proposal of marriage. She was not interested, and this was made very clear to Jacob. "You are not going to just give up because she kept saying she was not interested, are you?" asked Jonathan. "She is a Catholic and that makes it harder," said Jacob. Jacob could see the strength and stubbornness that Cecilia possessed. He knew that she would be a wise and strong wife and thought that they could be very happy together. He just needed her to change her mind and agree to marry him. Jacob was not sure if Cecilia's family and, indeed, Martin knew of his birth circumstances. He thought that if they did, it would surely go against him.

It was three years after the first meeting with Cecilia that a traditional marriage date between her and Jacob was set. In those three years, Jacob had won the heart of Cecilia. Cecilia's father was a carpenter and worked for the local council. He obviously shared a construction background with Jacob, and they had many conversations about building projects around the region. Jacob was spending most of his Sundays after worshipping at the Watchtower Society at Agbor, at Cecilia's home. Cecilia's parents knew of the difference in their religions but was willing to accept Jacob. "I am allowing you to marry my daughter because I can see that you are hardworking and honest; you are an ambitious man," said Cecilia's father. Like Jacob, Cecilia was never sent to school as her parents believed it was not necessary for a woman to gain any form of education. She was also required to support her poor household, as her father's income was not sufficient to care for a large and growing family. Jacob felt sorry for Cecilia regarding her lack of education, as he knew the importance of being able to read and write. Nevertheless, he could not be happier that Cecilia had agreed to marry him at last.

After the traditional marriage, Cecilia moved to Warri to live with her husband. However, it became obvious that the one-bedroom accommodation was not going to be ideal. Cecilia started almost immediately to generate income from the sales of firewood and other petty food stuff trading. Several months later, Jacob and Cecilia moved into a two-bedroom apartment. Cecilia being an affectionate person, decided that it would be beneficial to Jacob if his mother was living with them. Although Jacob's mother had gone on to have an additional daughter with another man, all her children, apart from Noah, were married and no longer living in the village. Jacob thought of his mother's pet goat. "There would be no space for the goat in this apartment," uttered Jacob. A few months later, Jacob's mother and his brother were living with them. Their landlord was kind enough to allow them to build a pen for the goat within the compound.

Cecilia was supportive and cooperative at all levels, which meant that she was willing to give up her religion and later became a member of the Jehovah's Witnesses. After a while, every member of the family, excluding the goat, was worshipping at the Watchtower Society every Sunday. They would also attend bible studies on some weekdays in the evening. In addition, Jacob and Cecilia were also required to knock on doors to preach the bible. For Jacob, being close to God was a fulfilment that he had always sought to achieve. He started to use his time in church to express his gratitude to God for sparing his life through the King. He would also thank God for the presence of Cecilia in his life, as she had turned out to be all that he ever wanted for a wife.

CHAPTER FOURTEEN

The Children

IT WAS IN THE EARLY month of May 1957, and the rainy season had already started in Nigeria. An early harvest of corn was a sign that there had been abundant rain, which had helped the farmers with crop enrichment and quality produce. Cecilia loved fresh corn and preferred them roasted. Cecilia was nine months pregnant, and she knew that she could give birth anytime soon. On this particular afternoon, she had eaten too many roasted corns than she could care to count. She was becoming fed up with the pregnancy, and it was leading to her being irritable. However, just as she was about to go and feed the goat with the cob of the corn, she started to experience labour pains. At first, she thought she was having a reaction to eating too much corn, but then, her water broke.

Cecilia was nineteen years old, and this was her first pregnancy. Although this was going to be her first experience of giving birth, she had witnessed and assisted her mother during birth labours that led to the delivery of some of her siblings. So, she thought that she could understand some of the challenges along the process of giving birth. Her mother had only just delivered a baby boy three months ago. The baby was the eighth child and the seventh pregnancy of her mother. Her mother did go on to have one more baby.

Realising that her water had broken was confirmation to Cecilia that her first baby was coming. Who would have thought that eating too much corn could have such an impact, she thought. Although her mother lived about seventy-five miles away and was unable to be at

Cecilia's side during her first birth labour, Jacob's mother was available and was ready to provide all the necessary support and comfort needed. Cecilia recalled her labour as being short, and a beautiful baby girl was born just a few hours after her water had broken.

"The baby is too white for a black child," mentioned Jacob's mother. Cecilia never forgot the look on Jacob's face upon seeing how fair in complexion the baby was. "She is definitely our baby," Cecilia screamed at Jacob. As a result of the large number of British men living in the country due to colonisation, it was a known fact that many children were fathered by the 'white man'; indeed, Cecilia's grandmother was most likely to be mixed race because she looked almost white. Cecilia and nearly all of her siblings were fair in complexion, and the new baby certainly looked 'too white.' The thought of having the neighbours and the public gossiping about the legitimacy of Cecilia's newborn led to the idea of darkening the baby's skin. Different types of herbs were mixed with charcoal and applied to the baby. However, with time, they realised that none of their efforts to darken the complexion of the child worked. The baby was named Joyce.

Initially, Cecilia had struggled to conceive after moving in with her husband. However, she was not concerned that anything could be wrong. She was confident that they would get it right eventually. So, after the birth of their first child, Joyce, Cecilia became pregnant again within a few months, and a son was born. The baby was about the right or expected skin colour, and therefore, no one was asking any questions about legitimacy. The baby boy was called Michael. There was a gap of sixteen months between the two children. Looking after two children soon became a challenge for Cecilia, and the rented accommodation was becoming inconvenient. It was again only a few months later that Cecilia became pregnant for the third time.

For Jacob, the birth of his two children with another on the way made him realise that he needed to make some significant adjustments to his living arrangement. Together, Jacob and Cecilia had saved enough money to buy a plot of land to build a sizeable home for a large family. They both decided to buy a piece of land in a new neighbourhood that was strategically located not too far away from the township of Warri. It was on a Sunday evening, and their children were already in bed. Cecilia and Jacob decided to discuss the type of future they would like to have. Although Jacob was unable to read and write, he had been exposed to different standards of living due to his work, building homes and commercial structures for the elite. Jacob was aware that his clients sent their children to good schools in the country and, in some cases, to the United Kingdom and the United States. "I would like to see our children attending one of the best schools and, if possible, send them to America to further their studies; that is my dream," said Jacob. "I share the same dream as you, and it is good to think big Jacob, but we must work extremely hard," Cecilia responded.

A few months had passed since Jacob and Cecilia bought their plot of land, and they had completed the foundation of the building. Jacob had designed the plan for the building and sought Mr Fisher's approval before he started the construction. "Jacob, this is a fifteen-bedroom house complex project. Are you out of your mind?" asked Mr Fisher. He added, "Are you planning on having a battalion of children?" Jacob smiled at Mr Fisher's remark and went on to say that although they wanted a large family, they had not planned on having a battalion of children. He went on to clarify that his family will occupy the three-bedroom self-contained apartment, his mother and brother will be allocated a bedroom each, and the remaining ten bedrooms will be rented out. He added that the income generated from the rent would contribute towards their cost of living.

Mr Fisher was impressed with Jacob's ambition and the entrepreneurial spirit he has started to see in him since he married Cecilia. "I believe you and Cecilia will make a significant difference in your lives," commended Mr Fisher. It had been nearly six months since Nigeria gained its Independence from Britain, and Mr Fisher knew that he might be required to relinquish his position and return to the United Kingdom. He was also reaching retirement age and would not mind leaving, he thought. However, for some reason not clear to Mr Fisher, he felt that his relationship with Jacob would continue regardless of which country he resided in. He had enjoyed the support that he had received from Jacob, and he thought that his fearlessness to act would lead him to greater opportunities in life. He was convinced that Jacob would be a great man as he could see the resilience in him.

Jacob's commitment on other building projects constrained the time he was able to invest in his home building. However, he was able to employ a few trusted masons and carpenters who worked on the project. In addition, Jacob and Cecilia were able to work on their house project most evenings and weekends, and as a result, led to the completion of the three-bedroom apartment just in time for the third baby's arrival. Another baby boy with an attitude, Jacob thought as he kept them awake all night for the first few months. The new baby was called Matthew.

It was exactly fourteen months later, and Cecilia had given birth to their fourth child, another baby boy. The fourth baby was named Alexander. Raising four children became very challenging for Cecilia and Jacob, even with the support of Jacob's mother. It was then decided that Cecilia's younger sister would move in with them to help lighten the demand of caring for the four children. Tina, who was about eight years younger than Cecilia, departed Agbor, the seventy-five miles journey for Warri. She would live with Jacob and Cecilia for some years as part of the family. She was aware that Warri was a much more vibrant and developed city than Agbor. The promise of a better opportunity in Warri to live and maybe acquire modern career skills contributed to Tina's decision to move. The presence of Tina had also allowed Jacob to be able to leave his family to take on construction projects outside the area. Jacob had bought a much-needed vehicle, which he used to commute with his workers for the out-of-town projects.

It was the beginning of 1965, and Mr Fisher had returned home to the United Kingdom, but with the promise to Jacob that he would come back to visit them. "Jacob, promise me you will be a rich and humble man next time I see you," demanded Mr Fisher. Jacob and Cecilia knew they were able to get on well in life, but the idea of becoming rich was outside their imagination. "Send me a telegram when the baby arrives,' again demanded Mr Fisher. At this time, Cecilia was pregnant with her fifth child. "This will have to be the last of it," said Jacob. He was not sure that Cecilia was paying attention to him. Cecilia went on to have a sound baby boy. Jacob was delighted and did not forget to send the telegram to Mr Fisher. It read, "A baby Boy! No more." The new baby boy was called William.

It was the year 1966, and Cecilia was not pregnant. It was the first time in several years that she had not been pregnant. Cecilia shared the same vision with Jacob, not to have more children. They had five children, one girl and four boys, and that was enough, they agreed. The first two children had started primary school, and Tina's help had proved invaluable. Cecilia was then able to invest time to discuss projects with Jacob and helped him in making better decisions. Jacob was doing well, and the construction business was growing. However, the demand was becoming challenging to manage. Jacob decided to reach out to Mr Dickson for some advice on how to manage his orders. Luckily for Jacob, he had caught Mr Dickson just as he was preparing to leave the country due to the recall of all British expatriates still remaining in Nigeria. "Mr Dickson, why do you have to leave the country?" asked Jacob on the telephone. To speak to Mr Dickson on the telephone, Jacob had to first send a telegram informing him of a date and time he would call. Mr Dickson had travelled to the nearest Post Office and Telecommunication (P&T) location to take Jacob's call.

"The British government believes that the country is becoming unsafe due to a high possibility of a civil war," uttered Mr Dickson. He continued, "So we have been advised to leave the country as soon as we possibly can." Jacob, feeling concerned, had asked, "How can I help you?" Mr Dickson explained that it was best for him to leave the country. However, he would travel through Warri to visit Jacob and his family for a few days before he departed.

CHAPTER FIFTEEN

The Civil War

IT WAS IN THE EARLY months of the year 1967, and Jacob had expanded his construction business. He had registered his construction business with the Federal Government of Nigeria and was now a limited company. This meant he was authorised to handle State and Federal building projects. He had converted two bedrooms that were initially rented at his home into an office for his construction company. He had employed a secretary and accountant. He had also recruited an architect, two site foremen, and ten additional masons to the six he already had as salaried workers, and he had also increased his carpenters from four to eight. Jacob decided that he needed to retain the service of a legal firm to help him interpret the terms and conditions of contracts. He also created a team to seek, lobby, and tender for projects.

As a result of these changes and improvements, for the first time, Jacob was able to see how he could become a rich man. For a moment, he thought about his village intentions to kill him because he was born with a tooth. "Only if they could see me now," he said to himself. He also wished his father was alive to see what he had achieved. Jacob and his construction company were ranked as one of the best in the area. ".. And we have only just started," he said to Cecilia.

"I am pregnant," uttered Cecilia. Shocked by the news, Jacob asked, "I thought we had decided we did not have any more children?" Cecilia, who had only just found out that she was pregnant because of the recognised morning sickness and the absence of her period for several weeks, was not in a good mood. "In this case, what you say and do are just two different things," uttered Cecilia. "I am not looking forward to the inconvenience of carrying another pregnancy," she continued. "Do not worry; we will get through it as always," said Jacob as he hugged Cecilia to reassure her. Cecilia knew that to grow the business, Jacob needed to take on projects far from their local area. The challenges of not having Jacob around during her pregnancy was something that did not excite her. However, her ailing mother-in-law had always provided much-needed support, and Tina remained a lifeline. Unfortunately for Jacob and Cecilia, Tina would be married in a few months' time and would be leaving to make a home with her new husband. Cecilia knew she had to find a way to adapt.

IT WAS JULY OF 1967, and the war between Nigeria and the acclaimed Biafra Republic had started. Although the build-up to the war had started a few years earlier, it was greatly intensified towards the last quarter of 1966. Jacob never thought his area would be affected. "The war will be fought in the acclaimed Biafra lands, and we are in Nigeria, so we have nothing to worry about," boasted Jacob. He was able to reassure his family to remain calm and carry on as normal. He also continued to work on his various projects across the Nigeria south region and was mindfully preventing travels into the southeast bordering the Biafra area. Even when the Nigerian military was operating in the Nigerian southeast bordering Biafra lands, Jacob carried on travelling to work on his project with his workers but had always returned home at the weekends to be with his family.

It was a Monday morning in October, three months into the war and Jacob had left home early to visit one of his project sites. The journey would take him about two hours' drive, heading east toward the bordering area with Biafra. Jacob was building a low-cost housing estate for the for the Nigerian government in the area. The project had started in January of 1966 with a completion date of November 1967. Although travelling from home to the project site had become intense since the civil war had started, nevertheless, Jacob did not envisage he could be in any danger. As he approached the town where his project was sited, he noticed a strong presence of the Nigerian military. They were carrying out a search operation looking for the Biafran soldiers, who they believed had crossed over into the region with the intent to ambush the Nigerian military.

Jacob was following the slow-moving traffic as they approached the Nigerian Army checkpoint. There were many military personnel and vehicles parked on both sides of the road, and the traffic seemed to be moving only eastbound. Jacob had not seen such military build-up in the area before and wondered what could have caused the traffic westbound to cease. He needed to know that he would be able to return to his family at the weekend or whenever he saw fit. So, he decided to ask one of the military operatives walking alongside the slow-moving traffic. "Good morning, officer; why are there no vehicles returning and heading west?" The officer responded that they had stopped all movements and travels from the eastern region towards the west. "For how long?" asked Jacob. "For as long as it takes to identify and kill all the Biafran militias that have already crossed over into this territory," replied the officer.

The thought of not returning home to his family at the weekend weighed heavily on Jacob's mind, as did the thoughts of the consequences of not being at the construction site for a while. He reassured himself that he had his foreman on site already and that he would be able to carry on with the project without him. So, Jacob decided it would be best for him to abandon that week's travel to the site and head home. He would then try again the following Monday. He knew his workers would be alright at the project sites across the region as they all lived on construction locations and had enough food to last for a few weeks. He was also aware that he would have to reach the workers to either provide them with additional food supplies or ask them to abandon the sites and return home for their own safety if the military intensified their search and hold operations.

Jacob decided to turn his vehicle around and head home. He started to manoeuvre his vehicle from the tightly sandwiched position to head westbound, and the movement alerted a few of the Nigerian soldiers. Jacob was quickly surrounded by the soldiers with their rifles aimed at him. "Stop!" demanded one of the soldiers, pointing his gun at Jacob and, with his finger on the trigger, ready to squeeze it. "Raise your hands up and keep them up!" instructed another military officer. Jacob complied while remaining inside the car. He was not sure why they had the sudden desire to restrict him. Although Jacob had instantly become anxious at the sight of five soldiers threatening to shoot him, he knew that the issue would be quickly resolved, and he would be allowed to head home once they realised he was not a Biafran.

Jacob was asked to get out of the car, and while he was being searched, one of the soldiers asked, "Where were you going?" Jacob explained the reason he had decided to turn back, but they decided not to believe him. "Why did you suddenly decide to turn back to avoid the search?" asked the soldier. He continued, "Everyone that is on the road must be searched and their tribe and identity verified." Jacob's vehicle was also searched, but they could not find any evidence that could tie him to the war. The military demanded his vehicle particulars and his driving license, which Jacob provided, but it was not enough to satisfy them that Jacob was innocent of their suspicions. "You are a Biafran; otherwise, you did not have to turn back to avoid the check," stated the soldier. Jacob was informed that he would be arrested and taken to their head office to be interrogated, and a trial in the military court would take place. Jacob could not believe what was happening to him. "You can take me to any of my building sites, and my workers can identify me," uttered Jacob. Unfortunately, everything Jacob was saying from there forward was ignored.

Jacob had arrived at the regional military headquarters not too far from where he was arrested. He was confined at the back of the army truck with about twenty other men suspected to be Biafran militias or informants. As Jacob and the other men were paraded through the compounds of the military base heading towards a holding cell, they experienced an execution of about fifteen men. "That will be you in a few days," uttered one of the army officers escorting them to a cell. Jacob could not believe he had worked so hard only to be wrongly accused of being a traitor and be executed. Three days later, the military Judges had listened to their cases, and each one of the men were pronounced guilty as charged. "You planned to destroy Nigeria by choosing the side of Biafra, now your luck has run out, and you will pay for your crimes," stated the main Judge. He continued, "You are now sentenced to death by firing squad."

The thought of dying by firing squad had remained on Jacob's mind for the following two days that he was in the cell awaiting execution. He realised that no one knew where he was, and news of his death would be unknown to his family. Jacob thought about his remains after the execution and wondered if the military would release his corpse to his family. Although he had always felt close to death as he was growing up, he never imagined that he would be frightened when the time came for real. He had been in the cell for five days, and they had been fed once a day. They received a portion of bread and water. Jacob had hardly slept since he had been arrested and was constantly thinking about his family. He remembered the joy he felt seeing Cecilia and the children when he returned home from his trips. He also wondered if he had remained as a rubber tapper and whether he would have avoided this unjust death at just forty-one years old. All the same, he knew that his time had run out, as he suspected that the execution would take place in a day or two.

It was Saturday morning, and Cecilia was surprised that Jacob had not returned. He would normally return on Friday evening, she thought. Tina was leaving that weekend to join her new husband, and Cecilia wanted Jacob to be available to present her with a gift and say thank you. Cecilia thought she would handle the gift presentation and that she and Jacob would have to visit her together on a weekend for him to formally express his gratitude.

It was lunchtime, and the children had thanked Tina and bid her goodbye. Jacob's mother was able to express her appreciation to Tina on behalf of Jacob. Saying goodbye to her sister was a daunting task for Cecilia. She could not imagine life without her for the last few years. She was also excited for Tina when she told her that she was pregnant. She would be giving birth a few months after Cecilia's due date. It was nearly dinner time, and there was still no sign of Jacob. Cecilia had started to suspect that something must have happened to Jacob, but she just had no way of finding out neither did she know how to go about helping him if he was in trouble.

CHAPTER SIXTEEN

The Execution

IT WAS ON TUESDAY EARLY in the morning, and Jacob was woken up by a loud noise. It had been eight days since Jacob was seized by the Military and about five days since he had been waiting for his execution. It was dark, and Jacob was not able to see what the noise was. "Did you hear that?" he asked, hoping that the other men in the cell had heard the loud noise. "What noise?" responded one of the inmates. "I heard a noise, and I think it is the wind blowing down the execution platform," uttered another inmate. "Our execution will be delayed further then," said another. "This is not a joke; I am innocent and should not be here," Jacob said. "I am innocent too; I know nothing about Biafra, and I have never met anyone of them," said another man. "Excuse me, are we not all innocents?" one of the inmates that had hardly spoken asked. He continued, "I have not heard any one of you speak the language of Biafra, so we are not one of them, so why would we help them?" Then they heard the noise again.

The Biafran military had advanced their position to push the Nigerian army west of their borders but had met fierce resistance. The loud noise heard by Jacob and the inmates were bombs launched at the Biafran positions. At sunrise, it became obvious that the Nigerian army had eliminated the threat posed by the Biafran military in the near region. However, they had also lost a significant number of soldiers that were ambushed by the Biafran militias. Returning to the military base after the operation with the dead bodies of their battalion comrades, the Nigerian army was in no sympathetic mood to their prisoners. They attacked the prisoners, beating them with their guns and helmets. "You will soon be executed," uttered one of the soldiers. He continued, "You are all lucky that the chief commandant has been absent on leave." Jacob knew that without the chief commandant of the military base, no execution order could be given. He realised he would have been dead already if he had been on the base. "When will he be back?" Jacob muttered to himself. All the same, he knew his living days were numbered.

It had been nearly two weeks since Jacob left his family home to visit his project sites. Heavily pregnant, Cecilia had run out of patience and decided to seek help. She decided to approach some of Jacob's previous clients that lived in the area. With their help, a search for Jacob was initiated. Information received from all of Jacob's project sites revealed that the last time he was on site was about three weeks ago. A trip to the police stations confirmed that Jacob was not on their arrest lists but had advised that the Nigerian military had been carrying out operations to arrest Biafran informants and supporters in bordering regions. Cecilia was not interested in that information as she knew Jacob was not a Biafran informant or a militia. A few days into the search, Cecilia was beginning to feel the stress and pain of achieving no credible information regarding Jacob's whereabouts. Although she was concerned about her pregnancy, she knew she had to carry on searching for her husband.

It was a few days later, and Cecilia, with the help of Jacob's mother, were preparing breakfast for the five children as they were not at school because of the intensifying war. "Cecilia! Cecilia!" Shouted one of their tenants. "It has been announced on the radio that the Nigerian army had captured many Biafran informants and militias," he continued. Before Cecilia could digest the information, he carried on. "The radio said that the military has executed many of the captured informants and militias, and they are still holding about twenty men, which they arrested three weeks ago and are awaiting execution." Cecilia was not sure why their tenant thought that such news of captured informants and militias would be of interest to her. "The radio mentioned that there were abandoned vehicles where the Nigerian military had captured some of the informants and militias and one of the registration numbers they read out was Jacob's pickup truck," said the tenant. "The military must have arrested Jacob," he continued.

The realisation that Jacob could be in the captivity of the Nigerian military for being a Biafran informant or militia did not make any sense to Cecilia. Jacob was well known in the region as a builder, she thought to herself. She knew that Jacob could still be alive, according to the radio, and she knew she must act fast to do whatever she could to save her husband's life. Cecilia immediately thought of the church, The Watchtower Society. Could they accompany her to the military base to prove Jacob's innocence? She thought. Cecilia explained her plan to Jacob's mother and sought the assistance of the tenant to help see it through. After a brief prayer, the church leader assigned two preachers to accompany Cecilia and her tenant to the military base. The trip to the military base was a challenging one. There were roadblocks and army checkpoints at nearly every mile. It was only because of Cecilia's condition that they were allowed through the checkpoints.

The captives at the military base could hear the talk amongst their guards that the chief commandant was due to arrive in the afternoon. This information was not the best news for Jacob, but he knew that the time would come eventually. The prisoners, including Jacob, were able to hear and see the preparation being made to welcome the chief commandant. "Do you think they will carry out the execution today?" Jacob asked the other prisoners. There was an instant silence as three soldiers armed with rifles were seen approaching their cell. The cell was a makeshift wooden barricade with a zinc roof. There were about two-inch gaps in the barricade, perhaps to allow for air circulation. The door, which was about five feet wide and six feet high, was made of wooden bars with about three-inch gaps. Although the cell may not withstand the strength of the twenty-men prisoners if they decided to break out, they knew that they were surrounded by armed soldiers, and they would be shot if they tried to escape.

The three approaching soldiers reached the wooden door of the cell and stopped. "Let them all out," said one of the soldiers. "You are going to tidy up the base as quickly as possible," continued the soldier. One of the areas that they had to tidy up was the execution point. There were two steel oil barrels filled with sand, one laid on top of the other, and there was a wooden pole measuring about six by four inches in thickness and nearly as tall as the height of the two steel oil barrels. There were eight of these, as counted by Jacob. The thought of eight men being executed at once led him to question in what order it would take place and whether he would be the first or second set of eight or amongst the remaining four. Jacob had now come to the realisation that any chance of him being rescued was lost, as it was now too late for him to be saved. As they tidied closer to the main entrance of the military base, Jacob thought he could hear a voice he recognised.

Cecilia, accompanied by her tenant and two of their church preachers, were at the entrance gate of the Nigerian military base. "We are sorry, but you are not allowed into the military base," uttered the security army personnel at the entrance gate. "You are holding my husband here, and he is not a Biafran, and we are here to prove it," said Cecilia. "Woman, you look like you will be having that baby any minute, and I suggest you go home as you will not be allowed in," said the security guard. "I am not leaving here without my husband; his name is Jacob," uttered Cecilia. The soldier continued, "We will have to remove you from the gate as we are expecting our chief commandant, and he will be approaching this entrance gate soon, so you must leave immediately." The preachers tried to reason with the army guard at the entrance gate but to no avail. "Jacob! Jacob! Shouted Cecilia with the anticipation that Jacob would hear her.

The tidying up of the military base compound was complete, and the group of prisoners were escorted back into their cell. Jacob was convinced that he had heard a voice that resonated with him but could not imagine that any of his family would dare to come to the gate of the military base. After all, he did not think that they would know he was even there. It was nearly four o'clock in the afternoon, and there was tension in the military base as they prepared to welcome the chief commandant back to his post. There had been a delay to his arrival as he was expected by two o'clock in the afternoon. There was an alert order for attention that came through the lone loudspeaker in the military base, and every soldier had to dash to their posts and official welcoming positions. The double-gated entrance into the military base swung open as a convoy of military vehicles emerged and sped their way to the office building. The Nigerian flag, which was flying at half-mast, was quickly raised to full-mast position as the chief commandant's vehicle door was opened by a soldier. The chief commandant emerged from the vehicle and stood at attention, and extended his right hand to his forehead to reciprocate a salute from the major. He later proceeded into his office, where he was being briefed on the progress of the battalion.

It was six o'clock in the evening, and the chief commandant had signed the execution order, which must be carried out with immediate effect. As the head and commanding officer of the one thousand two hundred strong battalion unit in the area, he was required to witness any execution being conducted in his military base. "Say your last prayers," uttered a soldier guarding the cell where Jacob and the other men were imprisoned. Jacob immediately started to pray but was interrupted as the cell door was opened, and they were asked to fall into line and head toward the execution point. Jacob thanked the other prisoners for their companionship and said, "We may well meet again together in heaven." Jacob noticed he was in the eleventh position as they marched them toward the execution point. "Keep moving," shouted the army officer escorting them. They arrived at the firing squad area, where they stopped. Then the first eight men were escorted to the position where they were tied to the wooden pole. They were facing a squad of ten soldiers with their rifles standing beside them as they stood at attention. Behind the firing squad soldiers was the major, who then alerted the chief commandant that he was ready for his inspection.

After walking about a metre from each of the eight prisoners, the commandant was satisfied and gave the order to proceed with the execution. Jacob closed his eyes as he heard the noise of several gunshots killing all eight prisoners. Jacob knew he was next. The prisoners were certified dead and were untied and removed from the firing line. The following eight men, including Jacob, were asked to move towards the firing line, and they were tied to the wooden poles. The chief commandant was again signalled to conduct his check. Jacob was tied to the third pole and was looking up into the overcast skies.

The chief commandant walked past Jacob heading to the fourth pole but then decided to return to him. "What is your name?" the commandant asked. "My name is Jacob Okwueze Oriahi," uttered Jacob in a trembling voice. "You are Jacob Oriahi, the builder, a native of Alihagwu in the Agbor region?" he asked again. Jacob, now looking directly into the eyes of the chief commandant, acknowledged he was indeed Jacob Oriahi from Alihagwu. "I know this man; untie him and take him to my office," instructed the chief commandant to the major. As Jacob sat and waited in the chief commandant's office, he heard the sound of multiple gunshots, and about fifteen minutes later, there was another.

CHAPTER SEVENTEEN

The Move

ALTHOUGH REMOVED FROM THE military entrance gate just in time for the chief commandant to arrive, Cecilia, her tenant and the two preachers returned and continued to demand the release of Jacob. "This pregnant woman, you are back again; return home!" Shouted the soldier guarding the entrance gate. He continued, "If your husband is inside here as a condemned Biafran militia or informant, then they will be executed shortly." A few moments later, they heard the sound of multiple gun shorts, then another, and another. "That's it, done!" uttered the soldier. Cecilia was confused but did not believe that Jacob was shot. "He is innocent, and you could not have shot him," said Cecilia. Then she shouted, "Jacob! Jacob!"

Cecilia continued to shout out the name of Jacob until a high-ranking officer who had witnessed the execution approached the entrance gate and asked one of the soldiers to provide an explanation as to what was going on. "Sir, there is a pregnant woman outside claiming that we are holding her innocent husband here," replied the soldier. He continued, "She says his name is Jacob." Cecilia carried on shouting for Jacob, which the officer could now hear. "Open the gate and let her in at once!" instructed the officer. The officer was surprised to see how heavily pregnant Cecilia was. He also noticed she was looking exhausted and frustrated yet determined. Cecilia and her aids were welcomed inside the military base and were offered refreshments. "I don't need any refreshment; I want to see my husband

and take him home," Cecilia demanded. Without uttering any further words, the officer excused himself.

A few moments later, but what seemed like an hour to Cecilia and her group, the chief commandant could be seen walking towards them. As he approached them, he called out Cecilia's name. Cecilia took a brief look at him and shouted, "Uncle Michael?" The chief commandant proceeded to hug Cecilia, and she broke down crying on his shoulders. "They are holding my husband, Jacob; please ask them to let him go," cried Cecilia. "Yes, we have Jacob, and he is getting ready to be released," replied the chief commandant. He continued, "It was a mistake that he was arrested." In a brief moment, Jacob emerged from the chief commandant's office. He was dressed in borrowed clothing that belonged to the chief commandant and was wearing a pair of military boots. It was getting dark, but Cecilia could see Jacob clearly. She noticed that he had lost a significant amount of weight and was looking dazed. "Jacob!" Cecilia called and ran towards him. She embraced him as she started to cry again. Jacob remained speechless as he could barely produce the strength needed to hold Cecilia.

The chief commandant requested for his vehicle convoy and informed Cecilia that he would be driving them home and would provide round-the-clock military protection for her family. "We will recover Jacob's vehicle, and I will have two armed officers protect him as he goes about his business in the region and beyond," uttered the chief commandant. "We will also station a couple of soldiers at your home for the protection of your family," he continued. Cecilia was thankful to her uncle. As the convoy of military vehicles headed out of the base, the chief commandant expressed his sadness regarding what had happened to Jacob. He carried on by offering his apologies for not attending their marriage ceremony. "I am looking forward to meeting the children; I hope they will not be asleep by the time we arrive," expressed the chief commandant. Jacob then broke his silence. "You have never mentioned that you had an uncle in the military, Cecilia," he said.

It had been nearly a week since Jacob returned from the military captivity. He had rested and had started to regain his weight. Although he was yet to visit his project sites, he had been informed that they had carried on working and were making progress in line the with the schedule. Noah, Jacob's brother, who had been working for the company for the past five years as a project coordinator, had ensured that all construction activities carried on smoothly during his brother's absence. After consulting with Cecilia, Jacob would be visiting Agbor to acquire a plot of land where they would build another home. Upon visiting all his projects in the region and ensuring that all was going well, Jacob and his security guards headed for Agbor. The military security meant that they were able to progress the journey through all checkpoints without any difficulties. Jacob managed to secure a piece of land and was quick to commission the building project.

Jacob had agreed with Cecilia that they would relocate to Agbor, where they would have more freedom and peace to raise the children and be safe. They agreed that the war had made it almost impossible to operate freely with ease of mind. Although Jacob had narrated his military captivity experience in detail to Cecilia, he had refused to speak about it again to anybody. The relocation to Agbor would take place as soon as the build was completed. Jacob had drafted the best of his workers to the Agbor house building project to ensure that it was completed in record time. To guarantee this, there were more workers, and they were also working on weekends. Jacob also planned to relocate the running of his construction company to Agbor. Noah, who had a wife and four daughters, had also agreed to relocate to Agbor. Noah's wife had only conceived two pregnancies; she had a daughter just after Cecilia had her fourth child and then a set of triplets twenty months later. Jacob promised to build a house at Agbor for Noah as part of his relocation package.

It was late October, and the war had been going on for just over four months, and it felt like they had only just started. Cecilia had maintained contact with her uncle, Michael, and she and Jacob were provided with progress updates regarding the war. The Biafran military had dug in to protect their declared breakaway territories from Nigeria at all costs. Their relentless resistance continued to cause headaches and pain for the Nigerian government. The Nigerian military advancements were quickly rebuffed by the Biafran army and militias. This had led to the deployment of extra reinforcements and brutal tactics, including blockade to starve the Biafran army to surrender. This had intensified the fighting in areas bordering the Biafra-claimed territories, such as Warri, where Jacob and his family resided and worked. Therefore, relocating to Agbor, which distanced the borders of the Biafra territories by around forty to sixty miles, seemed like a safe option to avoid becoming a victim of the war. Cecilia could no longer withstand the increasing frequencies of the sound of bombardment and gunshots, so she had decided to pack the family's belongings and was ready to leave at any moment.

It was November of that year, and Cecilia knew she had exceeded the full term of the pregnancy. She was aware that her water could break at any time, and the baby would be born. However, she was hoping that she would not go into labour until after they arrived at Agbor, where she would have the freedom to give birth at a hospital and have access to proper postnatal care. Jacob and the family decided to leave Warri on the fifth day of November for Agbor. The house at Agbor was almost complete but needed the electrical work to be finished in perhaps a couple of days. They would have to manage without electricity for a few days at Agbor as long as they left Warri before the window of opportunity to do so closed. The family arrived at Agbor safely with their military security provided by Cecilia's uncle. It was on the ninth of November, and Cecilia gave birth to a baby girl. There were no complications, and the baby and mother were fine. Jacob always made a conscious effort to check if the newborn babies had a tooth, and this birth was no exception. The baby girl was named Azuka.

Being away from what seemed like a battlefield brought so much relief to Jacob and Cecilia. They both had time to reflect on what had happened to them since they were married. They recounted their achievements and their traumas. They decided to agree that they were blessed, especially with the arrival of a beautiful daughter. Jacob thought about his ageing mother, Margaret. He knew that she was happy to have returned to Agbor. It was not her home village, but it was only about five miles away. She had informed Jacob that she would want to visit the village at some point, but Jacob was not sure if it was a good idea. He thought about the challenges his parents had to go through because he was born with a tooth.

He recalled all the attempts to kill him and the fact that he was seen as a curse to the village's progress and existence. "Jacob, you are now a much stronger man, indeed a successful man; you must return to the village and show them what you have become," advised Jacob's mother. "I hear you, Mama, but I need to think about it and come up with a good plan," replied Jacob. "What plan?" asked his mother. Jacob explained that he had heard that no progress of any kind had reached the village and wondered if they were right that he brought them a curse. "You left the village a long time ago, Jacob, and they should have progressed if they were destined to, so do not blame yourself for their lack of development," his mother reassured him.

CHAPTER EIGHTEEN

Dealing with the Curse

IT WAS THE FIRST CHRISTMAS at the new house, and all the extended family decided to use the opportunity to visit Jacob and Cecilia to welcome them back to Agbor. Cecilia had settled in well and was delighted that she was no longer pregnant. She was pleased that her parents, siblings, and friends were close by in comparison to the seventy-mile journey to Warri. She could drop in to see her parents daily as they lived less than a quarter of a mile away. The children had started school in the area and were making new friends. Cecilia and Jacob felt they had made the right decision to relocate to Agbor, where there was hardly any evidence of the civil war. Everyone was carrying on as normal in the region, and commerce continued to thrive. However, Jacob knew that he had to deal with the situation surrounding his birth in his village. He had agreed on a plan with Cecilia and his mother.

Jacob's construction business was doing well, and the building of a three-story office block had been commissioned. Jacob had designed the structure, which would also consist of living accommodations that would be rented. The construction for Noah's five-bedroom residence had also started on a purchased piece of land just behind Jacob's home. Jacob had become too busy to drive himself, and a chauffeur was employed. Cecilia also had a car and a chauffeur. Jacob had bought more vehicles required to aid the construction business so as not to rely on hiring. Therefore, he was able to set his own schedules for transporting building materials to project sites. In all, Jacob's mother was amazed to see her son, having defied death on several occasions, had become a rich and important person in society. Jacob was quickly becoming the richest man in the region. However, for Jacob, lacking education had continued to limit his ability to achieve more. In an effort to try to address this, Jacob had employed a personal assistant and a teacher to help him and Cecilia improve their numeracy and literacy abilities.

It had been over a year since Jacob and his family had relocated to Agbor, and the desire to confront his village continued to grow stronger. Although he had a plan, Jacob had become so occupied with his construction business that he continued to delay the implementation. "Jacob, for the sake of your peace of mind, we need to deal with your village issues," insisted Cecilia. "We need to review and re-evaluate the plan," said Jacob. After some discussions that went on for a few days, the final plan was agreed upon, and Cecilia and Margaret were going to initiate the implementation.

It was on a Sunday morning, and Cecilia had travelled the less than five miles distance with Jacob's mother to visit the head chief of the Alihagwu village. It was the first time Cecilia was making the journey to the village. The two-mile journey from the major road to the village was still not passable by vehicles. Jacob's mother was not surprised that this had remained the case. However, they both made it to the home of the village head. After exchanging greetings, Cecilia introduced herself to the head of the village. "I am Cecilia Oriahi, Jacob's wife, and you know Jacob's mother, Margaret." Cecilia continued, "We are here to initiate the process of resolving the issues surrounding Jacob's birth." Cecilia informed the head of the village that Jacob intended to return to his birthplace with full acceptance, and any curse or intended retribution must now end.

The village head, Chief Ajuma, had not forgotten about Jacob, the baby with the tooth. He knew that it had been over forty years since Jacob was born, and the views of the village had started to change their beliefs. He was in his eighties and answered to the Agbor

Kingdom King, that appointed him Chief of the Alihagwu village. This chieftaincy tile remains a hereditary prestige that passes over to the next of kin. Chief Ajuma looked old and frail in line with his age. He had done well for his age and continued to command respect amongst his people.

"Cecilia, you are welcome," uttered Chief Ajuma. He continued, "We have heard of Jacob's adventures and achievements, he is one of us, and we will welcome him to this village." Cecilia and Jacob's mother were delighted to hear the village Chief's proclamation. This visit was the beginning of the relationship-building that Cecilia had imagined. She continued to visit Chief Ajuma, bearing gifts at all times and made some promises to the village communities. As a gesture of reconciliation and acceptance, Cecilia requested that a piece of land should be awarded to Jacob and in return, she would make a goodwill gesture donation to cover the cost of the land.

Jacob was surprised by Cecilia's accomplishment in relation to his village issues. "You secured a large piece of land for us?" Jacob asked Cecilia. Before Cecilia could utter another word, Jacob continued, "Well done! But what are we going to do with the land when there is no road that is passable by vehicles to the village?" With a smile on her face, Cecilia said, "We will build a road to the village." Although Jacob was happy that his village no longer saw him as a curse to them, he was not sure if he would go to the extent that Cecilia was recommending. Why would he want to build a road to a village that wanted him dead, he imagined. However, Jacob knew that he would one day travel to the village to personally meet the village Chief and complete the reconciliation process that Cecilia had initiated.

In the meantime, Jacob continued to make a good name in the construction industry across the Midwest of the country. He had also built a good team in his construction business, so they continued to win almost all of the tenders submitted to build structures, including banks, hospitals, colleges, and housing schemes. Jacob knew he had secured his identity with several communities across the region through his building style and craftsmanship. Jacob's buildings were easily identified by their superior quality.

It was in the beginning of the year 1969, and Cecilia had agreed on a collaborative project with the people of Alihagwu communities and the Agbor local council authority to pave a vehicle-passable road from the major road to the village. Jacob and Cecilia would bear most of the financial cost. In less than a month, the road project was completed, and the village was no longer hidden from the outside world. The road also opened the opportunity to trade their farm produce to the rest of the country and encouraged visits to the village.

The people of Alihagwu wanted to thank Jacob in person, and he was invited to join in a celebration of the advancement. Cecilia worked behind the scenes to financially support the welcoming of Jacob to the village and to officially mark the road completion. The event was attended by state and local government officials as well as friends and family of Cecilia and Jacob. This was also an opportunity to officially conclude the reconciliation process between Jacob and his village people. Jacob was delighted to see his people cheering for him, as well as the warm welcome he received. He had maintained a good relationship with Mr Johnston, who was also instrumental to the success of the reconciliation. However, Jacob knew he must do more to elevate his village from poverty.

Jacob continued to visit his village to understand what they needed. From his assessment, he knew that the village was still lagging behind in many civilised infrastructures and basic utilities that support better living. So, collaborating with the village, Jacob built a modern town hall and a complex of chalets with hospitality amenities. The town hall comprised of venues for hosting events and parties, which attracted neighbouring villages to formally have a purposeful place to celebrate and enjoy themselves. There was also a restaurant that was managed by Cecilia. Jacob also built a maternity hospital where he recruited doctors from the United Kingdom through the government health scheme programme. Within a short period of time,

Jacob and Cecilia had almost transformed the village into a self-sufficient township.

"There is something missing," hinted Cecilia. Jacob could not believe his ears and said, "Cecilia, I love you so much for making all these things happen in my village, but I think we have done enough." Jacob recollected Cecilia saying, "There is more to be done; I just can't remember." A few months later, Cecilia and Jacob were back in the village building a general market with a capacity of about one hundred stalls. They also made provision for a water supply. The market became a commerce centre where on certain days of the week, numerous traders from across the region came to sell their produce and products and buy the local agricultural produce grown in the village.

Cecilia and Jacob knew that they had provided the village with something they could not have achieved by themselves. Hearing all that Jacob and Cecilia had done for the Alihagwu village, the King of the Agbor Kingdom summoned Jacob to his palace. "Who would have thought that a baby born with a tooth could change the lives of a village and its neighbouring communities," said the King. "Jacob, what you have done is rare in Nigeria," added the King. He continued, "As a baby a with tooth, my father, the King at the time, saved your life, somehow knowing you will be the one to elevate your village to prosperity." The King thought that what Jacob had done was astonishing and remarkable. "With your help, your village is no longer isolated, and the people can now have access to good healthcare, commerce, modern hospitality infrastructure, and a lifestyle of hope, and you did all this without government intervention," said the King.

The King went on to the speak of Jacob's forgiveness to his people. The people that never wanted him to exist and their short-sightedness had to be put right by an outsider. The King praised Jacob and presented him with the highest honour of a Chief of the Agbor Kingdom. "It is now obvious that Jacob came to this life with a tooth as a marker that represents goodness, and I hereby grant him the highest honourable title of Chief Ihienrinma of Agbor Kingdom," stated the King. [Ihienrinma means something that is good].

CHAPTER NINETEEN

The King's Dance

IT WAS THE FIRST WEEK of January in the year 1970, and the dry season was presenting some challenges to most people. The temperature had dropped significantly below average, and many people did not have the right clothing to keep warm. Most families had kept their children off school as they stayed at home to remain warm. The dry atmosphere and the wind blowing from the Sahara Desert carrying sand particles to the south of the continent made it difficult to be outside in the open. The unpleasant weather conditions had slowed down the fighting of the civil war, mainly taking part in the east of the country. It was rumoured that as a result of the blockade, many civilians including children, had starved to death.

"Jacob, I think the war is coming to an end," said Cecilia. She continued, "I heard it on the radio that the Biafran soldiers are laying down their weapons and that they have lost the determination to carry on fighting when their families and friends continue to die of starvation." Jacob, who was having his breakfast, could only nod his head to confirm he had heard Cecilia. "Oh, I am sorry Jacob, I forgot you never wanted to be reminded of the war," Cecilia apologised. Jacob had remained silent about his captivity experience and would not engage in any discussions about the civil war. A few weeks later, precisely on the fifteenth day of January, the civil war was declared over. The Nigerian military had succeeded in their strategy to blockade and starve the Biafran army to surrender. Although Jacob was delighted, he still would not discuss the war. However, he saw the war coming to an end as an opportunity to expand east of the country to help rebuild structures that were destroyed and construct new housing schemes.

The mood of the country had shifted from apprehensive to hopeful. The unification of the country once again, was a much-needed opportunity for all. There was a relaxation of some harsh government policies, and movement across all regions started to flow again. There was some cause to celebrate across the country, and specific reasons for this were not hard to find. Jacob and Cecilia did not need much justification to celebrate the development of the Alihagwu village that they had completed. However, Cecilia was not completely happy because the electricity company had no budget to provide supply to the village. This was a significant cost that Jacob and Cecilia were not willing to accommodate, given the extensive financial contribution that they had already made toward the completed projects.

"The electrification project will have to wait for another few years," confirmed Jacob. He continued, "Hopefully, the electricity board will have the budget by then." Cecilia was not too sure that waiting was the right thing to do and suggested, "We could provide them with a generator." Jacob knew that Cecilia's suggestion was good. However, this would require them to provide even more financial contributions towards the development project. Nevertheless, a generator large enough to provide electricity to the town hall, chalets, and the healthcare centre was ordered. Cecilia could now plan the celebration of the opening of the development.

Jacob's new three-story office building had been completed, and he had only just relocated the construction business headquarters there. He was in his office one Monday morning when a national newspaper journalist visited. "I am from the Daily Times Newspaper and here to ask you some questions for the article we want to publish about your development at Alihagwu." Jacob had not expected such publicity, but he was happy to oblige. "You need to get my wife involved, as she was the mastermind of the whole project," said Jacob. "We will be delighted to speak to your wife, too," confirmed the journalist.

A few days after the newspaper carried Jacob and Cecilia's transformation article of Alihagwu village on their front page, the Governor of the state decided to visit and see for himself. Jacob and Cecilia were congratulated and were invited to a dinner in their honour at the Governor's official residence. Jacob made new friends that included other state governors, ministers of different departments, heads of the police, judges, and magistrates. Cecilia was introduced to the wives of these high-profile individuals. It was also agreed that the Governor would attend the opening ceremony of the Alihagwu project as the guest of honour. Most of the high-profile officials were also invited as VIP guests.

Jacob and Cecilia were no longer ordinary citizens as they had friends that were state governors, judges, head of police, and other very rich people within and across other regions. Members of the media from television, radio, and newspapers also became close to Jacob and Cecilia. The pair had become a beautiful couple for the newspaper cover pages, as well as television shows. These publicities also helped promote Jacob's construction business, and the company was winning many projects on the basis that they offered good designs and a high-quality finish.

Cecilia and Jacob's fortune continued to grow. They decided to build a larger family home in a new and upcoming area, and they had the opportunity of having the street named after them, "Oriahi Street." However, Jacob and Cecilia did not forget their humble beginnings and especially how Jacob was born. Cecilia never forgot Martin the Butcher, that made the connection with Jacob possible. Jacob would never forget the King that saved his life. The pair jointly believed in the importance of people and, as such, had helped the less privileged achieve their dreams and had sponsored some individuals to go to the United States of America to further their studies. Jacob had realised that education is key to all things. He also knew that helping people to travel and study overseas would make it easier for him to provide similar opportunities for his own children when the time came.

The ceremony to commission the Alihagwu developments as fully completed and opened for use took place and was a successful event. It had attracted more media headlines and was attended by not only the people of Alihagwu but by the people of Agbor township. They all wanted to see what Jacob and Cecilia had done for their village. Although Cecilia was not a native of Alihagwu, indeed, she was an indigenous of Boji-Boji, Agbor; she had somehow adopted Jacob's village as her own. Cecilia was also seen to be the person that made the development of the village a reality. The opening event was also attended by the King of Agbor Kingdom. The King had become a good friend to Jacob and Cecilia.

It was during the event that the King announced he had offered Jacob the title of a Chief and one of his right-hand men. "I am therefore inviting the whole region, all citizens of this state and beyond, to attend a special ceremony at my Kingdom palace," said the King. Jacob was officially made a Chief as decreed by the King during the ceremony. The ceremony to celebrate 'the becoming of a Chief' in Jacob's honour was attended by a mass of people. The whole communities of Alihagwu and the neighbouring villages flooded into the palace at the event. "The King anoints one of our own," said the head Chief of Alihagwu. Many people from the Agbor township were present at the ceremony.

However, on the same day of Jacob's chieftaincy ceremony, the King had also officiated another traditional celebration called the "The King's Parade." This occasion is rare as it requires the King to walk some distance within his Kingdom in a celebratory mood. This meant that an even larger crowd was present to observe the event. What the crowd did not know was that the King had chosen Jacob to walk on his right side in addition to another well know Chief accompanying him on the left. This was a special honour for Jacob.

A moment before the procession started, the crowd had spotted Jacob on the right side of the King, and there was a huge cheer of admiration. The crowd was also in a celebratory mood as they saw their King step out into the open and began to walk. The King, who was in his late fifties, was about five feet ten inches tall, with broad shoulders and a well-built body that made him look bold and fearless in his well-decorated outfit. The King was wearing a moderate-size hat that fit neatly on top of his head. It was a unique and custom design for Kings only. The hat was made of golden materials, which gave it a bright and reflective feature. The King wore a gown that stretched to his ankles and just high enough to reveal his golden shoes. The gown was draped in gold threads that were woven into the fabric. This meant that the outfit glittered as it came into contact with the sun's rays.

To further pronounce the look of the King, he wore multiple traditional beads around his neck, dropping far down to his lower abdomen. There was an umbrella shading the King as he emerged to greet the crowd with Jacob on his right. Having Jacob on his right on this special occasion signified to the people that he was important to the Kingdom. Jacob, as a new Chief and according to tradition, must appear topless, exposing the might of his chest and shoulders. He wore a wrapper covering his waist down to his ankles. He was wearing a pair of shoes with silver effects. He had no hat on and was wearing a single strand of beads around his neck that also dropped to his lower abdomen. These beads, which are made of coral, remain status symbols as they signify prestige and authority.

Jacob would be turning forty-five years of age in October of that year. He had not reached his prime yet, but the challenges he had experienced in life had taken a toll on him. Jacob looked slightly older for his age and stood at five foot nine inches tall. He was of medium build and looked masculine. The procession carried on into the distance as the King danced with Jacob and the other Chief. There were constant gunshots fired into the air by the King's guards in order to create celebratory sounds that accompanied the traditional drummers.

The ceremony had lasted the whole afternoon and into the evening by the time the King and his Chiefs returned to the palace. There was a special party later on in the palace to celebrate the occasion with the VIPs. "You are now my Chief and a friend," uttered the King to Jacob. The King again went on to thank Jacob for his contribution to developing Alihagwu, which remained part of his Kingdom. Jacob's relationship with the King grew stronger as time went on. Cecilia, and Jacob's mother, Margaret, were present throughout the celebration. For his mother, the honour she had witnessed bestowed on Jacob was something she never thought was possible. Although she had believed that Jacob would achieve success in his life, she never expected it would come to the level she was experiencing.

Cecilia was also honoured with the King's gratitude and was thanked for her insights and support for all that she and Jacob had achieved. Jacob also used his speech to thank Cecilia, most especially for her remarkable vision of how best they approached life.

CHAPTER TWENTY

The Unwanted Child

I T WAS JUNE OF 1970, and it was the middle of the rainy season. The atmosphere felt refreshed as the rain had cleaned off the dust in the atmosphere as a result of the dry season. The temperature had risen, although it was in most cases, too hot in the middle of the day. Cecilia and Jacob had moved into their newly completed five-bedroom bungalow in the new and upcoming housing area of Agbor town. The new house was a lone building situated at the beginning of a bare track of road, called Oriahi Street in their honour. Jacob was proud to have a street named after him, although he had to invest in widening and levelling the road to allow vehicle passage. The street stretched about a mile and a half in length. The new accommodation was feeling adequate for the family of six children in addition to Jacob's ailing mother. Cecilia felt she was content with her family size; although she was not really expecting a sixth child, she was very happy with her family and loved all her children. They were all healthy and different in their own ways; she thought and felt she could not ask for a better family.

A few days later, Cecilia started to feel uncomfortable with her general body chemistry; although not completely unrecognised, she decided to visit her general practitioner anyway. Upon the doctor's examination, Cecilia was shocked to hear the doctor say: "Are you aware that you are pregnant?" Cecilia looked straight into the doctor's eyes and responded, "Not at all; I was not expecting to be pregnant at my age. I thought I was going through my menopause stage." The doctor was not sure why Cecilia would be certain of not being pregnant but instead going through her menopause and said, "Well, you are about four months pregnant, and it is likely that your expected delivery will be in November." Cecilia was not interested in what the doctor was saying as she felt she was not pregnant. However, the way she felt reminded her of the times she had been pregnant. "I already have six children, and I have had enough," said Cecilia with annoyance. "I think this one would be a boy," said the doctor as Cecilia was already leaving his office.

Cecilia was not excited by the news but, at the same time, could not see a way out of her situation. She was thirty-one years old and believed she had completed her family with a combination of two girls and four boys. Her last child was almost three years old. She was just not in the right mental place to carry out another pregnancy and go through the process of bringing up another baby. The news did not excite Jacob either, moaning, "I thought we'd had enough. Are you sure the doctor is right?" Well, the doctor was right, as Cecilia delivered a baby boy in November of that year without any complications. The labour lasted just over nine hours, and the baby weighed in at 9.9lbs. It was about five hours longer than any of Cecilia's previous birth labours. Jacob and Cecilia fell in love with the baby instantly at first sight. They were once again delighted to have another beautiful baby.

Six months after Cecilia had given birth, the baby became very ill and suffered multiple febrile convulsions. Every modern medical treatment was exhausted but did not cure the illness. Jacob and Cecilia were so scared that they eventually thought they would lose the child. The thought of losing a child was something they were not going to accept easily, so they were willing to do anything that they could to save him. In the meantime, the child continued to terrify them and all those that loved him with the febrile convulsions. The child would roll his eyes back in his head and pass out with a high temperature.

This carried on for a long time, and his older siblings became seriously concerned about their baby brother. However, as the illness continued, their desperation increased, and so Jacob and Cecilia decided to try traditional methods to help save the life of their child. This was suggested by Cecilia's parents and in agreement with Jacob's mother. As Christians, it was a difficult course of action for Jacob and Cecilia to allow a native doctor to examine and treat their child. The prognosis was that the underground gods wanted to take the child's life because they desired his beauty and wanted him for themselves. So, to prevent this from happening, the child would be defaced. The native doctor promised a minimum defacing would do the trick.

Defacing their beloved child was something Cecilia and Jacob completely rejected initially. There was a good reason for this. Jacob's father's family had a genetic condition of bone deformity called Multiple Hereditary Exostoses. This meant that all of Jacob's siblings possessed a bone deformity ranging from mild to severe. The exception was Jacob's half-sister. She was fathered by another man after Jacob's father had died. The bone deformity is clearly visible either on the arm or leg, or both. Jacob's bone deformity was very mild and hardly visible. Apart from the latest child, and their first son, Michael, all of Jacob and Cecilia's other children had some form of the bone deformity. They all had a mild bone deformity apart from their two middle sons, Alexander, and William, who had a more severe form.

Although the bone deformity was not life-threatening, the gene had been passed to the next generation. Therefore, with this in mind, Jacob and Cecilia did not want additional deformation on their latest child, although he had not shown signs of bone deformity at that time.

"It will only be a vertical marking on each cheek," said the native doctor. It was around the time when the baby was a toddler that Jacob and Cecilia gave in to having him defaced, as his illness did not cease. He was marked with a razor blade once on each cheek, and some herbal potion was applied to prevent the deep scar from fading. However, this did not stop the child from continuing to get ill, rolling his eyes back in his head and passing out with a fever. As the child aged, he outgrew the convulsions, and he never had any sign of the gene for the bone deformity either.

THIS CHILD IS ME. According to my parents and my siblings, I was growing into a handsome boy that they all envied. However, the teasing by my siblings became part of my upbringing. They would ask me to play dead, rolling my eyes back in my head and passing out to amuse them and their friends. I was known as the magic child because I could die and come back to life. Was this why one of my names is also Lazarus?

Today, you can see my facial markings clearly. I grew up hating them as none of my friends and siblings had such types of markings. Facial or any forms of markings are not common in the southern areas of Nigeria. My markings remind me of my struggle for life as a child, although I try to ignore them. It is also important to note that face marking in Nigeria can be done for many other reasons. Depending on one's tribe, you could have multiple long horizontal or vertical line markings. Some tribes will do this for beauty, identification among themselves, and also for spiritual protection, as in my case.

Early on into my childhood, I had noticed a really close bond with my parents, and this continued as I grew up. My name meant a lot to my parents, as they would often call me in a way that represented being praised. I felt that they believed there was something special about me. This can be interpreted from the names they called me and how they expressed it. I grew up knowing my name as Uche, which I now use as my middle name. My other names are Georgie and Lazarus, and my Catholic Confirmation name is George (after Saint George).

Uche means wisdom. My parents and grandparents would call me in a praise expression as follows:

Uche-Chukwu-Ka: meaning - wisdom of God is better/greater.

Uche-Ka-Egho: meaning - wisdom is better/greater than money.

Uche-Ile-Wehun-Elu-Uwa Nkei Ka Nma: meaning - amongst all the wisdoms in the whole world, yours is better/greater.

My maternal grandmother was my ally when I was a child, and we spent many times together. This included when I was at nursery, and I would only stay in class if I could see my grandmother through the window. She would also have my supply of milk, which I preferred, in my feeding bottle. I think I got more attention from my parents and grandparents mainly because I was quite a sick child. I continued to suffer from febrile convulsions until I was probably three years of age.

I did start nursery at a younger age. This was mainly because I did not want to be left out when everyone was engaged in some sort of activity. However, I did not want to partake in any activities without my grandmother being present, and neither did I want to stay at home. There was a three-year gap between me and my immediate senior sibling, Azuka, and the youngest of my playmates were over twelve months my age. This meant that they were already either in nursery or school while I was at home with no one other than my grandmother and our house assistants to play with when my parents were at work.

Although I was not happy to eventually learn that I was conceived by accident and that my parents were not really excited about the pregnancy that led to my birth, I was a happy child. I continued to grow up with overwhelming love and affection. Yes, I hated my markings, but I can forgive them, knowing it was done in an attempt to save my life. Overall, I was happy with the family I was born into.

CHAPTER TWENTY-ONE

The Secret

IT SEEMED NOW THAT MY mother was unlikely to have another child. She was fully content with her family size, and the thought of having another was completely remote. She was thirty-six years old, and her focus was to look her best and presentable as the wife of a rich Chief should. My mother had changed in her appearance compared to how she was before her last pregnancy. Although she remained beautiful, she looked heavier and with a more rounded face. She started to wear glasses to correct her long-sightedness. Her manner of dressing had become more opulent and sophisticated. She would only wear a dress once, and it may never be worn again. Her shopping habits had also changed. She would only buy top-end quality clothing and shoes from reputable shops.

The combination of her beauty and her sophisticated dress style helped me categorise my mother as elegant. Mrs Oriahi, as she was respectfully known to all in the region, carried some level of regard, which was recognised by the people. She was seen to be generous and well-behaved towards the public. To me, my mother, although uneducated at school level, was an intelligent woman, a wonderful mother, a lovely sister, and a good wife. She was fair in nature and never imagined gaining an advantage through immoral means. She was disciplined and always avoided any confrontation with the public, no matter the situation. She saw herself as the wife of the most regarded Chief in the region and, therefore, must be seen to be self-respectful. However, she was a woman that would not tolerate actions or behaviour from her family that she deemed unacceptable.

My mother believed that no one was above her criticism, not even my father or the King. My mother had respectfully told the King that his decisions about certain issues were wrong and politely recommended that he corrected them. I doubt that the King took any notice of her. It was one Sunday afternoon, and my father was having a lunch meeting with his group of friends, who were all Chiefs. There had been some dispute amongst them, and they agreed that my mother should be called to help resolve the issue. She did, but not before she pointed out the wrongs attributed to each one of them. My mother was seen as a pillar of support for my father's achievements.

My father, who gets chauffeured by his dedicated driver in his latest model of the E-Class Mercedes Benz, seemed to have forgotten his modest upbringing. He had ordered his Mercedes Benz through the A. G. Leventis Motor Company in Nigeria. A. G. Leventis had directly imported the vehicle from Mercedes Benz in Germany. The car was delivered to my father in a crate, which he left in his garage for a few months. It was on Christmas day of 1972 that my father unveiled the vehicle for the first time to the public eye.

The vehicle was rare in Nigeria and may not have been seen before by the people of Agbor. The car was cream in colour and looked sturdy and elegant. Even for the rich, it was an expensive car. The vehicle was only used to attend special occasions and therefore was hardly seen out as it was mostly locked up in the secure garage in the house. Like my mother, my father had become used to having the finest things in life. Therefore, they no longer felt uncomfortable enjoying their luxurious possessions. It appeared as though my father was enjoying life to the fullest. He had worked very hard indeed for his success. He was no longer satisfied with the standard; only high-end quality would do. As a man, my father was fair in his dealings with everyone and was generous too.

Helping others to achieve success became something he enjoyed. Perhaps he knew how he started life and wanted to give back. Later in life, he helped build a kitchen and a bathroom extension to my neighbour's house. They had only just moved in, and the property lacked a proper kitchen area and a bathroom. My father felt it was a decent thing to help as he could afford it. He also continued to acquire more landed assets in the nearby areas as well as in other regions, like Benin City, which was the state capital. Benin City was about forty miles west of Agbor. His business also continued to thrive.

The five-bedroom house became uncomfortable after I was born because it had become overcrowded. My parents owned the land beside the current house, and they decided to build a much larger home. The new home was a two-story house consisting of eight bedrooms and three lounges, which were compartmentalised into multiple apartments. It also had a large event area that could accommodate up to one hundred and fifty guests. There were two kitchens, which were situated one on each level, an office, a formal dining area, and two car garages built in. From the furnishings of the new house, it was obvious to see that the owners were rich. The furniture was imported from France, and the curtains were tailor-made in Italy. There were chandeliers visible on every ceiling and matching wall lights in every room of the house. There was the executive living room reserved for my parent's use only and to host VIPs. The finishings of the executive lounge were even more ostentatious, with a gold telephone clearly visible by the left of the sofa where my father regularly sat.

UNFORTUNATELY, IN 1973, MARGARET, a grandmother I hardly remember meeting, passed away in her sleep. She was about sixty-seven years old. Although my father was sad, he was glad that she was able to experience his achievements and successes. Most of all, she experienced reconciliation with his village people. My grandmother's funeral attracted many people, as well as some VIPs that were friends and business associates of my parents. My father decided to build a mansion in his home village in honour of his mother. Although Anna, my father's sister and his brother, Noah, remained very close, they both had their own families. My aunty, Anna, had married a man that lived in a village called Oki, not far from Alihagwu and had four children. Noah, my uncle, was living in the house that my father built for him in Agbor town with his wife and now had six children. He had set up a franchise with a football pool business, where he represented them as an agent. Initially, my father did not welcome his choice of a business venture as he disapproved of gambling in all forms. However, he had bought Noah a motorbike as a parting gift from his construction business.

My father's three half-sisters were also close to him, and they saw each other regularly. Again, two of his half-sisters were from his father, John's second marriage, and one from his mother. The half-sisters were married and were living a good life with their families. My father did occasionally play a supportive role in the upbringing of his half-sisters' children. My mother was very close to my father's siblings and visited them regularly. She would provide any support they needed and would also occasionally drop off home cooking and other foodstuff for them.

IN 1974, MY FATHER'S CONSTRUCTION BUSINESS continued to grow and had led to my parents acquiring additional strategic assets, including various land. As part of my parents' expansion programme, they built two adjoining double-story houses in Benin City, which was the capital of Bendel State at that time. The properties were semi-detached houses, each comprising of four bedrooms, two living rooms, with a kitchen and bathrooms, spread over two floors. There were also large balconies located on the second floor of each unit of the building. The property was surrounded by a large compound and also consisted of another four-room building, forming a self-contained service quarter. The location of the property was in a strategic area and on a prominent road in Benin City. The design of the building was advanced for its time and was clearly unique in the region. Although my parents had no intention of relocating to Benin City, it was obvious that they built the property to showcase their vision and innovation for construction. The properties were added to their existing rental portfolio.

Not too far from my family home in Agbor, there was a construction of a building taking place. The construction was peculiar as the perimeter of the land was boarded up, which prevented anyone from seeing what was being built. Normally, there would be signs that displayed the name of the construction company that was contracted to build the structure, but in this case, it was not obvious. The building materials were delivered by unmarked vehicles, and the workers were not from the area and did not speak the native language. There were also security personnel guarding the entrance and preventing anyone access onto the construction site. The construction became known as 'the secret project' to the locals as they could not determine what was being built and who the owner was. The project lasted for about six months, and when the boarded panels were removed, they revealed a beautiful bungalow.

It was a well-designed five-bedroom house with a terrace on the west side of the building on a second floor. The terrace was accessed by a set of stairs running by the side of the house. The terrace was large enough to hold a party for one hundred people. The house also consisted of a car garage built-in as part of the house structure. There was a large space at the front of the house that would not restrict moderate use either for a party or multiple-vehicle parking. The back of the house had a lovely outside patio that was accessed via the kitchen, and there was a well-designed garden that would enhance the living comfort quality of anyone or family that lived there. Just below the front apex of the building, there was an area that was approximately seven feet long by two feet wide that was covered with plastic sheeting material. However, it was obvious that something was written on the wall but was being hidden from others to see.

The perimeter of the land was finished with a combination of a brick fence of about four feet high and a metal railing of about three feet high. There was a double metal gate, which was slightly over seven feet high. The metal gate design matched those on the fence. The gate, which was also painted the same colour as the fence railings, was designed and positioned to swing open into the compound that looked onto a concrete paved driveway towards the garage. The over seven feet high solid perimeter fence and gate gave the bungalow slick security and some privacy protection. There were no similar good-quality properties other than my parents' home, which was near the bungalow. Although the building was complete and it was obvious to everyone, the owner and the contractor that built it remained a secret.

It was my mother's thirty-sixth birthday week, and my father had just returned from a business trip the night before. A surprise party had been planned by my father's secretaries with instructions to hide the preparations from my mother as much as they could. However, they were not as good as they thought, and I found it hard to lie to my mother. "What is all this fuss about, Lorraine?" asked my mother. Lorraine was the manager of the administrative team of my father's construction business. She had just turned twenty-five years of age and was married with two children to another employee of my parents' construction company.

Lorraine believed in loyalty and loved my parents. Therefore, she found it incredibly difficult to lie to my parents. Lorraine, who was slim and of average height, beautiful, and with a bubbly personality, was also a distant relative of my mother's. She was a Roman Catholic and continued to encourage my mother to return to the faith but was yet to succeed. She was aware that although my mother had converted to the Jehovah's Witnesses faith, her parents and siblings had remained with the Catholic church. Lorraine was also aware that my parents had not been attending the Jehovah's Witnesses meetings frequently since they relocated to Agbor.

"We are just following the instructions from Philip," she replied in response to my mother's question. "Then, ask Philip to telephone me to explain why my house is being decorated without my permission," instructed my mother. Philip was my father's business financial controller. He also administered my parents' personal budgets and expenditure transactions. Part of his responsibilities included liaising with banks and writing cheques. Given my father's numeracy limitations, he relied on Philip's guidance to manage his finances. Philip was responsible for paying my siblings' school fees and managing their personal financial needs. My siblings were expected to contact Philip for any issues that were related to finance.

Lorraine and her colleagues continued to decorate the house throughout the week as instructed by Philip. My mother received her call from Philip, and his explanation for the decoration was that my father was expecting some VIP guests. It was on the day that my mother turned thirty-six, and it was on a Saturday. My father would normally work until midday on Saturdays but did not wake up as early as he would have to prepare for the office. He knew that it was my mother's birthday but was not sure if all the arrangements were in place. That morning, he had stayed in bed longer than he usually does, and he had, as a result, slept a little longer than he would have liked. He got up when he realized it was nearly ten o'clock and reached for his bedside telephone.

After dialling a number, "Philip, good morning," he said. "Good morning, Chief," replied Philip. "I need an update in fifteen minutes; please ring my home office line," and he hung up the telephone. My father noticed that my mother was not in bed; neither was she anywhere he had looked. However, he proceeded to shower and get ready. Philip managed to ring him as instructed, and there was about ten minutes of discussion and my father appeared hopeful.

It was at about three o'clock in the afternoon, and my mother's driver had informed her that she was to be chauffeured to join my father at an undisclosed location. "What do you mean you do not know the location? How do you expect to get there?" my mother queried her driver. There was silence from her driver.

My mother's driver, Iyke, was about ten years younger than my mother and remained a dedicated member of staff to my family. He was of average build but had a beer belly. He shaved his head bald and had a bushy moustache. Iyke had been employed by my family for nearly five years, and my mother had no reason to distrust him. "All these secrets do not make sense to me; anyway, let's go," uttered my mother.

CHAPTER TWENTY-TWO

A House, a Car, and a Party

AFTER MY FATHER had spoken to Philip earlier in the morning, he had asked to speak to my mother's aid to enquire about her whereabouts and her plans for the day. "She has an appointment with her hairdresser at ten o'clock, and I believe she will be there now. She has no other engagements for the rest of the day apart from a visit to her mother at five thirty pm," said Kate, my mother's aid. Kate had been my mother's assistant for four years and had provided different types of support. The support included looking after us, the children when my mother was away, to shopping for the household, cooking, and maintaining the house. She also managed the other house assistant and remained a valued extended member of the family. Kate worked in the house from Monday to Saturday from seven am to three pm. She would sometimes work till late when required and was paid well for the extra time. She was twenty-two years old, was not yet married, and lived with her parents. Her house was about a ten-minute walk from ours, and she would mostly receive a lift home when Iyke was free.

Satisfied with the way that the entire birthday plan was unfolding, my father decided it was time he finished the tasks he had assigned to himself to ensure that the objectives of the day were delivered successfully. However, he was struggling to adjust to the day's routine. Normally, on a Saturday, my father would have left the house for the office at seven o'clock in the morning. He hardly ate breakfast and would start his morning by getting his usual daily business updates and then follow on with his schedules. He would finish at the office by four o'clock and would be home no later than five pm on weekdays, but would finish at twelve thirty pm on Saturdays and would be home by one o'clock in the afternoon. He would have home-cooked lunch unless he was out of town on business, in which case, he would eat at a restaurant.

Although my father had not been frequenting the Jehovah's Witnesses Kingdom Hall, he had been attending the early morning service at a nearby church. The service started at five thirty in the morning for only half an hour. This was convenient for my father as he was an early riser. My father would shower as soon as he woke up and then got dressed. He would then kneel by his bedside and pray for about five minutes.

My mother and father had different bedrooms, although my father preferred to sleep in my mother's bed daily. Their bedrooms were linked by an opening, with each of their rooms consisting of an identical super king bed built-in wardrobe, and they shared a bathroom. There was also a room within their apartment that was nicknamed 'the strongroom.' The strongroom, which had no window, could only be accessed through my parents' apartment. The strongroom also had a complex door lock mechanism, making it more secure than other doors in the house. Inside the strongroom were my parents' high valued possessions and including clothing, handbags, shoes, and expensive jewellery. The key to the strongroom never left my mother's side.

Knowing that the plan of the day was going as expected, my father got dressed for the occasion and left the house. His driver was waiting outside with the clean and shining Mercedes Benz. Without much of a delay, they were on the move. The driver had been briefed on the tasks at hand, which must all be delivered on time and as specified. It was at exactly ten minutes past three o'clock in the afternoon that my father's car pulled up by the side of the road at the scheduled location. He stepped out of the vehicle, and the driver drove off.

There was no sign of anyone at the location where my father was standing. However, he did not seem to be in a hurry and was happily standing and looking up the road as if he was expecting someone to appear. He looked at his watch, and it was about fifteen minutes past three pm. Just as he raised his head after looking at his watch, he saw my mother's car approaching his location. There was a smile on his face when he noticed my mother in the back seat of the car. Iyke slowed the car down as he parked near my father. My father approached the car and opened the door for my mother. He lowered his upper body to smile at my mother as she was still sitting in the car. He extended his hand towards my mother, hoping to help her out of the vehicle.

"What is going on, Jacob?" my mother asked. "Well, get out of the car, and we shall both find out together," replied my father. "Your hair looks nice, and as always, you look gracefully beautiful," continued my father. "Thank you! I can tell you are definitely up to something, Jacob; tell me what it is," my mother responded as she stretched her hand to meet my father's. Gently, my father pulled her hand and she followed and stepped out of the vehicle. My father continued to hold her hand as he guided her away from the roadside.

By the time Iyke and my mother were driving off from the house, there were a few lorries parked nearby, waiting for my mother to leave. The lorries were carrying live band entertainers' equipment, canopies, chairs, and tables. They only had an hour to set up before my mother returned. My auntie, Tina, and my mother's other sisters had been busy preparing food and chilling drinks for the surprise party. My father had contracted my mother's favourite musician as the key entertainer for the party, in addition to a few other local drummers and dancers. Just soon after Iyke and my mother had left the house, Auntie Tina and my mother's other siblings had appeared from their nearby hiding locations to drop off the food and drink. There was also instruction from my father to Kate to have all my siblings, including me, ready to leave the house by five minutes past three. Although the destination was never revealed, it was just a five minutes' walk from the family house. Iyke was only given the location details five minutes before three o'clock and to ensure he took my mother out of the house no later than three pm. He was also instructed to do a detour and only arrive at the location no earlier than three fifteen pm.

"Where are we going?" asked my mother. "Just follow me and stop asking too many questions," replied my father with a smile. It was just a twenty-yard walk, and they arrived at the front gate of a house. The gates immediately swung open, and before my mother could say a word, over one hundred people started to make their way out of the house and headed towards my parents as they stood by the gate inside the compound. Simultaneously, the happy birthday song was being performed live by two drummers, a saxophonist, and a singer on the second-floor terrace of the house.

My mother was motionless as she could not believe what she was experiencing. As the song continued, a five-layer cake nicely decorated and placed on a round silver table was being rolled out from the house and towards my mother as she held her right hand to her mouth. She remained motionless and speechless. Just before the cake could reach her position, my father pointed his finger to the apex of the building and said to my mother, "Cecilia, look up there!" Everything was happening too fast for my mother as the drummers and the saxophone grew louder with the happy birthday song. My mother then looked at the direction of my father's finger. The plastic sheeting was being removed, and an inscription was revealed. It read "Cecilia, My Love." My mother was not sure why her name was on the house. "What does that mean?" she asked. "It means it is your house," replied my father. He continued, "It is your birthday present and happy birthday!" My mother could not believe what was happening. The cake had reached her position at this time while the music continued. There were thirty-six lit candles on the cake, with piped icing lettering that read "Happy Birthday Cecilia." Before she could finish admiring the cake, the garage door started to open, revealing a brand-new Peugeot car. There was a temporary number plate on it that read "Cecilia 36".

My elder siblings sat inside the new car as my mother approached to have a closer look. "Is this for me too?" she asked. Before my father could answer, Joyce, my eldest sister, shouted, "Yes, mummy, it's your new car. Daddy bought it for you." My mother opened the driver's door of the car and looked inside and was amazed at the modern features she could instantly identify as different in comparison to her current vehicle. She was called out to cut the cake before she was able to explore the capability of the new car. "Can I look inside the house first?" she asked my father. "No, no, it will take you forever; just cut the cake now, and you can do that later," interjected my father.

As she stood behind the cake with the candles flickering in the breeze, she managed to look into the crowd and could see her parents and siblings; she could also see her friends, my father's friends, and the majority of their employees. "Again, 1..2..3, Happy birthday to you…" the singer carried on. My mother was asked to make a wish as she blew the fire out of the candles. She was not able to blow the thirty-six candles out at once. It was at the fourth attempt that she succeeded. She then pushed the silver knife that was handed to her by my father into the bottom layer of the cake, cutting it from the top to the base. The cake was then taken away as she started to meet each one of the guests, thanking them for their wishes and receiving hugs from them.

The weather on the day remained dry and sunny. It was coming to the end of the rainy season, and there was the possibility that it could rain. However, the blue sky did remain free from any clouds, and the temperature of the day was twenty-six degrees centigrade, which was about average for that time of the year. It was nearly five o'clock in the evening when my mother had finished meeting every one of the guests. She had not forgotten that she had yet to explore the house.

As she walked into the bungalow, she noticed that there was a ribbon with a bow that was tied horizontally across the main entrance door. As she started to wonder how that was possible, as she had seen the guests leave the house through that door when she arrived at the compound, my father approached her and said, "Cecilia, your father wants to make a speech." The music had stopped, and my grandfather was handed a microphone.

My grandfather was a tall man with an average build. He stood at nearly six feet in height. He was sixty-four years old and looked his age. He wore a short-sleeved safari suit with a pair of well-polished black shoes. My grandfather liked his tobacco and preferred to smoke with a pipe. However, occasionally, he would smoke a cigarette when he did not have the time to prepare his pipe. Although my father had bought my grandfather smoke pipes as gifts, he did not like smoking and had prevented anyone from smoking near him, and definitely not inside our home. My father had tried smoking in the past, but only briefly, before he quit and had hated the practice since then.

With my grandmother beside him, my grandfather started to speak into the microphone. He did not need to introduce himself as he was well known to all the guests as Cecilia's father. "It is with pleasure that I welcome you all to my beautiful daughter's thirty-sixth birthday celebration," my grandfather continued after telling a joke. He spoke for about five minutes before handing the microphone to my father. "Friends and family, it is a lovely feeling to have you all to witness Cecilia, my beautiful wife, turn thirty-six years old." He continued for another five more minutes telling the guests how my mother had remained the pillar that supports him. Finally, he said, "For the love I feel for my wife, Cecilia, I would like to present this house to her as a gift and to thank her for being a special person in my life." A pair of scissors was handed to my mother as my father guided her towards the ribbon at the main entrance of the house. My grandmother was standing behind my mother as she took the pair of scissors in her left hand. "Mother, come stand with me," my mother instructed as she appeared tearful. My grandmother then moved forward beside my mother, placing her left arm around her; she said, "I am here with you, my daughter."

My grandmother was a shy and quiet person. She was generous and would do almost anything for anyone. She was not as tall as my mother, standing at about five feet one. She had a skinny body and was considered medium in complexion as she was not as light-skinned as my mother. It was obvious on her face that she was dealing with a challenging issue as she was not smiling as much as she used to. My mother was aware that she was having a rough patch with her husband, my grandfather, that may lead to a breakdown of their marriage.

"It is with great heart and respect that I accept this house as my own, which will be open to you all," said my mother as she spoke into the microphone and then cut the ribbon. There was cheering from the guests as my mother proceeded to open the door. She entered into a lobby that opened into the main living room of the house. "Everything is on one floor," uttered my father as he walked behind my mother. "Where is the kitchen?" asked my mother. "Right at the back," replied my father.

My mother continued to explore the house for another half an hour before my father politely intervened, "You can come back tomorrow and spend as much time as you need, but we need to attend to the guests now." My mother suddenly realised that she had made no food or drink in preparation and said: "Jacob, what are we going to do to host all these people? I have not cooked as I did not realise this was happening." My father responded that it was alright as it had been taken care of.

"It is time to proceed to the next stage; come with me, Cecilia; let's go home," uttered my father. Extending his hand towards my mother, they walked out of the house together and headed home. The musicians, other VIP guests, as well as the neighbours and people from Alihagwu village, were already being entertained by the time they arrived home. The party carried on until midnight.

CHAPTER TWENTY-THREE

The Money

IT WAS A FEW days after my mother had celebrated her thirty-sixth birthday party, and she was in her new car being chauffeured to the market when the thought of her religious faith came to her mind. She felt she was certain that she had left the Jehovah's Witnesses faith by default. She knew that going forward, she and her family would not be returning to the faith. She felt sorry about the situation as she had enjoyed her time with the people she had met as a Jehovah's Witness. She was also aware that my father had been attending a different church for a few years, and she wondered if it was time to formally return to the Catholic faith and take her family with her.

Lorraine would be delighted by her decision, she thought. Her thought also reminded her of her love for my father. She thought back to the first time she had seen my father and had refused to want anything to do with him. She wondered what her life would have been like if she had never married my father. She felt reassured of my father's love for her after the house present that she received. The car and the party were just a bonus, she concluded. She felt that she had nothing to worry about regarding my father losing his affection for her, not that there was any reason to doubt his feelings. She was also confident that my father had realised and appreciated her participation in their wealth creation and happiness. Iyke had reached the market drop-off zone and had waited for my mother to leave the vehicle as normal, but she remained in the car. It was about five minutes later

that Iyke decided to alert her, "Madam, we have reached the market."
My mother was so deep in thought and did not realise that they had
reached the market. Also, the new car was quiet and had air
conditioning on that required all windows to be shut, and therefore she
did not hear the usual market noise distraction. "Thank you, Iyke,"
replied my mother.

As she started to walk into the market, she met one of my father's
friend's wives. She had been at her birthday party. They exchanged
greetings, and she thanked my mother for the good reception at her
party. My mother was aware that all of my father's friends had married
more than one wife. She recollected seeing them with more than one
woman companion and with a few men sitting with three wives.
However, she was confident that my father would not consider a life
of polygamy. She knew that my father believed in the value of 'one
man, one woman,' and had the reassurance that my father was not
capable of betraying her in that way.

All over the country, it continued to be accepted as a cultural
practice that a man could marry as many wives as he could afford.
Affordability being the ability to provide accommodation for the
wives. The wives would, in return, be required to raise money to care
for themselves and their children. The husband would be expected to
provide financial support for education and a handful of justified
major expenditures, while the petty living expenses would be
expected to be covered by the wives. There were the occasional
instances where the wife remained a full-time housewife, and the
husband would be expected to cover all costs of living.

To further reassure my mother that he had no interest in living a
polygamous lifestyle, my father had publicly denounced the need to
marry more than one wife.

It was a couple of months after my mother's birthday, and
unfortunately, my grandfather had decided to take another wife. My
mother was also aware that her father had a son with another woman

while he was married to my grandmother. He did not marry the child's mother and did not contest her being the sole parental guardian of their son. The son was living with his mother in a different region of the country. The situation was neither resolved nor was it accepted by my grandmother. This had led to the fracture of their relationship and had, for the past few years, left my grandmother worried about her future.

Sadly, the news had reached my mother that her father was divorcing her mother and that a new wife was moving into their family home. My grandmother had to leave her home with my mother's three youngest siblings. However, it was not long before my grandfather demanded the return of the children. It was customary and the law that children were in the legal custody of their biological father and not their mother. It was also traditional that the man or husband retained full ownership of any property or assets acquired during their marriage. Although this was an assumption and could be challenged in a court of law as the Matrimonial Act legislates for equal ownership. However, my grandmother was pushed out of her home and marriage without any financial gain or support. My grandmother later moved into my family home, where she was cared for and loved. She also took on a significant role in looking after me.

I had formed a strong bond with my grandmother as a result of spending much time together. We had a good and loving relationship, which was made possible as she had to keep an eye on me as a result of my febrile convulsions condition. It was also helpful for my parents to leave me in the care of my grandmother while they attended to their various business commitments. According to my grandmother, I would always prefer to spend time with her, and when I was tired, I would fall asleep in her arms. It was obvious I was spoilt by my grandmother, and she would not hesitate to protect and defend me from any of my older siblings' teasing.

MY FATHER HAD RETURNED from a business trip to find that Philip, his financial controller, could not be reached. "Lorraine, I need an update about Philip; please come to my office," my father had requested through the telephone. My father had thought that Lorraine, as the manager of the administration team, should be able to provide insight about Philip's whereabouts.

"Sir, I believe Philip has left the country for the United States of America," uttered Lorraine. "Is this a joke? Why was I not informed about his plans?" asked my father. "Philip has been stealing from the business, sir," said Lorraine. "What do you mean he has been stealing from the business? How?" said my father. He continued, "Philip has been a loyal member of the staff, and I trust him. What evidence do you have to prove he was stealing from me and that he has now left for the United States?" Lorraine knew she must tread carefully with her responses. She went on to inform my father that she had noticed some manipulations on some cheques that the bank returned after processing the payments.

"Why would the bank return cleared cheques to us? Since when did they start doing that?" asked my father. "Since I was informed by Mike, the clerk in the finance team, that the amounts on our ledgers were not corresponding with the bank statements. So, I approached the bank and requested that they send us every copy of our cheques after they have processed the payments." Said, Lorraine. "I don't understand what you are saying, Lorraine," uttered my father. He continued, "Are you telling me that Philip had manipulated a cheque? How was that even possible? I sign all the cheques as managing director of the company."

"Not just one cheque, sir, but several," Lorraine responded. She went on to inform my father that Philip was drawing up cheques with amounts that represented higher values than the business intended, and he had been pocketing the difference. She explained that the practice only affected cheques addressed to Philip to withdraw cash for business use. "So how was he able to do this?" asked my father.

Lorraine explained that upon reviewing the cheques, nothing seemed obvious as the amounts in words corresponded to the amount in figures. However, she said that she believed Philip was inflating the value of the cheque in words and representing the figure amount with the correct numbers, which he later changed before he presented it to the bank. "Can you show me in practice what you are saying, please," requested my father.

Lorraine returned to her office to collect the photocopies of the cheques provided by the bank, the ledger that contained all cheques prepared, the paperwork that supported the expenditures, some bank statements, and a cheque book. Lorraine returned to my father's office and showed my father that the amounts on the ledgers and the paperwork that proceeded with the cheques did not match. She also showed my father that the cheques did match the bank statements. "So, what is the issue then if the cheque and the bank statement matched?" asked my father. However, before Lorraine could answer the question, my father realised that he was missing a trick.

"I see. He was altering the cheques after I had signed them, but how? Was he able to erase the cheques and rewrite them?" he asked. "I will show you what I believe he had done," said Lorraine. Reaching out for a blank cheque, Lorraine wrote 'two thousand eight hundred naira' in words on it at the appropriate section, and then in the figure section, she represented the amount as N2,000.00. She then handed the cheque to my father and asked him, "Sir, can you tell me the value of this cheque, please?" My father took the cheque and examined it, and said, "Two thousand naira" and handed the cheque back to Lorraine. "Sir, that is because you have read the figure; however, the amount in words says two thousand eight hundred naira," said Lorraine.

My father, who was sitting on the edge of his chair, decided to stand and walk away from his desk and headed towards his office window. There was silence in the office room for about five minutes as my father pondered. He used his hand to pull a section of the window's horizontal plastic blind down as if he wanted to see something, but there was nothing there.

My father later walked back to his desk; while Lorraine was watching every step he was making, he reached for the phone and dialled a number. A brief moment later, "Hello, Kate, can you please ask my wife to come to the phone? Thank you." As he waited for my mother, he moved the phone receiver from his left hand to the right and was still standing. "Cecilia, I need you to please come to the office; I need to speak to you about something," my father said. "Jacob, you sound worried; what is the matter?" asked my mother. "Please, do not worry, it is nothing bad, but come as quickly as you can," my father responded and replaced the phone receiver.

There was another brief silence in the room, but the noise of the wall cabinet opening as my father reached for a bottle of Gordon's Dry Gin and a glass interrupted the tranquillity. My father then poured himself a slightly larger-than-average gin than he would normally drink at that time of the day. He looked at the clock on the wall; it was ten minutes past one in the afternoon. Walking back to his chair, he sat down and said, "So he was changing the zeros to eight, and this had not affected the appearance of the cheques?" asked my father. "That is correct, sir," replied Lorraine. She continued, "He was not only doing it for zeros but for any number he could easily alter without them looking like they had been changed, as that would have required additional signature."

"I get that now, and thank you for your explanation," said my father. He continued by asking Lorraine when she heard last from Philip and when did he leave for the United States of America. "How did you find out he had left for the United States?" my father added to the other questions he had asked. "Sir, I started to investigate this issue as soon as it was brought to my attention, and I have so far only managed to look back to the last six months' records," said Lorraine. She continued, "I believe he must have been doing this for the last two years, as it would have been picked up by the audit that we did three years ago." Lorraine went on to explain that she had confronted Philip three days earlier, and she found out from his family that he had left for the United States the following day. "So, he would be arriving in the United States today?" asked my father. "That will be correct, sir," replied Lorraine.

"Cecilia, thanks for coming so quickly," uttered my father as he welcomed my mother into his office. "Lorraine, can you please brief her on all we have encountered regarding Philip, please?" my father requested. Nearly half an hour later, my mother was as distressed as my father, and both realising one common issue. "Lorraine, please leave us, and thank you for your efforts, and I will be making an announcement about this and the way forward shortly," uttered my father. Lorraine thanked my parents and then left for her office. "Only if I could read and write!" My father uttered, making his frustration visible.

"Jacob, do you know how much in total he may have stolen?" asked my mother. "Well, more than enough to travel to the United States and do whatever he had planned over there," replied my father. He continued, "We need to go back for another two years to check on the record." My father noticed my mother had gone quiet, and he knew that she must be thinking of something, so he stood up and headed into the corridor that led to his office bathroom. A few moments later, my father emerged and asked, "What's on your mind, Cecilia?" Looking straight into my father's eyes, she said, "Nothing! That's what we will do, nothing."

My father could not believe what he was hearing and responded in annoyance, "Nothing? Are you out of your mind? Someone stole from us, and you suggest we do nothing? Then you are inviting everyone to come and steal from us." Standing up from the double sofa chair where she was sitting that was strategically positioned in the office room, my mother said, "Jacob, I am equally as angry as you, given the love and trust we have for Philip, but we must now handle the matter in a way that does not make us look bad to the public."

CHAPTER TWENTY-FOUR

Business Diversification

A FEW WEEKS HAD passed since my parents had found out about Philip's deception, and in accordance with my mother's suggestion, nothing was done. However, the whole company staff was informed, and Mike, who alerted them to the fraud, received a cash gift and a brand-new Honda motorcycle. Lorraine also received a cash gift and a promotion. My parents had invited Philip's family to inform them of the theft, to which his parents acknowledged that they had received a confession from their son that he had stolen the funds to further his education in the United States. They pleaded for forgiveness and provided confirmation that Philip was in the United States of America and was registered as a student in a community university. My parents informed them that no case would be brought against Philip and that the stolen funds would be considered a parting gift.

Although my father remained disappointed that Philip had broken his trust, he was delighted that he was putting the money to good use. My father went on to tell Philip's family, "He did not have to steal from me, as I would have been pleased to sponsor his studies in the United States." My father continued, "I hope that what he managed to steal from me will be enough; I wish him well and the best." A few months later, my father had recruited a new financial controller.

It later became known that Philip's idea to study overseas had been a result of him being asked by my father to research good universities in the United States of America that could be considered for my eldest siblings, Joyce, and Michael, to attend. Although they were due to complete their secondary education the following year, my father wanted my two eldest siblings to leave for the United States as soon as it was feasibly possible. My father had made his intentions known to Philip since the year he had joined his business. "I want all my children to get the best possible education, and I believe the best universities are in the United States," my father recalled telling Philip. Philip was also aware of the study fund accounts my father had maintained in the banks for this purpose. However, my father continued to miss Philip and would have wished that he had asked him to send him to the United States to study.

This would have been a good outcome for my father as he thought that Philip being in the United States a year or so before Joyce and Michael arrived would have helped them in many ways to settle in the foreign country. My mother had noticed that my father had often remained in deep thought and in a depressed mood since Philip left. "I know he had the education you didn't have, but you will get on fine with the new financial controller, and who knows, he may be better than Philip," my mother uttered. My parents both agreed that it was best they did not contact Philip and to let him get on with his life. "We will find a way to get our children there, and they will be protected by God," said my mother in an attempt to reassure my father.

THE NEW FINANCIAL CONTROLLER had settled in fine after intensive training about my father's business operations. My father had travelled with him extensively to show him projects the company was working on and was also introduced to the family. "Victor, meet my wife, Cecilia, and my children," said my father. He had brought the financial controller to the house so he could start to familiarise himself with everyone's progress plan. "This is Victor, our new financial controller, he has replaced Philip, and he has reassured me that we are in better hands. So, welcome him and feel free to express your ambitions to him," continued my father. Although my father felt some level of confidence in Victor, he remained cautious and a little reserved with him.

Victor was thirty-seven years old and had completed his financial management studies at the University of Benin. He was married with two children who were still in primary school. His wife was a petty trader, selling all sorts of food items in their home kiosk. Victor, who also farmed and grew yam for sale to supplement his professional job, also tutored mathematics in the evening school for adults. Victor was of average height, standing at about five feet eight inches tall, and of medium to small build. He had a peculiar laugh that most people found irritating, and his eyebrows seemed overgrown. Victor used a bicycle to travel to work in his previous job as an accountant at a large bakery. The bakery, a successful business, delivered bread across the state and beyond and was considered the best quality by the majority of people. Victor had worked there for the last five years before resigning to take on a more challenging and rewarding position in my father's construction company.

It was now nearly three months since Victor joined my father's company. The relationship with Victor had grown in the right direction since then, and my father continued to relax his cautiousness about him. However, there was a new process in place that ensured integrity and reduced fraud. Lorraine's new position as head of operations meant that she oversaw the activities of every unit in the business. This was a big task, which was supported by Mike, the former clerk that worked under Philip. He was instantly promoted during the course of developing the new process. The new process also ensured that all cheques were verified by two staff with documented evidence before it was brought to my father's attention. There was also an agreement with the bank to provide copies of paid cheques on a monthly basis. Victor needed faster and more reliable mobility to effectively execute his role, and a new motorcycle was purchased for him. Also, as Victor's role increased to attend to my father's personal business, he was paid more to forfeit some of his other side jobs.

"Victor, we are to expand and diversify," uttered my father. "Listen to my vision and let's discuss the pros and cons," continued my father. "The King has offered to sell me a strategic piece of land on which I plan to build a luxurious hotel that is better and of a higher standard than any in the region. It will comprise of five floors, with a swimming pool and an outside bar." In addition, my father mentioned that part of the land would be used to produce construction blocks until the hotel was ready. He added that the block factory would produce all the bricks used for his construction and also be open to the public to buy. The block factory will be relocated to a different land nearby once the hotel is complete. "This sounds like a good idea, and I will put a financial analysis together for the land acquisition and draw up a budget plan for the block factory and the hotel projects," said Victor.

The land size seemed ambitious; however, it was within the scale required for the hotel building and the outside amenities. The purchase of the land asset was completed without any issues because the King had approved the sale. The location of the land was strategic as it provided an attraction for travellers crisscrossing the country from the east to the west. The land location also lies on a major road connecting the south to the north of the country. This put the land at a prominent junction, making the proposed hotel an important location. My father's foresight for this business opportunity was rather beyond the scope of someone that had no formal education. His thought of diversifying into a different sector was a move to secure his financial growth for the future. It was also an opportunity to invest his cash assets into tangible entities that provided a better return ratio. It was a week later, and the budget plan for the block factory was ready. Victor had travelled across the country to research the best possible machinery needed to mould high-density blocks of various sizes. My father's ambition was to deliver a block moulding facility that was able to triple the capability and capacity of any existing operator in the industry and in the region. "There would have to be multiple production lines to achieve the level of capacity that we need," mentioned my father to Victor.

It was about another month when the machinery and equipment for the block moulding facility were installed, and trial runs commenced. One of the competitive advantages incorporated in enhancing the business model of the factory was the massive drying capacity for the moulded blocks and the ability to keep operating when it is raining. Another advantage was the flexibility to move moulding machinery and equipment to the customer's project sites. This meant that a remote moulding team was set up with the specialism to mount and dismount equipment and shelters at project sites. This model added value to my father's construction business, where the most consumed material was blocks. There were also savings to be made from the self-production of materials required for construction, reducing the transportation cost for delivering blocks to sites, my father had believed.

My father had also planned to relocate the head office of his construction business to the site of the block moulding factory. This was made possible due to the large size of the land. He was able to build a temporary office block that did not constitute any obstruction to the moulding factory, and neither was it constricting the area for the proposed hotel building. Besides the office block, he had built a restaurant and an office for my mother. My father enjoyed quality meals, which he believed my mother was second to none in providing.

"Cecilia, you know you are now as good as my mother at cooking delicious meals; thanks for learning from her," my father would say to my mother. My mother did learn to cook different meals during the time she lived in Warri. Different regions specialised in a variety of meals, and perfecting the best taste required a detailed understanding of the recipes and the cooking methods. My mother went a little further by only using the best quality ingredients money can buy. She was prepared to travel as far as possible to buy high-end quality ingredients needed to cook meals. She would also try to create her own sauces and bases from scratch, ensuring that they were produced under the best quality process. All this enriched the flavour and taste of my mother's cooking.

"All my friends speak highly of your meals, and I think you should open a restaurant," my father would say to her. A month later, my mother's restaurant was fully functional. It quickly became a place where members of the public regularly visited to enjoy the taste of rich good cooking. This also meant that my father's lunch did not have to travel far to get to him on a daily basis. The restaurant was also a meeting location for my father's friends to conduct their business over a lovely meal. The restaurant, which was open from seven am for breakfast and served lunch till four pm when it closed, was well designed with dining tables and also sofas for easy and relaxed sitting. There were also alcoholic and soft beverages, as well as tea and coffee, on offer in the well-decorated air-conditioned environment.

Kate, my mother's aid, had recommended her cousin, Joy, who was employed as the restaurant manager. Joy was in her early thirties and was very fair in completion. She was beautiful and stood at above average height of five feet ten inches tall. She was slim. Most customers were drawn to the restaurant by Joy's attraction. Amongst the favourite meal eaten, there was the fresh fish pepper soup with yam. There was also the moi-moi dish that most customers ate for breakfast, and many believed the quality and taste were second to none.

My father knew that he had a beautiful wife and made no apologies for showcasing her to the nation. The quality of my mother's outfits was not just based on affordability but also on her vision and desire to look the best at all times. The combination of her attractiveness and elegant dressing put her on the radar of jealousy amongst my father's friends and, indeed, anyone that admired beauty. My father was also aware that his relatives were jealous of his loving relationship with my mother. "When are you going to take a second wife?" my father's siblings would ask him. "Cecilia is too proud and arrogant; she cannot be the only woman in your life, as it makes you look weak in the eyes of your friends that have two to four wives," they would continue.

My father continued to ignore them, and my mother, knowing their thoughts and wishes, never stopped to provide them with gifts and support whenever they requested for it. My father was well aware that nearly anyone that was rich in the region had more than one wife. He knew this was expected of him. However, he never felt the interest or the desire of wanting another woman. My father would attend the Chief's meeting for the area, and they would tease him with jokes like, "Let all the men with more than one wife rise," uttered a member of the Chief's association.

My father would respond in the same joking manner, "Let the only one strong enough to have four wives in one sit." My father would then say to his chief mates, "My one beautiful wife provides for me what even four of yours couldn't." They would laugh together before carrying on with their meeting business.

CHAPTER TWENTY-FIVE

Old Friends

IT WAS IN THE beginning of 1976, and I had continued to watch and learn from my parents. I was joining my father on business trips across the country, and we continued to spend time together during my school holidays. I also noticed the special bond between me and my parents and especially how my father shared his thoughts with me. It was during my summer school holiday, which was normally from May to September, and my parents decided I would be joining them on a business trip to Lagos. It was the rainy season, and I tend to dislike the fact that most plans are dependent on whether it was raining. Although I had been to Lagos before, when I was younger, I really could not remember it.

I was nearly six years old, and I believed I was wise for my age, and my parents were always interested in my views about everything. Although I was very young to understand most of my father's dealings, my constant exposure to his activities, business and otherwise, increased my knowledge and intelligence about the way things work. At that time, Lagos was the capital city of Nigeria, and it was also the most commercialised state in the country. My father's business had a direct relationship with the Nigerian government, and he did have to visit the federation housing authority at its head office in Lagos to discuss new and existing construction projects. "We will take a few days to explore Lagos. We will take you to the beach and also show you the tall buildings," my father told me. I was also asked to bring my Polaroid camera so I could capture photos to share with friends that had not been to Lagos.

We left for Lagos on a Monday with a convoy of three vehicles. I was in my father's Mercedes Benz, sitting in the front passenger seat, and my mother and father sat at the back. We were being chauffeured by Iyke. My father's driver was on another assignment to the southern region, just on the outskirts of Warri. Our journey started at about five-thirty in the morning, and we arrived in Lagos just before nine thirty am. We made a couple of stops to relieve ourselves and enjoyed some packed breakfast cooked by my mother the morning before we left.

I was impressed with Lagos and did not understand why we could not live there. "I hope we can set up an office here in Lagos, and we could make a home here," uttered my father. However, my mother was not too sure about relocating to Lagos. "I am not sure I can learn the Yoruba language," my mother responded. After my father had conducted his business, we had a couple of days to spend, and we went to Bar Beach, and it was the first time I experienced the natural beauty of the ocean. I was delighted that the sky remained blue and there was no sign of the rain. Bar Beach is located at the Atlantic Ocean shoreline of Victoria Island in Lagos. It has a sandy beach, which we walked on barefoot, and I also had the opportunity to ride a horse aided by the owner. I took many pictures with my Polaroid camera and a few with a professional photographer. I particularly liked the one that was taken with me on the back of the horse by a professional photographer.

On our departure day from Lagos, my father informed us that we were going to find an old friend before leaving for Agbor. He informed us that he had hired a local driver that could help us locate the address of where his friend had lived. "Daddy, how are we sure that your friend will still be living there?" I asked. "Hopefully, we will get another lead from that address that could take us to him in that case," replied my father.

We stayed at the Federal Palace Hotel located in Lagos, Victoria Island. It was one of the best hotels in Nigeria, and the suite we stayed in had a view of the Atlantic Ocean. Travelling from the hotel to our next stop took about an hour and thirty minutes. The traffic was heavy and not what I expected. "There are too many vehicles on the road; where are they all going?" I naively asked. "Just like us, everyone wants to go somewhere; we have to be patient," responded my father. We arrived at the location, and after checking for my father's friend, we were told he had moved, and we were given another address, which took us about an hour to reach.

The roads leading to the house were not well maintained as there were more potholes than I could count. We had parked in front of a modest house and waited for confirmation that my father's friend was living there. "I will be right back," my father said as he exited the vehicle. It was about ten minutes later that my father returned with an old man looking so eager to meet me and my mother. My father opened my door and said, "Peter, meet my last born, Uche." I stepped out of the car, and at the same time, I could hear my mother opening her door and starting to run towards us. "Good morning, sir," I greeted him. Before he could reply, my mother had reached him and embraced him.

"You must be Cecilia," uttered Peter. "Yes, I have heard so much about you, and we have been searching for you for a very long time," replied my mother. Peter turned to my father, and then he started to cry. "Jacob, I told you that you would make it" Peter said, sobbing. My father hugged him, and we all went inside his house. Peter started to tell my mother and I how he met my father. "He looked determined, yet he was heading nowhere when he asked me what was wrong with my lorry," said Peter. He continued, "I liked him the moment I laid my eyes on him, and I felt something good and spiritually right about him." Peter went on to describe my father as a teenager and how he wanted to adopt him as a son or a brother. He spoke about my father being a rubber tapper at Mr Dickson's plantation and how he knew that his future was a bright one. "Jacob, you are honest and hardworking; you were so determined to learn even though you could not read and write," added Peter. Peter had aged and was looking weak for a sixty-two year old. He did not seem to be particularly happy, still looked underweight, and his eyes appeared to be drawn into his head more so than normal. Perhaps he was experiencing some difficult times.

My father and Peter had left my mother and I in the living room while they went to another part of the house to speak in private. We later said our goodbyes and left. We had spent about two hours with Peter before we started our journey back home. My father had decided he would drive, and Iyke was asked to join one of the other vehicles. I was asked to sit at the back while my mother moved to sit in the front passenger seat. "Why is your friend a lot older than you?" I asked my father. "He was older than me when we met, and it was because of him I became who I am today," replied my father. "I know you are still a child, but I want you to do all you can to remember the things I tell you. They may not mean a thing to you now, but you will learn from them when you become a man," advised my father. I nodded and listened as my father narrated his story from when he was a child until meeting Peter and becoming successful. He later said that he wanted us to have privacy in the car; hence he asked Iyke to join the other vehicle. "Are you going to mention the incident during the war?" my mother asked. "Let's leave that for another day," replied my father. My father's story fascinated me as a child, and I became even more interested to know more as I grew older.

We had driven over three hours and were less than halfway home. My father was driving in the middle position of the convoy. "You must all be feeling hungry he said," and without hesitation, I made it clear that I was very hungry and needed food as a matter of urgency. "Great thing I asked then," my father responded to my comment. "Where are we going to eat?" I asked. "Don't worry, we are stopping soon," my father replied. I noticed him looking in the rear mirror, then he turned his head left to gaze at the wing mirror and quickly at the right one. He then turned the signal on and pulled out of the lane, and accelerated the car faster. He overtook the first vehicle leading the convoy, which was carrying Victor, Lorraine, and Mike. My father was now leading the convoy, and I was excited about that.

"Go faster, Daddy?" I demanded. "No, don't!" My mother shouted. "A little bit of speed won't harm," replied my father, and I could feel the vehicle accelerating and could see the speedometer rising from 80km/h to 90km/h and then 100km/h. "That's enough," uttered my mother. I turned back to see if the other two vehicles were catching up, and to my surprise, they were right behind us as if our acceleration had never happened. My father later reduced the speed to 70km/h, which was the maximum national limit on that road. After another ten minutes' drive, we pulled off the road onto the driveway of a restaurant with the two vehicles following behind.

We were seated at a different table from the rest of my parents' staff. Each table in the restaurant could only accommodate four people. We placed our orders for late lunch, and as we sat waiting for the food to arrive, my father left to speak to the rest of the group. Everyone seemed happy as they laughed at my father's joke. "I think Iyke should drive now as I may be caught breaking the speed limited," my father commented and laughed. He then returned to our table and sat down.

"Cecilia, Peter has some serious challenges," said my father. He went on to speak about Peter's situation and that he had given him some money and had promised him more help. Peter had lost both of his parents in a motor accident, and his wife had left him. Peter's parents had left a significant amount of debt, of which Peter had paid the majority, but still had a lot left to settle. His children were struggling to gain a good education due to a lack of financial support. "I have promised to pay all his children's cost of education, and I will clear all his debt and upgrade his house to a better liveable standard. I will also arrange for Victor to buy him a suitable vehicle," said my father. My mother, looking into my father's eyes as she paid attention to him, took his hand, squeezed it, and said, "Thank you, Jacob." I felt that was not enough and asked, "But how will he feed himself, he needs food as he looked too skinny." My father turned to me and said, "I am glad you are listening and paying attention to all things around you; keep it up. We will pay him a monthly salary, and that will help him feed himself in addition to his pension." I was not sure what a pension was, but I thought I would ask on another day. We had all finished our meals just over an hour after we had stopped and were making the final part of the journey home. Iyke was driving and was telling me a story while my parents, sitting at the back, had fallen asleep.

"BEN, HOW WAS YOUR TRIP?" my father asked his driver just after we had arrived home. "It went well, sir, and I was able to deliver the items in person to the manager of the shipping company." Ben had been my father's driver since nineteen sixty-nine and continued to enjoy his job. Ben was a big size man. Everyone apart from my parents called him Big Ben. He was also the friendliest man amongst my parents' staff. He would go the extra mile for anyone, and he hardly complained about anything. He was renowned for saying, "It is what it is; why the bother." Ben stood at about five feet eleven inches tall, with a chest size of fifty-two inches wide. He wore size twelve shoes and always carried a white handkerchief in his pocket. He was always looking clean, well-dressed, and presentable. Ben had a wife and four children. He never liked to talk about his age, but we knew he was forty-four years old. Ben was seen as a family member and carried out my father's instructions to the best he could. His best had always met or exceeded my father's expectations.

There was a cargo ship that departed Warri every fortnight, heading to Southampton, England. My father needed some precious locally sourced food items to be delivered to Mr Fisher and Mr Dickson. My father had always used the shipping company for importing furniture and other overseas-made items. Mr Fisher and Mr

Dickson had left Nigeria just at the time the Biafran war was starting. My father had promised to continue to send them the locally made gin, plantain, mango, yam, and sometimes dried fish, which they enjoyed during their time in Nigeria. The best of these items would be sourced and prepared for shipping by my mother.

In addition to the food items, my father had a special gift for both friends. It was a bank draft addressed to each man, with enough value to buy a brand new 1975 Model Citroen DS. There was also a note that accompanied each of the bank drafts, "Thank you for making me the person that I am today."

My father could not imagine that he would have become as successful as he was without the help and support of Mr Peter Omon, Mr Dickson, and Mr Simon Fisher. They gave him hope, insight, and confidence for aspiration. They had all said that they saw something special in my father and that he had been destined to be successful.

CHAPTER TWENTY-SIX

The Harmattan

IT WAS AT THE beginning of 1977, and the dry season was upon us as always. The dry weather that started around October the previous year felt like the most severe to everyone. The local people were worried as the harsh weather was so dry that we started to notice lines of cracks on our skin, in some cases leading to skin fissures. However, this was something my grandmother could solve. She must have experienced even more intense harmattan seasons and had survived them without too much discomfort. My grandmother made a concoction of a moisturising lotion that rehydrated the skin and kept us comfortable. The potion was made from the seeds of palm kernels.

Palm kernels are fruits produced from a certain species of palm oil tree. The palm kernels are usually extracted for the oil that is contained in the outer fibrous tissues, which is used in producing palm oil, and the nuts of the kernel, when cracked open, contain another edible hard seed. This seed is then dried or fried before being ground into a paste. The paste is then squeezed under high pressure to release its fine oil content. It is this oil that my grandmother used as the base of the moisturiser. We used the moisturiser to alleviate our dry skin issues caused by the harmattan seasons. My grandmother would usually produce more than we needed and was able to sell some of the potions to generate some income. So, although the weather was harsh, we always managed to stay resilient with the help of our grandmother's moisturiser.

It was the first dry season that was experienced by the block factory. Moulding the blocks required wooden pallets, which were manually inserted into the machines. These wooden pallets, which were made from fresh and untreated wood, act as a base to which the blocks are moulded onto. The blocks would remain on the wooden pallets until they were set and dry. In the normal rainy season, it would be about two days maximum for the blocks to be dried in the open air, and the wooden pallets would be removed, cleaned, and examined for defects before being reused. However, the harsh dry season had dehydrated the untreated wooden pallets, rendering them uneven, and they were not able to be inserted into the machine. The dry atmosphere also affected the curing process of the block. The blocks were setting too quickly and, as a result, would make them crack when dry.

This was a major setback for the business, and the factory had to suspend production. Although the sales office remained open, customers were given future dates of up to three months before delivery. The three months were leading to the beginning of the rainy season, where conducive weather would favour production. However, my father launched an investigation and researched how other block moulding facilities in the country dealt with the impact of the harmattan season. Part of the solution was for my father to create a new mini sawmill and a carpentry workshop within the grounds of the block factory. They would treat the wood used in making the pallets and were on hand to repair any pallets almost immediately. The sawmill was also open to the public for all wood preparation services for a charge.

It was around March in the same year, and the dry season started to ease off its intensity. We reduced the frequency in which we were applying the palm kernel moisturiser. The dusty wind power started to calm down, and the haze that clouded the atmosphere and reduced vision began to clear away. As we were preparing to enter a new weather season, my family was also getting ready for a change.

My eldest two siblings, Joyce and Michael, were preparing to leave for the United States. This was something my parents had always hoped for since they started to raise a family. They wanted their children to receive the best education possible no matter where it would be found. For several years, my parents had researched the best country for my two eldest siblings to attend for their university education. To my parents, not attending university was not an option. They had not even contemplated a situation where any of their children would refuse or be unable to gain the highest form of education.

The issue of financing education was never an issue for my parents. They were aware that there were different levels of education. To my father, it was simple. He had seen the level of advance knowledge and skills Mr Fisher and Mr Dickson have displayed. They both studied in the United Kingdom. "Why do they seem to know better than us in everything?" my father would ask in his usual conversation to justify his case for pursuing foreign education studies for his children or, indeed, anyone. "I just simply believe that with the best education, you will be better equipped to contribute to future advancement in life," my father would continue.

It was five o'clock on a Sunday morning, and I found myself waking up on a sofa with my parents. My head was resting on my father's lap, and my feet were on my mother's as they both sat on opposite ends of the three-seater sofa. I could not remember how I got there as I knew I had gone to sleep the night before on my father's bed. I was able to hear voices that I recognised speaking as I opened my eyes. It's a family meeting, I reassured myself as I could see all my siblings in my parent's private living room. I always enjoyed the family meetings, albeit they started very early in the morning. "Why was I not woken up?" I asked. "I am part of this family, and I have things I could say and things I am supposed to know," I added. "Yes, so you can run your mouth about our plans to your little friends in the neighbourhood," responded William. "Enough, let's focus on our discussions," interjected my father.

The family meeting carried on for another two hours, and there was an update about my eldest siblings, Joyce and Michael's, travel to the United States, the university they would be attending, and where they would stay. They also received caution from my parents to behave well. I remember my brother, Michael, saying, "I will need a car!" My father's response was, "That is all being arranged, and you will get the funds to buy a small car, but nothing extravagant." The takeaway from that meeting, for me, was the car. Nothing extravagant, I believed, was definitely the opposite of what my brother would go for. So, I asked him just as the meeting was finishing, "What car will you buy?" To which he replied, "You will have to wait and find out, my little brother."

Joyce and Michael, being the eldest children, were special to my parents. My sister, Joyce, being the first child of my parents, was cherished so much. My parents adored her for many other reasons, in addition to being their own child. For my parents, a first child signified the beginning of the many to come, and they saw that position as an extraordinary one. She was the head and would watch over the others to come in good faith. Joyce was also beautiful and had grown into a teenager, becoming the prettiest girl in town. I believe my parents were delighted she was leaving for the United States to prevent the possibility of potential suitors seeking her hand in marriage. I think my parents believed that hardly anyone in the country was good enough to marry her. Joyce was taller than average height, slim built, and very attractive. She was also intelligent and wise. She would discuss business ventures with my father since she was ten years old. My father had encouraged her to study a degree in business administration in the United States.

I found Joyce to be funny, a caring person, and could be very understanding and relate to people's situations well. Her empathy meant that she was always willing to help anyone. I also liked her group of friends. They would mostly spend their summer school vacations at our family home. We would have about four of them staying with us for several weeks at a time. They all thought I was cute and would always want me to hang around them. I was able to learn at a young age how girls think. They would share their innermost thoughts and secrets amongst themselves with nothing spared. I have, on certain occasions, passed on information to my parents, which backfired on me, and for a few weeks, I was excluded from hanging around with my sister and her friends. I know they adored me, though, as they eventually forgave me and continued to take me everywhere they went.

The other reason my two oldest siblings were so important to my parents was because their second child, Michael, was a boy. The culture would favour a male child for succession. The oldest male child is seen as the next leader of the family after the father. Therefore, Michael was nurtured from his early years as a leader in waiting to take over from my father. Michael had grown up into a handsome young man. He measured six feet in height and had a slim build. Again, like my sister, he was very intelligent and loved mathematics. "You are to become a civil engineer," my father would say to him. Like Joyce, he was at boarding school and would return home during the holidays. I would share my time between the two of my eldest siblings during their school holidays.

My brother, Michael, took me everywhere he went. There was a time that I followed him to a party. It was on a Saturday evening, and my parents had retired to their apartment. Normally, I would be with them on the sofa watching a programme on the television with my head resting on my father's lap and my feet on my mother's. My parents were also aware that my eldest siblings liked to take me out when they were home, so they hardly worried if I was missing for a while.

The party was a long drive away, and my brother's best friend, Zigga, was with us. I sat in the middle seat in the back of the car. This gave me a clearer vision of the road ahead. I was obviously the youngest at the party, and I knew for sure I was not supposed to be in there. I believe my family name and status was the main reason I was allowed in. It was late, and long past midnight, by the time we left the party with my brother's girlfriend, Penny. We were going to drop her off at her home, and the road to her village was unpaved and winds through woodland without streetlights. All I could see ahead of us were our car lights as I sat at the back with Zigga while Penny sat in the front passenger seat.

We managed to reach Penny's home to drop her off. Zigga and I remained in the vehicle as Michael and Penny left the car and closed the doors. I could see they were kissing, which lasted for at least ten minutes before they parted and my brother got back inside the car, and we started to drive home. As we were driving through the woodland, we noticed a huge tree had fallen across the road, preventing us from going through. There was no sign of any possible help we could reach out for in the middle of the woodland, and it was not possible to move the tree. Going back led only to Penny's village, which did not have any motoring road access to anywhere; therefore, it was not a viable option.

As time went by, Michael became increasingly concerned that my parents would be worried that we were not home. I know for sure that my parents would be sitting up on my father's bed, staring at the clock on the wall and listening out for the sound of a vehicle pulling onto our front drive. I also knew that it did raise my parent's blood pressure. On many occasions after midnight, I have sat awake with my parents, waiting for my elder siblings to return home. This issue got discussed at most family meetings, but compliance levels remained significantly poor. My father would sometime telephone the police chief and ask for the patrol units to search for them. My elder siblings were aware of the police search for them after midnight and knew how to avoid being caught.

As I sat in the car waiting for Michael and Zigga to figure out the next course of action for getting us home, I noticed the time on the car dashboard. It was twenty-six minutes past two in the morning. I knew this would have past the critical time when my parents would ring the police chief. For over half an hour, Michael and Zigga had tried to move the tree trunk to no avail. I opened the door and stepped out to join them, but Michael noticed me coming and said, "Go back inside the car where you will be safe." Ignoring him, I continued walking towards them. "Shall we go back to Penny's house and borrow a machete to cut the tree trunk off the road?" I asked.

We were shortly back at Penny's house and explained our problem to her father. Penny's father expressed that they were used to the trees falling across the road and went into his shed to produce a chainsaw. He got onto his motorbike, and we followed him to the woodland road, where he effortlessly sawed the tree trunk into chunks that we were able to move. We cleared the road and headed home. It was nearly four o'clock in the morning by the time we reached home. There were two police vehicles in front of my house, and my parents could be seen looking helpless and distressed as I approached them. "Are you all alright?" asked my mother. "Yes, we are fine," Michael uttered, knowing he was in big trouble.

It was in the middle of May of that year that we all said our goodbyes to Joyce and Michael as they prepared to leave to catch their plane to the United States. My grandparents and my father's relatives were at my house to wish them well. A few of my father's friends also came to wish them well. The church priest was invited to say a prayer and to offer some words of advice. For us as a family, it was a challenging time as we said goodbye to the two of them at the same time. We knew we would never be the same again as a family.

A few days later, we were on a telephone call hearing about their new environment and how it felt to be in a strange country. Michael asked to speak to me, but the only thing I could think to ask him was, "What car did you buy?"

CHAPTER TWENTY-SEVEN

The Missing Son

THE RAINY SEASON was at its peak in the month of July in 1977. One of the most consumed fruits or vegetables in Nigeria during the rainy season is corn. Corn is usually the first crop to be cultivated just after the first rain of the rainy season. The land would usually be prepared for cultivation at the end of the harmattan season. Many Nigerian farmers adopt mixed farming as the most sustainable method of agriculture as it allows them to cultivate several crops simultaneously in one piece of land. The corn, which is usually planted first, will mature for harvest after ninety days. It can be harvested from May till October. The corn is mostly consumed when roasted from fresh and eaten as a snack. The most popular way to consume roasted corn is when eaten with the purple bush pear or the African Pear. The scientific name for the bush pear is Dacryodes Edulis. It grows on trees, and when soaked in hot water for a few minutes or placed near an open fire, it softens and is ready to eat. The combination of roasted corn and bush pear remains a favourite snacking meal in Nigeria during the rainy season.

It was just after seven o'clock in the evening and my father and I was sitting on the sofa of his living room, watching the television and enjoying the corn and bush pear. We had already had our dinner together not up to an hour before my mother presented the roasted corn and bush pear as a substitute for dessert. My mother joined us, and she started to tell us about her busy day. We tried to listen as we consumed the corn and the bush pear with the television on. "This is delicious," uttered my father. "Are you listening to what I am saying?" asked my mother. "Cecilia, you know not to speak to me when I am doing this corn and pear justice; let's talk later, please," my father responded. How do you do justice to a corn and bush pear, I wondered. However, my mother rested her back on the armchair where she was sitting and then placed her feet on the coffee table. She seemed relaxed as she started to watch the television.

There was a television programme I often watch with my parents at eight o'clock on Wednesday evenings before I went to bed. The programme only lasted for thirty minutes, and it was always joyful for me to see my parents laugh together. We had finished our corn and bush pear by the time it approached eight o'clock, and the programme was about to start. My mother moved to join us on the sofa to get a better front facing view of the television. Then I did my usual, placing my head on my father's lap and feet on my mother's.

At about ten minutes into the programme, there was a scene that was hilarious, and I could not really laugh lying down and decided to sit up. However, I could only hear my mother laughing, and it seemed my mother noticed that my father was silent at the same time as me, and we both looked at him almost simultaneously just as I was sitting upright. My father's head had fallen back on the sofa, and he was motionless. My mother immediately got up and rushed to my father.

"Jacob, Jacob," my mother shouted at my father as she continued to shake him, but he was not responding. "Call the doctor," my mother shouted at me. I rushed to the telephone to dial the number of the doctor. "Dr Memeth's Residence, how can I help you?" responded the doctor's wife. "My father needs Dr Memeth urgently," I shouted into the phone receiver. "Uche, good evening; what is wrong with your father?" asked the doctor's wife, who was a nurse. "He is not breathing, and we need Dr Memeth now!" I replied. "I will get him to come up immediately," she responded, and the phone line went dead. Dr Memeth was a tenant who occupied my parents' bungalow that shared a boundary with our new family house. Dr Memeth, who worked as a physician at the general hospital, also had a private clinic, which he ran from his bungalow during his free time. Dr Memeth became our family doctor because of our proximity, and we maintained a good relationship with him and his family. His wife also worked at the general hospital as a nurse. They had two children, a three-year-old boy, and a one-year-old girl. Mrs Memeth was pregnant with their third child.

Dr Memeth arrived in my parents' living room less than ten minutes after I had spoken to his wife. He was carrying his work bag, dressed in his pyjamas, and was wearing flip-flop slippers. Dr Memeth was slightly shorter than an average man, standing at about five feet four inches. He was thirty-six years old that year and looked his age. He was also of average build and always looked decent and tidy. He had a white saloon car, which always looked sparkling clean, and he would park it in his locked garage every time he was not driving it. There was a teasing rumour within the neighbourhood that he was so obsessed with his car that he treated it like a human patient. As quickly as he arrived, he attended to my father.

By this time, everyone in my household was in my parents' living room, looking concerned but helpless. "I need privacy at once," uttered Dr Memeth. However, I never expected that included me as I would normally be anywhere and everywhere with my father, and Dr Memeth was aware of this close relationship. "Uche, I need you to fetch me a bowl of water and a clean cloth," said Dr Memeth. My mother was sitting beside my father, holding him upright. I left to attend to Dr Memeth's request and returned to see my father lying on the sofa and had an intravenous fluid fixed into his right hand. My mother was holding up the intravenous fluid as she stood beside my father. "We need to take him to the hospital at once," said Dr Memeth. Calling the ambulance was something we could not do at that time as it just was not available. There were no drivers at that time of the day as they had finished their contracted hours and had gone home. My mother could drive, but I believe Dr Memeth was not too sure how quickly she would take to get to the hospital. To my surprise, Dr Memeth said, "I will get my car ready." He immediately left to pull his car out of the garage, and my father was taken downstairs and into Dr Memeth's waiting vehicle.

It was the following morning that I was woken up by my mother to tell me that my father was responding to treatment at the hospital and that he had asked for me. It was during the summer holiday, and I was free to follow my mother to the hospital to see my father. My mother had made breakfast, which I ate with my father in his private hospital room. "What happened to you, Daddy?" I asked. "The doctors said I was exhausted as a result of working too hard. They want me to reduce my travels and rest more," my father replied. "I have many things to do, I have told them, and they will give me medication to reduce and maintain my blood pressure," he continued.

It was three days later that my father was discharged from the hospital. Although he would continue with his working pattern, he was to allow more time for resting. I had agreed with my father that we would spend two weekends monthly in our country home in the village. "We will go hunting, have barbecues and visit relatives and friends within the village community, just you and I," stated my father. I was delighted and looked forward to our first trip. "Can I take my chopper bicycle with me?" I asked. "Of course, but let us buy you another chopper, and we can leave it at the country house, so we don't need to inconvenience anyone transporting it there and back," replied my father. "Can I get a blue one this time?" I asked. "I will inform Victor to arrange this and drop it off at the house in the village," replied my father.

Summer holidays meant that the rest of my siblings in Nigeria would return home from their boarding schools. They would often return with a friend or two to spend the holiday with us. This tended to make our house a little busier than usual. My brothers, Alexander and William, had returned from school with a friend each. Alexander was fifteen years old. He was fair in completion and very intelligent.

He was about five feet five inches tall and was of average build. He was kind and always cared for everyone. However, he did get easily annoyed and had a low tolerance level.

My father had informed us that we would be travelling to Lagos, and Alexander and I would be accompanying him. On the day of the trip, we left early for the nearest airport to catch a flight to Lagos. It was Benin City Airport, which was about forty-five miles away from home. My father did not see the need to drive all the way to Lagos, especially after he had been asked to rest more to maintain a lower blood pressure. My mother's driver, Iyke, had driven us to the airport, and he was asked to return later in the evening to pick us up. We took the first scheduled flight from Benin City to arrive in Lagos for eight o'clock in the morning. On board the flight, Alexander thought my father was talking too much about life, and he wanted to find another seat away from us to have peace. "It is only a fifty-minute flight; can't you just stay?" I asked Alexander as he stood up to look for an empty seat in the economy cabin.

We then chartered a taxi that chauffeured us across the city of Lagos to attend my father's various business meetings. We stopped for a late lunch as my father would always aim to complete his dealings before taking time to rest. Having travelled with my father on many occasions, I knew he hardly stopped for lunch. He would carry on, determined to achieve his set objectives before he thought of breaks. On this occasion, I had to remind him, saying, "Daddy, remember that the doctor had asked that you take breaks and rest during your day, and we are hungry now too." It was only after this reminder that my father decided we stop for lunch.

It was a long and busy day for us. Even with the lunch stop, Alexander and I felt exhausted. I became really concerned for my father, given that he would do similar trips often. I felt we needed to find a way to remind him to stop for lunch regardless of the number of tasks he was planning to achieve. I also thought he needed to spread out his tasks so that he was able to reduce the stress involved in getting things done. His business continued to grow, and this required him to be present at certain Federal government meetings, mostly scheduled in Lagos. In addition, he had to attend the State level development project meetings.

I realised that I needed to speak to my mother about this so she could discuss it with my father and perhaps with Dr Memeth. We were later dropped off at the airport by the chartered taxi, and he was delighted with the tip my father gave him in addition to his charge. We were catching the five o'clock evening flight back to Benin City. As usual, I followed my father into the first-class cabin, and although we could not see Alexander, we felt he was perhaps sitting away from us to read his book. The plane landed as scheduled, and as we started to disembark, I started to look out for Alexander. It was after we had reached the arrival hall that we realised that Alexander was not on the flight.

My father immediately became anxious and determined to be reunited with Alexander. We went to the airline desk and informed them of my missing brother. "My son is missing. He was supposed to be on the flight from Lagos with us," my father told the airline staff. They requested for Alexander's full name and flight details, which my father provided. "Please take a seat, and we will reach out to Lagos Airport to locate him," informed the airline staff. As we waited, my father decided to reach for the pay phone and called my mother. The news that Alexander was missing did not go down well with my mother. I could hear her shouting on the receiver that my father must not return home without her son. "How was it possible that he was not on the flight with you?" my mother shouted. "Can you calm down? You are adding to my stress," my father responded. I continued to hear my mother shouting, and I saw my father replace the receiver without saying goodbye. I noticed my father's face had changed, and I became more concerned for his health. It was about another twenty minutes later that we were asked to return to the airline desk. "We have your son on the phone, sir," uttered the airline staff. My father was offered the phone to speak to Alexander and after a short conversation, he replaced the receiver, but not after I heard him shout, "Do not move an inch from where you are. Do you understand me?"

"Unfortunately, sir, we do not have another flight from Lagos into Benin City until seven o'clock tomorrow morning," uttered the airline staff. "That is not good enough," replied my father. "Sir, we can accommodate him at a nearby hotel to Lagos Airport, and he will be picked up in the morning to board the seven am flight tomorrow," replied the airline staff. "I am sorry, but I need him here before I can leave this airport today," my father responded. "But there are no flights from Lagos to Benin City until tomorrow morning," the airline staff reaffirmed.

My father asked that I follow him as we left the airline desk and headed into the administrative area of the airport. We walked through a set of glass doors with a sign that I could not read. I knew that my father could not read the sign either, but I thought that he must know where he was going. There was a lady sitting behind a desk that appeared to be a reception area. Following my father's lead, we approached the lady, and my father asked for Mr Williamson. "Please tell him Jacob Oriahi would like to see him," my father requested. "Welcome, Chief Oriahi, I know who you are, and I will get Mr Williamson immediately," responded the lady.

After what seemed to be a short wait, Mr Williamson was ushering us into his office. He seemed to know my father very well, and he looked at me and said, "You must be Uche, the last born; how are you?" There was a short delay to my reply as I took a minute to wonder if he was someone I should know. "I am fine, thank you," I replied. My father started to explain the situation about Alexander, and after a brief conversation, my father asked, "Is there any airline that I can charter their plane to fly my son from Lagos to Benin City?" After another short conversation and a telephone call, "I have a plane ready to fly your son and can depart in the next one hour," uttered Mr Williamson. "Yes, yes, please get him on that plane," replied my father as he reached for his briefcase and produced a cheque book. "Please, Chief, don't worry; we will get the airline to send the invoice to your office."

"Have you just chartered a plane?" I asked my father. "Yes, it is the only way to get him here tonight," my father replied. We were made comfortable in Mr Williamson's office as we waited for my brother's chartered plane to arrive. My father was updated as the flight was prepared and took off from Lagos with Alexander, heading to Benin City.

It was about one hour later that we were reunited with Alexander, and we left the airport to head home. Alexander had explained on the way home that he had decided to go and use the toilet, and he could not find us by the time he returned. "Perhaps if you were not reading your book, you would have paid attention that we were being asked to board," I uttered, to which I received a bad look.

CHAPTER TWENTY-EIGHT

The Clean Shot

IT WAS STILL THE summer of 1977, and my family home remained rowdy, filled with my siblings and their friends from school. Although my parents never took notice of the noisy situation, they realised that it was their responsibility to care for my siblings' friends. Twice a week, my parents would release their drivers and vehicles to chauffeur my siblings and their friends to visit attractions as well as shopping and other entertaining activities outside the area. They would travel to Benin City, which is about forty miles away west, and other times to the east to visit Onitsha market that is about fifty miles from our home. I was never allowed to join any of the trips as I was too young. Occasionally they would bring me a gift and tell me about their trips. I did find it annoying that I was not allowed to join them.

On one occasion, I knew that the trip was planned, and I got myself ready and hid in one of the travelling cars. I got into the back of the car and squashed myself as small as I could by squatting and burying my head between my knees. I had the impression that my siblings would not have any issues letting me join in on the trip. Unfortunately, I was easily found, and an attempt was made to get me out of the car, which I resisted. I was not prepared to leave without a fight, and I was holding onto the seatbelt of the car and refused to let go. It was only after my mother had intervened with promises that I would follow her on a trip to Onitsha in a few days' time that I let go of my grip on the seatbelt. I had heard so much about Onitsha but had never been.

Visiting Onitsha was a good experience. As promised by my mother, it was a couple of days after my protest to be allowed to travel with my siblings and friends to Onitsha that we were making the trip. I was delighted I was going somewhere with my mother, that had shopping activities, and not the office visits and meetings that I was used to when I travelled with my father. On the morning of the trip to Onitsha, as usual, I had followed my father to the morning mass, and on our walk home, he enlightened me briefly about Onitsha. "Onitsha is a very busy place, and children tend to get lost," my father said. "Why would children get lost?" I asked.

"Onitsha has one of the largest markets in Nigeria, and many people all over the country will visit to buy goods," my father replied. He continued, "Promise me that you will always stay by your mother's side and do not wander away to look at anything by yourself." I immediately thought about my brother missing in Lagos, and I knew it had caused some issues between my parents. My father was annoyed with my mother's approach to the matter and did not appreciate the way my mother spoke to him on the phone and even when we returned from that trip. My father felt that my mother was becoming aggressive towards him, and he did not like it.

"Yes, I promise to stay at Mummy's side at all times," I responded. I continued, "I have noticed that you and Mummy are not as loving to each other as you used to be, why is that?" Although I was not expecting any detailed response as we were about to reach the house, my father went on to say, "I am so proud you pay good attention for your age. Yes, I feel your mother is getting more aggressive by the day, and it is adding to my stress level. Do not worry, though, as we will sort things out." Although I was aware of this, there was nothing I could do but to watch and hope that they resolved their issues and got back to being nice and loving to each other.

It was some minutes after nine o'clock in the morning, and Iyke was already approaching the halfway point to Onitsha as I continued to ask, "Are we there yet?" This was the first time I was following on a journey towards the east. Having heard of my father's incident during the Biafran war, the eastern part of the country did not really bring me any comfort. However, I was excited to be going somewhere new. Onitsha is a large commercial city that is located in the Anambra State of Nigeria and has a current population of about one million five hundred thousand people.

Onitsha market remains one of the commercial hubs in the country that serves the region and beyond with goods made locally as well as those imported from foreign countries. Although the market is open to regular public shoppers, it mainly caters for the wholesale trade. Anambra State shares a boundary with Bendel State, my State, which was later divided into two states forming Edo State (the west) and Delta State (the east). Anambra State now shares a common boundary with Delta State. I was amazed by the size of the market and how busy the traders and customers were in going about their business. We spent several hours in the market buying all sorts, including expensive and sophisticated clothing materials and gold jewellery. Unlike my father, we did stop for breaks and had lunch, and at no time were we feeling exhausted even though we had covered a lot of areas by walking to visit shops. It was the first of many visits to Onitsha that I continued to enjoy as I grew older.

IT WAS ON A SUNDAY, and we were having our usual early morning family meeting. Summer months, as a result of the school holidays, did ensure that we had all the family members present in the meeting. However, my eldest siblings, Joyce, and Michael, who were now living in the United States, would obviously not be able to attend, well not in person, as my father did sometimes, on a few occasions, had dialled them in through an international telephone call. During this particular meeting, we heard from Joyce and Michael via the telephone. My father had bought a special telephone set that enabled the speakerphone, and we could speak to them as though they were in the room. They gave an update about their studies and progress on other activities that they were working on. My father then informed us that he would be visiting the United States soon. He also discussed the weekend trip to the country home in the village as well as other activities he was progressing within his construction business. Each one of us was invited to speak of our personal issues and any extra support we may require. I spoke about being left behind all the time by my siblings, as they never wanted me to participate in their events. I was surprised to hear my father say, "It is better that way; you are too young to get into their activities, most I don't agree with anyway."

My father had finished work early on this particular Friday, and he had returned home just after lunchtime. "Your mother did not visit her restaurant today; where is she?" I remember the stressed look on my father's face that afternoon, and I did not want to add to his frustration that I did not know where my mother was. "I do not know, but I think she may have gone to the local market as she usually does?" I responded. "Alright, go pack a few things, and we are leaving for the village," uttered my father. "We will leave a message for her that we have left for the village," said my father with a rather unhappy tone. I was excited that I was getting to enjoy a wild weekend with my father, so I went to pick up some clothes and a few items that I needed. In less than half an hour from the time my father arrived from work, we were ready to leave for the village.

"Ben, you can take the rest of the day off, and that includes Saturday as well, and spend it with your family," said my father as he handed an envelope to him. We were taking the Mercedes Benz, and that excited me too. We tried to say goodbye to my siblings, but they were nowhere to be found. "I told you, you don't want to follow them anywhere," said my father. He continued, "Where could they have gone this afternoon? Instead of doing something useful, they are probably out and about with their friends chasing women and drinking." I did not say anything even though I knew he was right. I had also seen some of my siblings and their friends smoking cigarettes, but I knew that I dare not tell my parents. I thought that was what teenagers did anyway, although I hated the taste of alcohol as well as the smell of cigarettes being smoked.

We had stopped at a supermarket on the way to our village house, and we bought a few tins of the Queen of the Coast tuna and a freshly made loaf of bread. We also bought a carton of twelve 70cl bottles of Gulder beer and a crate of twenty-four bottles of assorted flavours of coca cola soft drinks. It was nearly four o'clock by the time we reached the house at the village. As we approached the compound, Sunny, the head of our security staff, opened the gate, and we drove in. The first thing I noticed was the number of overripe guava fruits that had fallen from their trees. I knew I was in for a treat as I love guava.

As soon as my father pulled up the car in the driveway and I was able to get out, I reached for the guava trees, ignoring the fallen ones as they looked mostly rotten, and plucked a few well-ripe ones. I did not wait to wash them and started to eat the fruits. "Well, you need to wash them first!" Shouted my father. "Come and help Sunny take some of the stuff from the car into the house," he continued. Sunny was one of the few trusted people my father was close to in the village. He oversaw most of my father's affairs in the village and looked after our house. He had his own family house just opposite ours. Sunny was older than my father but looked fit and tough for his age. He was formerly a soldier and had served during the second world war and the Biafran War.

Sunny was about five feet, eight inches tall and had a medium size build. Although his chest seemed large, his waist was on the smaller side. He was not really skinny but could appear so when seen from a distance. Sunny's eldest son worked in my parents' construction business as a truck driver. Sunny lived with two wives and had children, but I had no knowledge of how many.

My father and I checked that everything in the house was functioning well and that everything we needed for our weekend stay was available. There was no telephone, as there was no line connected to the village area yet, and therefore we were unable to reach anyone to request for supplies, but we preferred it that way as it added to the adventure. After a brief catch-up with Sunny, we had the generator working, and the air-conditioning units were switched on to cool the house. The fridge was turned on, and I loaded it with the drinks we had bought. "There is something missing," my father said. "What could that be?" he asked. I was not sure what could be missing, I thought we had everything, but suddenly I remembered. "The cartridges for the shotgun," I said.

"Follow me," my father demanded. I followed him into the garage through the utility room, and he flipped the light switch on, and there it was, a blue chopper. It was still wrapped in plastic, and I could not wait to rip it off. "Thank you, Daddy," I said. My father had walked toward the outside garage door and pulled the shutters up. As the shutters gave way to allow the natural light into the garage, the beauty of the chopper bike became more visible. I jumped on it, moved the gear into the first position, and I stepped on the peddle. It was a smooth ride along the driveway to the gate. "Alright, that is enough now; we need to go into the village and visit a few relatives," I heard my father shout at me. I knew I had the whole weekend to ride the chopper, so I turned back and headed into the garage, where I parked the bike.

My father and I then got into the car and drove into the village. It was a good feeling to see the village with a little bit more grown-up mind, as I tried to imagine my father being born there and the challenges he had faced. The village looked peaceful but was smaller than I had thought, and there was one main long street that cut across it and another road that linked to the back of the village. Both streets were motorable and linked to the major road that connects to other villages and the Agbor town. We met many relatives and friends in their homes who received us well. We later returned to the house, and we had our tuna sandwiches for dinner.

It was the following morning, and we were preparing to go hunting. My father had taken me hunting before, and I had enjoyed it. My father believed in the idea of a clean shot. I really did not understand what he actually meant by giving a clean shot to the hunted animal. I felt I should pay attention a little bit more this time, as I was slightly more mature now compared to the previous hunting visits. Therefore, I would hopefully be able to understand and remember what a clean shot really meant. I looked at the time, it was just past six o'clock in the morning, and my father wanted us to return from hunting before ten am when my mother would be arriving with our breakfast. "Good morning, Sunny," my father said. "Good morning, Chief," replied Sunny as he proceeded to help us load the shotguns, cartridges and the other gear and snacks we were taking with us in the vehicle. It took us about ten minutes to arrive at the spot where we parked the vehicle and carried all our gear, and headed into the forest.

It was lonely, and all we could hear was the noise being made by different animals. It was nearly half an hour's walk into the forest when my father located a spot we could use as our base, and we dropped our excess gear and snacks. We rested for about fifteen minutes, and we were geared up and ready to hunt. My father had two shotguns, each hanging on his shoulders, and I had the cartridge belt and a neatly folded sack tied to the right side of my waist. "You must stay by my side at all times so I can see you," my father uttered. "Ok, Daddy," I replied. "Not behind me, but beside me," my father reaffirmed. I decided that it was the perfect time to ask my father to explain the term 'clean shot' to me. "It means that I must be effective and efficient," said my father. Although I was impressed to hear my father speak the English words that made him sound educated and intelligent, I was not sure what it meant. So, I asked him to explain. "It means that I must aim at my target precisely at the spot where my first shot can kill it and that I must not miss," explained my father. It was after about twenty minutes of searching that my father located a potential target. "Slow down," my father whispered. He gently removed one of the shotguns from his shoulder and rested it on a tree trunk. Then he started to lower himself to the ground and, at the same time, used his right hand to signal to me to do the same.

We were now both on our knees, and I noticed my father had kept his eyes on his target. He then removed the other shotgun from his shoulder, which was at this moment half laying on the ground. He repositioned the shotgun on his right arm and signalled for two cartridges. My father used his finger to request the type of cartridge he needed, with the thumb signifying the heaviest of the grade to the pinkie finger denoting the least-sized cartridge. My father showed me the thumb twice. I knew I must stay as quiet as possible as I reached for the two requested cartridges and handed them to my father. He slowly snapped the shotgun to release the loading bay and inserted the two cartridges.

My father then used his finger to point out the target to me. I looked forward to the direction of his pointed finger, and I noticed a bush pig grazing at about twenty yards from us. I thought that it was a large animal and was not sure if my father could deploy the right firepower required to kill it. Then I remembered his explanation of the clean shot. I knew I needed to stay motionless as my father positioned himself to take the clean shot. I had confidence in my father and believed he would always do the right thing at the right time.

 I watched my father as he slid the safety of the shotgun to the off position, and he closed his left eye. I know he was ready to shoot, but suddenly, we noticed another smaller bush pig that appeared and joined the larger one. At first, they seemed irritated with each other, with the larger bush pig displaying some angry behaviour. I noticed my father had slid the safety back to on but remained motionless. He did not speak as he continued to focus on the two animals as they seemed to have accepted each other's company and started to graze again. I could see that the bush pigs had moved and, as a result, may have compromised my father's line of sight. Just as I realised this, my father shifted his position and rested his body against a tree trunk. He was now aiming at the target from a different angle. My father used his right hand to signal that I should move closer to him. I gently moved with as little distraction as possible. My father again pointed at the target, and I followed his finger, which led me to believe he was still aiming at the larger bush pig. I remained motionless as I watched my father slide the safety of the shotgun to the off position. Again, he closed his left eye, and I saw him squeeze the trigger, and I heard a loud noise echo through the forest. Just as my ears were struggling to recover, I heard another shot.

I could hear birds flying off from the treetops as a result of the loud noise. My first instinct was to look up so that I could see the birds. Then my anxiety quickly overwhelmed me as I thought about the bush pigs. My father had started to get to his feet as he snapped the shotgun cartridge chamber open to remove them from the barrels. I then jumped to my feet, and simultaneously, we looked in the direction of where the bush pigs were, and we saw nothing. I looked at my father's face with thoughts that he would be as disappointed as I was feeling, but instead, I noticed he was cautiously smiling.

"Come, I think we had two clean shots," my father said as he started to walk towards the location where we last saw the bush pigs. "There they are," said my father as we saw the two bush pigs lying helplessly dead. "How did you manage to shoot the two of them?" I asked my father. "I managed to get two clean shots," he replied. The sack that I had was of no use as the animals were too large. So, we had to drag them to our temporary base, and after a rest, we carried them, one after the other, into the vehicle. We then drove to the house of the village head chief, and we presented him with one of the bush pigs.

My mother and my sister, Azuka, had been waiting by the time we arrived at our village home. My sister, who was exactly two years and three hundred and sixty-three days older than me, could not wait to see if we have had a hunting success. I was delighted to show her the bush pig and gave her a detailed encounter about our hunting trip. The weather remained pleasant that morning, and we were able to have breakfast outside under the mango tree. Sunny joined us for breakfast and decided that he could prepare the bush pig for our Saturday dinner.

My brothers arrived to join us for dinner as my mother had used the bush pig for cooking a lovely meal, which we all enjoyed. We all stayed up late by the fire after we had our dinner under the beautiful sky of the village. It was peaceful, and I remember asking my father, "Why can't we move in here?" But before my father could respond, "Who wants to live in the village? I don't," said my brother, William. "The plan is for me and your mother to move in here after you all have left home," my father said, and added, "This is our retirement home."

The following morning my mother cooked breakfast, which we all enjoyed. I played with my sister as we climbed nearly all the trees in the compound, and we took turns riding my chopper. It was about one thirty in the afternoon after we had all eaten the leftovers of the bush pig for lunch, that we packed up and headed home to our residence in the town.

CHAPTER TWENTY-NINE

Christmas

IT WAS DECEMBER OF 1977, and the dry season seemed to have started earlier than usual. The rainy season was expected to last till October, but it had not rained since September. Due to the lack of rain for four months, the December month climate condition had become uncomfortable. It appeared that the harmattan seasons were getting harsher by the year, and all the vegetation looked dry and dying earlier than it would have been. The harmattan wind blowing from the north of the country toward the south had reduced the temperature to an average of eighteen-degree centigrade from the usual twenty to twenty-one degrees centigrade. This average temperature during the rainy season would normally be thirty-four degrees centigrade between March and October. We were therefore experiencing a colder, dryer, and windy environment, but it would be Christmas soon.

The thought of Christmas, regardless of the harsh climate conditions, created a different type of mood that made people become happier more than in any other month of the year. It put everyone in the planning mode for the festivities to come at the end of the month. Therefore, it would soon be time to do Christmas clothes shopping and buy decorations for the house. Food shopping tended to follow just a couple of weeks before Christmas day.

It was the first Christmas that I can remember well, and I was just seven years old in the month of November. I was tall for my age, and

I felt that I was liked by everyone. I had also learnt a lot from my parents as I continued to be around them most of the time. I would listen to their dealings and conversations with people, including business and personal friends, and this made me more mature in my views. My siblings thought I talked above my age and in most cases, did not like my smart mouth. Going Christmas clothes shopping with my mother at that age remains a vivid and joyful experience in my memory.

It was simple, really. There was a boutique in town called The One Stop that sold the best designer outfits, and that was the only retail shop we would visit. The boutique was the only shop that sold high-end designer clothing, including shoes, underwear, and aftershave. The owner of the boutique became a family friend because he was my father's dresser. My father hardly went to shops for clothes. Instead, his dresser would bring his new season wardrobe to my father's living room, where my mother and I would help him choose what best suited him. All the outfits my father would buy from Nigeria were supplied by The One Stop Boutique, other than a few sophisticated pieces of clothing that my mother would buy from the Onitsha market. Therefore, being dressed in quality clothing to the same standard as my father excited me. As a young boy, I loved the way my father dressed, and I thought he looked cool and a long way apart from his friends. My father's favourite outfit was the safari suit with a classic fedora hat. This he wore to the office and for business. However, he would wear traditional outfits for non-business occasions and events.

As a Chief and a kind man, my father was one of, if not the most valued and cherished man in the region. His businesses continued to increase my parents' wealth, and as they became richer than almost anyone in the region, they were also popular, and my father was one of the most liked Chiefs in the region and highly regarded by everyone. It was not long before I started to notice that I was privileged, as I had access to many things that most children my age could only dream of having. I then recognised that it was a pleasure being a son of my father. It was a gratitude that I did not take likely. Although my father was a very successful man, he was humble and not too sophisticated. I believe that my father had earned a good reputation in business because of his refusal to cut corners or use substandard materials in construction. The block factory also maintained good customer feedback because of its quality and reliability.

So, Christmas for us was like a project. My mother would be the senior responsible officer, and she would have five dedicated staff, excluding her own aide, that would help coordinate and manage the Christmas project. I would act as deputy to my mother's aide. I was indeed a helpful and considerate child. My father's aide and secretary would also work part-time on the project. Christmas was also a period when my parents gave back to the communities, including relatives and staff. There would be Christmas gifts for the state governor, judges, other political and public officers, residents of our street, schools, hospitals, and churches. The gifts included live cows, turkeys, goats, and chickens. In addition to rice, beans, salt, whisky, wine, eggs, etc, and cash in envelopes. My parents believed in giving and especially to those that had contributed in any way to their achievements and success.

The delivery of these various items to their recipients posed some significant challenges. My father's aids, Victor and Lorraine, would provide a list of names and towns but no proper addresses. My mother had to front the delivery of the gifts in person as a mark of respect to the prestigious high-ranking individuals in their society. As deputy to my mother's aide, I would accompany the entourage to deliver the gifts, and I always got a pat on the head and a five naira cash note. By the end of the delivery period, I would be employing friends to help me count my cash.

The focus would then move on to my family once my mother was satisfied that every external recipient of our gifts was going to have a good Christmas. My parents had a love of rearing their own poultry, so we had a poultry farm in the back garden. Thinking back now, I know we had been cruel to the poor birds, as they were sadly all kept in a cage; there were about two hundred chickens in the cage laying eggs for our consumption and to give to our neighbours and friends. We also consumed the chickens for food. There were also fifty guinea fowls and fifty turkeys. The guinea fowls and turkeys are allowed to roam in separate specially built enclosures. I was never a fan of the turkeys as they were too big and able to poke my eyes. The guinea fowls were uncontrollable and always looking for the opportunity to escape. It was on one Saturday morning, a few months earlier into the year, during feeding of the birds, that two guinea fowls managed to escape their enclosure. We later found them in one of our neighbour's trees.

My parents were out of town that weekend and certainly did not want to be disturbed with the petty and annoying news that two guinea fowls had escaped. Therefore, my elder brother, Matthew, and I took charge of the situation. After much deliberation, I followed my brother to my parent's apartment, thinking he had a solution that would help us lure the guinea fowls down from the trees and into their enclosure. My brother headed towards the gun cabinet and reached for my father's double-barrelled shotgun. I thought he had abandoned the idea of capturing the escaped guinea fowls and now wanted to play pretend shooting with the guns like we used to do. So, I asked him, "What are we going to do with the shotgun?" Matthew was about thirteen years old at that time. Therefore, I was surprised when he reached for the ammunition compartment and said, "Watch and learn, little brother."

Although I had followed my father's hunting and had watched him aim and shoot birds on trees with accuracy and success all the time, I had no idea that my brother could actually use a double-barrelled shotgun for real. We had played with guns without my parent's knowledge, but we had never ever imagined going near the bullets and cartridges, not to mention inserting any into the shotgun. My brother was tall for his age, but even then, not more than a foot taller than the length of the particular shotgun he was holding in his two hands with support from his elbow. "I have seen Daddy shoot birds from the trees, and we are going to do exactly that," Matthew muttered. Pretending I did not hear him correctly, I asked, "Are you actually thinking of using the shotgun to kill the birds?" I stood with my two hands positioned at my waist as I looked into Matthew's eyes for a sincere and realistic answer. "They are better dead than escaped," Matthew responded. Filled with apprehension yet a little bit of excitement, I agreed to the venture, even though I did not have a choice.

Although I knew we were going to be in serious trouble when my parents returned, being part of the "combat team" to capture our two escaped guinea fowls, dead or alive, seemed more intriguing at that moment than to worry about my parent's reactions. After all, I was not going to be the one taking the bulk of my parent's scolding when they returned and found out what we had done. I was asked by my brother to pick up the cartridge belt, which I did and loaded it with twelve rounds of the right cartridges. I knew the right pellet size cartridge for shooting larger birds like guinea fowls, as my father had taught me this when we went hunting. I had the cartridge belt tied round my waist, although it was too large, and I had to hold it in place with my two hands. I thought we were going to speak with the neighbour that owned the tree, but my brother had a different plan.

We would aim and shoot the guinea fowl from our back garden without the permission of our neighbour. "They would not see us coming," my brother hinted. I was not sure if he meant the birds or our neighbour; whatever the case, I decided to stay quiet as I could see my brother was trying to find the best position to execute the kill. He requested two cartridges, which I handed over. He loaded the shotgun, and he took aim, and in less than a minute, I heard the first shot, and before my ears could recover from the sound shock, I heard the second shot. To my surprise, yet excited, I saw the two birds dropping from the trees into my neighbour's compound. The sound of the gunshots had alerted everyone in my household, and the neighbourhood was out to investigate what was going on. My parents were the only ones that had the license to own and use firearms in my area. Our security guards did not carry firearms, and the neighbours knew that my parents were not at home. So, they wondered who could be shooting and at what. My brother and I quickly returned the shotgun and the cartridges and headed out to retrieve our kill. We had during the process of retrieving the two dead guinea fowls ignored every question that was posed to us by the neighbours. We later invited a few friends and had a pre-Christmas feast with the help of our cooks and Jane, my cousin.

It was five am on a Sunday, and my parents were hosting the usual family meeting. Every family member in the household, including my cousins, had to attend this time due to some concerns my parents wanted to discuss. Employees were exempted. It was a week before Christmas, and without a doubt, an update of where we would celebrate Christmas and the New Year festivities would be discussed, and final arrangements would be ironed out during the meeting. Just as usual, it was agreed that Christmas would be celebrated in the family house in the town where we were, and on the thirtieth of December, we would travel the five miles distance to our country home in our village to celebrate the New Year.

To my parents and indeed all my siblings and including me, the house in the village was considered a lovely mansion. It consisted of two driveways, in and out, with a roundabout just in front of the house. Initially, my father did not want to have anything to do with his village of birth due to the terrifying intention to have him killed after he was born with a tooth. The property consisted of larger grounds in comparison to the house that we lived in the town, and the compound was big enough to fit two football pitches in, so there was plenty of space to roam around. The construction was completed in 1975, two years earlier, and had remained the largest home in the region. There were all sorts and multiple species of fruit trees, ranging from cashew, orange, mango, grapefruit, lime, and lemons, to guava, avocado, papaya, and coconut trees, etc. There was also a section for pineapples and bananas. Then there were the flowers that lined the driveways on both sides and along the fence perimeters. The trees and flower plants had special lights connected to them, and it really excited me when they were switched on at night.

Just below the apex of the house roof lay a sign that read, "If God is with you, nothing is hard." You could find this sign on most of my parent's buildings anyway. For me, it meant that my parents had a strong relationship with God. I loved it there and was thinking I could not wait to ride my chopper again at top speed along the driveways. Once more, we had a poultry farm at the back of the house. There was a larger enclosure for turkeys and another enclosure for roosters to roam. For some reason, the enclosure doors were not as reinforced as those at the town residence. The turkeys often breached the door, and they would be found roaming around in the compound but unable to escape due to the ten feet high fence perimeters. It was normally my task to usher them back into their enclosure with the help of our dog, Bistoff. Bistoff was a German Shepherd and became scared of the turkeys after losing a few fights.

As always, the purpose of the family meeting would be to get an update about my parent's ventures and to inspire us to stay on the right track of life. Some of my siblings spoke about the challenges they were facing in school and in life in general, and my parents provided some understanding and discussed potential solutions and subsequently addressed the problems. As usual, my parents stressed the necessity to behave well, especially in public. There was also the advice to not smoke or drink excessively. One of the essences of the family meeting would be for my father, especially to highlight the importance of education. The family meeting would start with a prayer by my father with our eyes closed. However, I had seen eyes that were not closed. When I raised that issue with my father, I was shocked by his reply, "How did you know they had their eyes open?"

Although I continued to see opened eyes during prayers on subsequent family meetings, I refrained from alerting my father because I did not receive a positive reward from him when I did, in addition to the telling off I got from siblings and cousins for telling tales. It took me a while to be able to answer my father's question of how I knew they had their eyes open during prayers. This particular meeting did not close without the mention of the shooting of the guinea fowl. My brother received a one-week grounding and a lecture with the police force to understand the danger of firearms, while I received a verbal warning. The family meeting would close with another prayer by my mother.

Looking forward and counting the remaining days before Christmas excited me. My mother had bought me an expensive suit, and a pair of quality Italian shoes. These were my main Christmas day outfit, and I would also have another new set of clothing for Boxing Day and a made-to-measure traditional garment for the New Year celebration. My mother had hidden the new outfits in my father's closet, but that did not stop me from showing them to my friends when my parents were out.

Watching the cow being slaughtered in the early morning on Christmas day left me with mixed feelings. It was sad to see a large animal being killed, but I was glad to know that we would share meat with our neighbours and, therefore, bring a joyful Christmas celebration to those around us. There was also the turkey and chicken on the Christmas menu. Just after we had our Christmas meal around 1 pm, there was various entertainment throughout the day. There were different masquerade dancers arriving during the day to entertain us and our neighbours, and in turn, they were rewarded by my parents with food, drinks, and money. I was allowed to stroll out with my friends to visit nearby relatives and family friends – mine and theirs. We would stay for about ten minutes at each visit, just enough time to drink a bottle of coca cola with some biscuits and hopefully receive money gifts. The purpose of the visit was to collect cash presents and move on to the next relatives.

The New Year celebration included a party at my country home with the slaughter of two cows and a few turkeys and chickens. There were live bands entertainment, and everyone in the village, including family, friends, and well-wishers from nearby towns and cities attending. Christmas and New Year celebrations as a child remain some of the most enjoyable times of my life.

CHAPTER THIRTY

Cousin Jane

GROWING UP IN THE seventies amongst my siblings that are closer in age to me and my various cousins now living with us meant that I was always learning new things daily. It was the year 1978, and there were twelve of us living in the house during the school holidays. As well as the strong bond I had with my parents, I noticed I was more protected than my other siblings and even compared to my neighbourhood friends. I was not allowed on the streets to play and definitely not allowed outside after six o'clock in the evenings. I also became fond of my siblings and cousins. Just like Joyce and Michael, now living in the United States, my other siblings, Matthew, Alexander, William, and my sister, Azuka, as well as my cousins, still took me out to show me off to their boyfriends and girlfriends. My parents also continued to take me to parties whether I was invited or not. The fondness I shared with my parents continued to grow stronger even as I matured. It felt as though my parents could not be happy without my existence.

Given all the attention and love I continued to receive from my parents, it was difficult to imagine they never wanted me when my mother found out that she was pregnant. At the age of eight, although I had my own bedroom, I had always slept in my parent's bed, sandwiched in between them. Initially, I would go to my father's bed to sleep for the night, hoping that he would be in bed after watching the nine pm news. However, most of the time that I had woken up in the middle of the night, I noticed that my father never came to his bed.

I did find out where he goes, though, my mother's bed. So, I would join them. I later decided to save myself the hassle and would go straight to sleep in my mother's bed as my father would join in later. That was when I started waking up in my own bedroom, wondering who had the audacity to remove me from my rightful place between my Mum and Dad. William and Azuka, who were five and three years respectively older than me, never stopped short of teasing me that I was still being breastfed by my mother, even though they clearly knew that it wasn't the case.

The home I grew up in remains one of the largest family houses in the region. However, it did become less lively during school terms, with reduced shouting and quarrelling due to the absence of my elder siblings and cousins at school. This did present some level of loneliness when I returned home from school, even though there would be a couple of staff working in the house. Their job was not to look after me, so my grandmother would be home to receive me as my parents remained busy with work. My primary school was just across from my home and about three minutes' walk. I was delighted when my cousin Jane did not have to attend school anymore. Jane was about ten years older than me. She had finished secondary school at this time and was deciding what to do next. So, she was mostly at home, and my grandmother did not have to be there anymore.

It was just before the school term, and my father had left for a two-week visit to the United States, and I was missing him. Although the house was more than large enough to accommodate us all, there were continuous conflicts of interest that went on and sometimes would lead to a physical fight. My brother, William, tended to be involved in all the fights. He was inclined to be stubborn and to some extent, fearless. However, he would always succumb to the wrath of my mother. Unfortunately, he tended to forget quite quickly the fury of my mother and then got himself into more trouble. On one day, William decided to pick a fight with my cousin Jane, who was five years his senior. My money was on my cousin Jane to win the fight, but my mother had returned home before the fight became physical. What a shame, as I was hoping for William to be finally taught a lesson. However, my mother did not disappoint, and William was tied to a pole in the garden. I thought it would be funny to get all his friends to see him tied up on a pole, but I did receive my own little punishment for alerting them.

My cousin Jane was upset after the ordeal, and I felt sorry for her as I knew she did not deserve the heckling and abuse she received from my arrogant brother. So, I hung out with Jane, and we later walked to the shops to buy sweets. I saw Jane as a protector. She would look out for me and shield me from any unwarranted attacks from my siblings and cousins, that liked to poke me for telling their secrets and behaviours that fell short of my parent's expectations. I think they could not stand me sometimes, as they would ask my mother to take me with her when she would be going out. However, I was, on a few occasions, seen as an ally when I had done favours such as giving them loans after they had blown their allowances, even though they never paid it back. So, it was necessary to rely on the protection of Jane, especially when my parents were out of town. I became fond of her and trusted her completely.

It was during school term time, and my siblings, including my cousins, except Jane, had left for boarding school. Again, the house suddenly became peaceful, and although I did not miss the different personality views that often led to clashes and even fights, I wished they were back home. I missed the games we all played after dinner and the stories told by my cousins from their different upbringings. Living with my cousins, that had come from different backgrounds and upbringings, somehow helped me to build up my confidence. I was able to see life from a whole different point of view because my cousins had experienced a much harder life in comparison to me and my siblings. So, I gained more confidence to want to walk to school on my own and challenge the bullies that teased me because I came from a privileged home. However, our family dog Bistoff had decided to start accompanying me to school. Bistoff would sit outside my classroom and wait patiently and quietly. I normally walked home during breaks, and the long one-hour recess times, so Bistoff never had to stay out alone for too long. My primary school head teacher was a friend of my mother and never bothered me about Bistoff accompanying me to school. Jane was mostly home and would make me Ovaltine during my breaks and my favourite lunch of fried plantain with scrambled eggs. Bistoff would have tuna fish, his favourite. My school session was from 8 am to 1 pm, Monday to Friday. I was eight years old then and was in primary three.

One day, my Physical Education (PE) teacher was selecting pupils for a particular sports activity that required tall boys. He did not hesitate to call me out and asked my age. I told him I was eight years of age. He insisted I was lying about my age, and he would always discipline liars. I told him it was against my religion and my parents' rule to lie. Therefore, I couldn't lie to him about my age. I mentioned he could go and ask the head teacher. The education system in Nigeria is simply based on your capability to pass your term exams and progress to the next class year. Unfortunately, there was no extra support during my time, which meant that less capable pupils would repeat their current class year until they passed. Therefore, it was not unusual for a pupil to be twelve years old while still in primary three.

My PE teacher decided to punish me for lying to him. I was flogged six times on my palms – three strokes each. I telephoned my father when I got home and told him what had happened. My parents returned home immediately to check I was alright. After examinations and questioning, my father spoke to the head of education ministry for my area, and my PE teacher was suspended. My PE teacher felt the wrath of my father in addition to his suspension, but as Christians, he was forgiven after several apologies to me and my parents. My father called off his suspension on the condition he would never flog anyone for the rest of his life. That was the first time that I experienced the power and influence my father had. I started taking my father more seriously.

It was the end of school, and I walked home with Bistoff. Our house helps were not home, and I wondered where they may have gone. Jane advised she had asked them to visit the local market about a mile away to get some food shopping. We never used to lack any foodstuff as we did get fresh deliveries daily, and my mother tended to stop at the market on her way home to pick up whatever we may be lacking. My grandmother was no longer required to be home for when I returned from school, as Jane would be home. So, it was just me, Jane, and Bistoff inside the house at the time I got home from school. As usual, my lunch was waiting, and Bistoff was excited with his meal and went off to relax at his favourite location, the stairs landing. It was peaceful, as hardly anyone uses the stairs in midday during school terms.

Cousin Jane called me into the family lounge on the ground floor and asked that we play a special game. I noticed she had her lounging mattress, which was three feet wide by two inches thick, on the floor beside the sofa. I had seen her lay on the mattress a few times in the family lounge while watching movies or reading a novel. I was excited to play a game. However, I needed to promise her that I would not tell anyone about the game as it would be our secret. I agreed and could not wait for the game to begin. Jane asked that I join her on the mattress, which I did. Jane started to undress as we lay on the mattress, which was a surprise to me. I knew that my mother would ask me to leave the room while she changed into different clothing. All the same, I was eager for the game to start. Jane proceeded to remove her underwear, and at that stage, I knew I was not supposed to be in the room with her, and I started to get up to leave to allow her the privacy to change her clothing for the game. But she caught my hand and asked me not to leave. I told her she needed her privacy to change, but she said it was part of the game. She asked that I had to undress too, to play the game.

It was not unusual for me to undress and run around naked in the house. Especially when it rained. I would be completely naked, attempting to catch the raindrops. Torrential rain is mostly the norm in Nigeria. Especially after the dry season, the first few rains are more powerful yet the most exciting. Sometimes, my friends would join me in the back garden of my house, and we would all be naked, running around and messing about in the rain. My mother would ask Jane to drag me inside the house after I had been out in the rain for too long. Jane would provide me with a towel and even help to dry me. Therefore, I was not embarrassed to undress in front of Jane. However, I was reluctant because I felt that the circumstances were different. She was naked, and I have never seen her without clothing on. She noticed I was uncomfortable, but I felt relaxed after she asked that I should trust her and that I would love the game. So, I undressed. Jane proceeded to touch my penis and asked that I touch her private area. I wasn't sure how touching and playing with our body parts could amount to a game. However, I trusted her and continued to allow her to touch me as she guided my hand up and down her private area. I noticed she was feeling something I did not understand, but whatever it was, I felt she liked it.

I want to win the game; I told Jane. "Yes, I will let you win, but you need to know how to play the game first." With her hand still holding and rubbing my penis, I noticed that it became stiff. So, I told her I had to go and urinate. As a child, I noticed that some mornings when I woke up with a rigid penis, I also felt the urge to pass urine. However, Jane insisted that it was part of the game that I was stiff and that I did not need to urinate. She then told me that it was part of the game to insert my penis inside her, and the first to urinate would win the game. So, Jane pulled me on top of her and proceeded to use her hand to guide my penis inside her. It was out of interest that I asked her why she had hair there, to which she replied that I would get hair too when I am her age. I was not sure if I liked the hair for myself, but I decided to try to focus on winning the game by urinating. Jane used both of her hands to hold my hips and guided me up and down. I was not sure if that was her helping me to urinate quickly so that I could win the game as she promised.

The process carried on for a while, and I started to feel the game was boring. I pulled myself off Jane and told her that I could not urinate. To which she said it does take longer sometimes. I really felt awkward about the game, but like she said earlier and reminded me, it would be our secret, and I must never tell anyone. I then got dressed and left the lounge. I headed outside to look for my friends to play. It was a weird feeling, although I did not tell anyone.

It was perhaps a week or so later that I returned from school that Jane had called me into the lounge. I noticed it was just the two of us inside the house, and I could see her lounging mattress on the floor. She asked that we play the game again and that I should try to win this time. Perhaps I had gained some level of maturity within that week or so after the incident that made me feel that the game was not right. I still could not understand it, but I felt it was a silly game. I, therefore, refused to play the game again with Cousin Jane. I believe she felt I knew that whatever it was, I just was not comfortable with it. I started to reduce my contact with Jane. I struck a deal with my mother to ask her driver to pick me up after school and take me to her office, just beside my father's construction company headquarters.

Cousin Jane later moved on to further her education in a different state, and I hardly saw her again. It was a few years later that I heard she was getting married, and I declined to attend. The marriage took place in a different state, and my parents never pressured me to attend. As I aged, I became aware of what had happened between myself and Jane. However, I was too ashamed to speak about it, and I also felt it was incest, and the disgust I felt remains with me. Although I nearly kept to my bargain with Jane, never to mention it to anyone, I did tell my eldest sister thirty-five years later after the incident.

I could only imagine what my parents would have done if I had told them immediately after the incident. I know that my mother's heart would have been broken.

CHAPTER THIRTY-ONE

The Way It Is

IT WAS JANUARY OF 1980, and we had returned from our village home after spending the new year holidays there. It did become obvious that my parents were quarrelling amongst themselves more than usual. There would be arguments in the middle of the night that would wake the whole household up. It was challenging to see them quarrel. My father and I continued our fortnightly weekend trips to the village house, and we usually went hunting. It was on one weekend trip that my father's half-sister visited. She brought some foods and drinks, which we accepted, but we had our fresh baked bread and the Queen of the Coast tuna sandwich to look forward to for late lunch/dinner.

Furthermore, my parents had warned us not to eat other people's food. I felt the reason for this was understandable, as there was an enormous difference in quality, taste, and presentation between my mother's cooking and others. Therefore, I would rather bear hunger till my mother's cooking was ready. "How are you, Uche-Ka-Egho?" asked my aunty. "Good afternoon ma; I am fine, thank you," I replied. After I had exchanged greeting pleasantries with her, I decided to take the food and drinks she brought to the kitchen and place them in the fridge. On my way back, before I could enter the living room where my father and aunty were sitting, I could hear her mention the name, Cecilia. I decided to wait and listen to their conversation. "You know that Cecilia is just growing too much confidence, and she needs to be controlled," said my aunty. She continued, "I heard she does not respect you anymore and fights with you most of the time." I realize the only person that would tell her what goes on in my house could be one of my cousins, her son, who lived with us. "Who is providing you with all this information?" my father asked. "You don't need to concern yourself with how I hear what goes on between you and Cecilia. I just want you to deal with it and be happy," expressed my aunty.

"I am dealing with my problem in my own way, and I don't see how a little quarrel with Cecilia would concern you," uttered my father. "That wife of yours is too proud and arrogant, and you must marry another one to put her in her place," said my aunty. "She's in her place, so why would I want to change that?" asked my father. "As a Chief, you must have more than one wife; this is how you command respect. Look at all your friends, they all have two to four wives, and they all respect their husbands," responded my aunty. She continued, "Cecilia cannot continue to be chauffeured across town and spending all your money as if she were a godsend and, in the process, continue to fight with you. You need to put a stop to it."

I was astonished to find out how strongly my aunty felt concerning what she considered to be my mother's pride. "You need not concern yourself about me and Cecilia," responded my father. I then walked into the living room, and the conversation about my mother ceased. I had the feeling that my aunty was looking for another wife for my father regardless of his interest in it. My father and I continued our peaceful weekend, and my mother arrived with food as usual, and there were no arguments between her and my dad.

"YOUR BROTHER IS GETTING MARRIED," my father said. It was time again for the family meeting one early Sunday morning. I looked around the living room but was not sure to which brother my father was referring. The eldest brother I had in Nigeria, Matthew, was sitting about ten feet from me and looked unconcerned at the thought of the news, so I could tell he was not the one getting married. After all, I could barely tell which of his many girlfriends he wanted to marry.

After what seemed to be a long pause, but was actually about two seconds interval, came my father's follow on comments. "Your mother and I have decided, and we have reached an agreement with her family," my father continued. "The marriage ceremony will take place next month," said my father. I really was dying to interrupt my father to ask the obvious question, but I knew he would find that annoyingly disrespectful and may ask me to be quiet, so I waited for the right moment. "For obvious reasons, it will not be an elaborate marriage ceremony, so only close friends and family will be invited," my father continued.

I looked at my mother's face to gauge how she was feeling about the announcement, and it seemed she was absolutely in agreement with everything my father was saying. Just as I thought my father had finished speaking and it was time to ask my question, my mother spoke. "I have already made arrangements for the light entertainment for the occasion," she said. I was no longer able to hold my patience and was feeling restless, but then my sister got her words in before me. "Is she a lovely girl? When are we going to meet her? Hopefully not on the day of the marriage," she uttered.

I was becoming furious at this stage. It appeared that everyone knew of the marriage plan except me, and why was no one asking who was marrying this girl? I was also disappointed to find out that my parents did not always tell me their plans beforehand.

"She is your brother's girlfriend, and I can tell they love each other very well," my father said. He continued, "She is a lovely girl and well-behaved, and she is from a good family too." So, it was settled then, one of my elder brothers was getting married, and I had no say about it, and it did not matter if I had met the girl, not to mention if I liked her or not. For the first time, I was annoyed by everything that was said to that point during the family meeting. Finally, there was a window of opportunity to ask my pressing question.

"Well, just so I remind you, Father, I have four elder brothers; which one of them is getting married, and how come I am just hearing it for the first time?" Matthew was just eighteen years old, and I wondered if that was the right age for someone to get married. "Your eldest brother, Michael, is the one getting married, and you are too young to be discussing the matter as you do not have the maturity for such conversations," said my father. Alright, I thought with a slight relief. However, it still did not make any sense. So, I asked again, "How is my eldest brother, Michael, who is in the United States, going to get married to his girlfriend, that is here at Agbor?"

I noticed my father was looking at me as if I was a toddler that had just wet his nappy. "Will Michael visit home to attend his marriage?" I asked. He had to be at his own marriage. Otherwise, there cannot be one, I thought. "No, he does not have to be here, and Matthew will stand in for him," said my father. I turned my face to my older brother sitting about ten feet from me, and I asked, "Are you happy to do this? It will seem you are marrying her; what would all your other girlfriends think?" As if I had said the unthinkable, he responded, "Be quiet, little one, you are just too annoying; go find your feeding bottle and lie on mother's lap."

It was about seven weeks later, and Michael in the United States was married. His new wife, Lydia, had moved in with us. Although she had lost her mother before she became a teenager, her father and older siblings looked after her well. She was fair in complexion, about five feet nine inches tall, and medium size. She was about the same age as Michael, and I had met her before when my brother was still in Nigeria. She quickly settled in with us in the family home, and we became good friends. She would go out with me to the shops and to meet her friends too.

Although I believed my parents knew the answers to my new questions, I felt that my brother's new wife might be able to answer them too.

I had imagined that for couples to be married, they must be living together. So, I asked, "How come you are living with us and not with my brother?" At first, I felt she was going to avoid the question when she said, "Come with me. I am going to show you something." I followed her into her room, and she pulled down a suitcase from on top of her wardrobe. "Come and see these cards and letters; they are from your brother," she said. She read the letters and cards to me, and then she said, "Although your brother is not here, we are in love with one another, and I will be travelling to the United States to be with him very soon." I was impressed with all the evidence she had shown me to prove my brother's love for her. "How soon would you leave for the United States?" I asked. "As soon as my passport and visa are ready, I will leave," she replied. "Perhaps in two or three months' time," she continued.

ANOTHER SUNDAY MORNING family meeting was upon us, and the agenda was not as friendly as anyone would have imagined. The meeting was to discuss the future of Matthew. My parents were surprised that he had no intention of progressing his studies in the United States. "I want to work in the family business," said Matthew. I could not help it but to remember the last time my parents scolded him for using the shotgun to shoot dead the two guinea fowls that escaped their cage. I recognised the look on his face and realised he was serious about his future. "You need a university education to be able to work in the construction business or even the block factory. You need to go to university, then you can join the business if you still wish," responded my father. "I have decided I will not study anymore as I do not have the interest to do so," said Matthew. He continued, "You would be wasting your time and money asking me to further my studies as I will not do it." I took a good look at my father, knowing that my brother's decision was going to hurt him. My father tried to reason with him and explain why furthering his education was important, but he was wasting his time. There would be several more family meetings, including private one-to-ones with my parents, before it was settled that my elder brother would not continue his education and would instead join the construction business. A couple of weeks later, Matthew was training to become a project manager, working for the construction company. He received a brand new company car and earned a good wage. My parents also decided that they would build him a house as a form of compensation for him not gaining a university education.

Michael's wife, Lydia, was preparing to leave for the United States. She had now lived with us for a period of no more than six months, and I believed she could not wait to see her husband. I was delighted when the house phone rang one evening about a week after she had left. "Hello, Uche speaking," I spoke into the telephone receiver after picking it up. "It's me, your sister-in-law, Lydia; how are you?" I was delighted to hear from her. She sounded a lot more cheerful, and I could understand why. "Do you like it over there?" I asked. "It is lovely but getting cold," she replied. It was in the early fall season over there, and it had started to get cold. "I heard the months of November and December are the frozen months; you can always come back, though," I said. Everyone in the house took turns speaking with Lydia, and we also spoke to my brother, Michael, who thanked us for looking after his wife. My father had to say the last word before he replaced the telephone receiver, "Don't keep me waiting long from being a grandfather!"

As if my parents could not wait to get everyone that had finished secondary school to start university, it was announced in the family meeting that my brother, Alexander, who is about seven years my senior, was leaving for the United States shortly. It was a few weeks later that Alexander arrived in the United States. I started to wonder if I would be ready to leave my parents when it came to my turn. Nonetheless, the family house was becoming less busy as Lydia and

Alexander had departed for the United States within three months of each other.

I was growing up and understood life from a different perspective. I was at the same time keeping an eye on my parent's relationship, and I was not sure if I liked what I was noticing. All the same, I was just beginning to be mature enough to realise that no matter what one does, sometime things will just be the way they will be.

CHAPTER THIRTY-TWO

The Becoming of Grandparents

"WAKE UP! WAKE UP!" I heard as I started to wake from my deep sleep and opened my eyes to see my sister, Azuka, shaking my right leg. "Leave me alone; I am sleeping," I said. "Wake up now; Daddy is being taken to the hospital," said my sister. I quickly pulled myself to an upright sitting position but was still on my bed. "What are you talking about?" I asked as I rubbed my eyes and was trying to wake myself up fully. "Daddy was taking a shower, and he collapsed in the bathroom," my sister uttered. "How was that possible?" I asked again. "Shut up and get up, and I need you to follow me," my sister responded. I realised she could be telling the truth, so I jumped out of bed and quickly followed her out of my room.

We arrived in my parent's living room, and my father was lying on the sofa with Dr Memeth attending to him. "His blood pressure is too high, and we need to take him to the hospital at once," uttered Dr Memeth. I looked at the clock on the wall, and the time was quarter past ten at night. I would only imagine that my brother, Matthew, would take my father to the hospital in his car. Unfortunately, we could not find my brother as he was yet to return home. My other brother, William, was turning fifteen and could already drive, and I expected he would drive my father in my mother's car to the hospital. My father was carried downstairs by my mother, sister, and brother, with the guiding assistance of Dr Memeth. "Let's rest him here, and I will get my car ready," uttered Dr Memeth. "My brother can drive him using my mother's car," I shouted. "He has no driving license," responded my mother. I took a look at my brother and wondered how he was able to drive around town in my mother's car when she had been out of town with my father. I knew it was a tale I had to tell my mother later.

My mother had followed my father to the hospital, and I found myself sitting with my brother and sister in the lounging area downstairs of our home. My cousins had joined us at this time, and they all looked worried. They had all returned home from school for the Easter holiday. "Will Daddy be alright?" I asked. William looked at me and said, "Of course, he will be fine; he is just stressed." I waited for him to continue or, indeed, for anyone to say something more, but there was silence. "What is stress, and how did Daddy get it?" I asked again. My sister looked at me and said, "Be quiet." Although Azuka was three years my senior, I was not in any way scared of her. I know she dare not raise her hand to me as she would have to answer to my mother. "I won't be quiet; I just want to know what stress means and how Daddy got it," I uttered. "Well, we don't know," responded one of my cousins, that was about four years my senior.

"Mummy and Daddy were quarrelling in the kitchen upstairs, and I could hear them. Daddy left to take a shower, and he collapsed in the bathroom," my sister said. The kitchen was not far from my bedroom, and I thought I should have heard them. "Well, if that was true, why didn't I hear them from my bedroom?" I asked. "Because you were snoring your head off," my sister replied. "I don't snore," I quickly said. "Oh yes, you snore; we can hear your snoring from across the street," said my brother. "I don't believe you; you are just saying that to annoy me," I replied. I continued, "Anyway, where is Matthew?" I could not get any response to my question. Then I asked again, "Why is he not home yet?" Of course, I knew he came back home late at night from socialising with his friends. I knew he would either be catching up with his friends over a few beers, or he would be watching a movie at the cinema. He had taken me to meet his friends on a few occasions, and one time we went to a bar and went to see a Bruce Lee movie afterwards at the cinema. We were late home, and my mother was concerned and gave a warning not to keep me out too late. I had not been to the cinema again with him since then. We stayed up and waited for my mother to return from the hospital.

It was a few days later that my father returned from the hospital. We did visit him daily and could see he was feeling better. He was asked to stay home for a week to fully recover before returning to work. The following day after my father had returned from the hospital, he was preparing to go to his office. "Daddy, I thought the doctor advised that you rest at home for at least one week; why are you going?" I asked. "I have a bed in the office, and I will rest there," he replied. "Is that really a good idea, Daddy?" I asked, and before he could respond, I continued, "You will be dealing with business matters for sure while you are in the office." My father walked close to me and put his arm around me, and said, "Don't worry about me, my son; I will be fine." I put my arm around him and hugged him. Yes, I was worried about him, as he could tell. "We will go to the village and spend a nice and quiet weekend there; what do you say?" I loved being alone with my father, so I would always welcome the opportunity to spend time with him no matter where we went. "Yes, that would be great, Daddy," I responded.

My father had spent most of his rest leave days at the office. Although he had a bedroom in his office, he was hardly on the bed. I could see that my mother was looking after him while in the office, and I started to feel that it was better he was at the office than at home. My mother was able to use her restaurant kitchen to prepare delicious fresh catfish pepper soup with yam, and my father would enjoy it for his lunch. On one occasion, my father had finished his lunch, and he said, "Cecilia, I know I keep saying this, you are the best cook ever, obviously after my mother." My father would comment on my mother's cooking frequently, and I could understand why. Although I ate some of the pepper soup and yam, I don't particularly have the same satisfying feeling for fresh catfish. I find them slimy and too soft for my liking. I would prefer them roasted. My mother did know how to prepare delicious traditional Nigerian meals that my father loved. We also loved our mother's cooking, and our friends had made satisfactory comments after we had shared meals with them.

IT HAD BEEN OVER SIX MONTHS since my father was discharged from the hospital, and he continued to do well. I noticed some changes to his work pattern. He was no longer leaving for the office as early as he once did, arriving at seven o'clock in the morning and leaving by four pm. Instead, he was arriving at the office by nine am and leaving by three o'clock in the afternoon and would avoid going to work on two Saturdays in a month. I also noticed that his relationship with my mother was better as they were getting along well with less fighting.

It was approaching the rainy season in the year 1981, and I was hearing some rumours that my sister-in-law in the United States was pregnant. I wondered why the news was not announced during the subsequent family meetings. So, I felt the need to confront my parents about it to get confirmation. However, I decided now was not the right time to ask such a question. I am also aware that I may be asked to shut up if I do not ask the question at the appropriate time. Nevertheless, I was not too happy that I heard about the possibility of Lydia being pregnant by others outside of the family.

It was on a particular Saturday morning, and my father was not going to the office. He had called me to his private dining room. "Yes, Daddy, I heard you wanted me to come and see you," I said to my father as I entered the extravagantly decorated dining room. The private dining room was reserved for my parents to entertain only very close friends to use for special occasions. However, I would often use it as my study room, but my father had started to use it to study his building plans. "Come in and sit down here," my father replied and was pointing to a particular dining chair beside him on the right.

"We are going to design a hotel building," said my father. He continued, "It will be the largest hotel in the area, and it will be the tallest building in Agbor." I was not sure what to say as I was excited that we were going to own the biggest hotel and the tallest building in the area. However, I was not sure how I could assist my father in achieving his plan. I thought about his architects and engineers and wondered why he was not seeking their input. "I want this to be our task, and we will own the design without anyone claiming ownership to the concept," said my father. My father reached for his briefcase and opened it. He then produced a few basic instruments, but they looked complicated to me. "Open that cupboard and bring some drawing papers," said my father as he pointed to the wall cabinet opposite where we were sitting. As I stood up to walk to the cabinet, I remembered that my father had no formal education, and the concern of how he was going to draw a multiple-story hotel building gripped me. However, I trusted my father, and I knew that he understood his limitations.

After a few Saturdays spent working on the hotel plan, my father was satisfied with our design and illustration of the entire complex. In addition to the hotel building, the grounds comprised a large swimming pool, an outside bar, a fire pit, and a car park. It was a few weeks later that our concept was translated into a construction plan, and the project was started. I watched the digging of the foundation of the hotel building. I knew I was tall for my age, but I was surprised to notice that the depth of the foundation was more than my height. The hotel was situated on the same land where my father's construction business head office was located and beside the block factory. My father's plan was to relocate the block factory to a nearby land he had recently purchased.

It was midweek, and I was still on summer break from school, so I had continued to accompany my father to supervise the hotel building project. We would normally take our lunch at my mother's restaurant. "Fresh fish pepper soup for Chief," instructed the restaurant manager to the chef as my father and I approached the restaurant. I wondered if my father wanted fish pepper soup for lunch as I did not hear him place an order. "Why would they assume you want fish pepper soup for lunch?" I asked my father. "This was because I told them this morning to place an order for the best catch of the day to the fish supplier," my father replied. "What would happen if there was no catch for the day?" I asked sarcastically. "Then I will have you for lunch," responded my father as he rubbed my head.

"We need to visit the barbers this Saturday as you need a haircut," continued my father. I disliked having a haircut, as my father's barber never cared to give me a trendy style cut, and I normally got teased by my friends. "No, Daddy, you can have your haircut this Saturday, and I will have mine done just before the school term begins," I said. "Rubbish, we will do it together as we usually do," uttered my father. The fish pepper soup was delivered and placed on the table in front of my father. I was sitting opposite him, and I could feel the eyewatering pepper as the steam evaporated from the dish into the atmosphere around us. "That must be very hot," I said. I received no reply, but the jollof rice I ordered had arrived and was placed in front of me.

As we started to eat, I asked my father, "Is it true that my sister-in-law in the United States is pregnant?" I watched my father as he chewed and swallowed his mouthful. He then reached for the glass of water beside his food dish and took a sip. "Yes, we are expecting the baby in a few weeks," replied my father. The child would be my parent's first grandchild, and he carried on expressing his joy in anticipation of the arrival of the baby.

What was actually a few weeks seemed like several months to me before the news was announced that my sister-in-law had given birth to a beautiful baby girl. It was around seven o'clock in the evening in the third week of August that my father received the news during a telephone call from my eldest brother, Michael, in the United States. Finally, my parents had become grandparents. As my father replaced the telephone receiver, he called out to my mother and broke the news to her.

My family home atmosphere turned into a celebratory mood in an instant. My father reached for his shotgun. "Uche, come here," my father instructed. I ran to join him in the strongroom, and he handed me the cartridge belt, which I placed over my shoulders. "Follow me," my father instructed again. I followed him outside as I wondered what he was going to do. We were now on the street and in front of our house, and my father gave me the sign requesting two cartridges. I handed him two of the least weighted cartridges, which he checked were the right ones he needed before inserting them into the shotgun chambers. My father pointed the shotgun towards the clear sky and depressed the triggers. There were two shots with almost no delay between the first and the second. He requested two more cartridges, which I presented, and in no time, there were another two powerful sounds close to each other. We continued to discharge the cartridges into the atmosphere until I was holding an empty ammunition belt. At this time, the whole neighbourhood was alert and was wondering what was going on.

"I am a grandfather," my father shouted. There was a round of applause coming from every corner, and in a short period of time, the street in front of our house was filled with people. "Tonight, we celebrate the birth of my granddaughter," my father uttered. As if it was planned, drinks were being offered to the crowd around my house, and in no time, jollof rice and grilled beef followed. Matthew took one of his loudspeakers and placed it in front of the house, piping music onto the street. It was as if we were having a street party. Some of my uncles and aunties arrived, including my grandparents, and they stayed till nearly midnight when the party ended. However, before the crowd dispersed, it was a tradition, according to my father, as he carried me up in the air, turning me upside down, and gently lowered my head to touch the ground. He then said, "Uche, my son, you have kindly shared your good spirit with a new generation." I had no clue what that meant, but I was happy that I was significant in the celebration of my parents becoming grandparents.

A week later, my mother left for the United States to see my new niece. She would stay for three months.

CHAPTER THIRTY-THREE

Don't Be Like Your Siblings

MY MOTHER WAS REACHING the end of her three months stay in the United States as she got to know her granddaughter. My father and I had just finished a telephone conversation with my mother, and she would be returning in a week's time. It was on a Saturday, one of the non-working days for my father, so we started to watch the wrestling programme on the television. I had always watched wrestling on the television with my father on Saturdays. The programme finished with our long-lasting champion losing the match and relinquishing his belt. We were not feeling cheerful, although the thought of my mother returning home in a week's time excited me. I had so much to tell her in relation to my siblings and cousins behaving badly. I knew there would be punishments to be handed out to nearly all of them after I had made my documented cases known to my mother.

My father, on the other hand, had reached for the intercom on the side table beside the sofa and pressed the call button. A short moment later, the voice of Kate could be heard over the intercom. "How can I help," Kate said. "Hello Kate, we did not know you were here," my father spoke into the intercom. The intercom was connected to the shared living area, where we all hung out together, and to the kitchen. My parents would use the intercom instead of getting up from their sofa to call on us. I don't think my father was expecting Kate, my mother's aide to answer the call. "Where is everyone?" asked my father. "I don't see anyone here, and there is no one in the kitchen either," Kate responded. "Anyway, do you mind bringing me a chilled lager, please?" requested my father. "And a Sprite, please," I shouted from where I was sitting, hoping she would hear me. "Ignore that, Kate. He can go get himself a drink if he wants one," uttered my father.

My father looked at me with raised eyebrows as he ended the intercom call. "You are the youngest in this household, and nobody works for you; remember that," my father uttered. Before I could respond, he continued, "Can you keep a secret?" I felt that my father should know the answer to that question as I have told him my sibling's secrets. "If you ask me not to tell anyone something, then I won't," I replied. "Alright, listen to me," uttered my father as Kate entered the living room. She had brought my father his favourite lager, Gulder. At first, I thought she had listened to my father as I did not see the Coca-Cola Sprite that I requested, but surprisingly, she produced my drink request. "Thanks a lot, Kate," I said. "You are welcome," she replied as the approached me and rubbed my head. She then left the living room. As usual, my father would expect me to pour his lager into his large 75cl mug.

My father had taught me how to limit the frothy foam when pouring the lager to ensure that the whole bottle content was emptied into the mug. So, I opened the bottle using the large bottle opener that lay on the bottom shelf of the side table beside my father, and I held the mug with my left hand, bending it at a seventy-five-degree angle towards my right. I then started to pour the lager into the mug and gently reduced the angle by moving it towards an upright position. This process ensured that less bubble gas was generated, leading to significantly less frothy foam on top of the mug, thereby allowing room for the entire 75cl bottle to be contained. I knew my father was satisfied with my pouring of the lager as he continued with the discussion. "The secret I want you to keep is that we are going to buy your mother a brand-new car," uttered my father. "Sure, I can keep that a secret," I replied. "Ok, let's do this," my father said. He picked up the telephone receiver and dialled a number. It was one of my father's friends that owned a vehicle dealership on the line. Although my father was not all that close to this friend, he would buy his vehicles through his dealership. After a brief conversation, it was agreed that the new vehicle would be delivered on the day that my mother would arrive home from the United States.

My father took a mouthful of his lager, and I watched him as he gently swallowed the liquid with some sense of appreciation. Just before he set the mug back on the side table, he held it slightly below his chin level and took a refreshing and satisfying look at the mug as if he was drinking a different lager. "This tastes good," my father said with a smile on his face. I wondered why he would say that, as he had always drunk the same type of lager for at least a decade. "Let's phone your mother," my father continued. He reached for the telephone receiver again, and after dialling a few numbers, he was speaking to the operator, who connected him to an international line. He was shortly speaking to my eldest brother, Michael. I later spoke with my mother, and I managed to remember not to tell her about the new car.

For some reason, I was able to control my excitement as I normally could not keep a secret. My father went on to have a brief conversation with my mother and then replaced the telephone receiver. "Thank you for not telling your mother about the car," my father uttered. I was not sure what to say as I thought to myself in silence, "Was that not what the deal was, and we must not tell anyone?" I realised then that my father never trusted me to keep secrets at my age. My father again picked up the mug containing the lager he was drinking; he took a look inside as he swivelled it. I could tell he was seeking some form of confirmation that he was drinking the same lager that he had previously drunk. "Give me the bottle of this lager," my father requested. I reached for the empty bottle and handed it to him. I watched him as he closely examined the bottle. I knew he could not read, so I said, "Do you want me to read for you?" He continued to examine the empty bottle as he rotated it to see the wording on the label. I was not sure what he was looking for, but I felt he was not going to find it as he could not read. "There it is!" My father exclaimed. "This batch was produced two months ago," he continued. I was not surprised he could identify the batch production date as he was educated enough to write and read dates. "What does that mean?" I asked. "Because it was only produced a couple of months ago, it tasted more refreshing compared to the one I drank previously," my father responded. I was not all that impressed with the taste of beer and therefore was not interested.

My father later finished his lager over a football match we watched together. "I need to show you something," my father said to me. "Follow me," he continued. He stood up and headed into his bedroom, and I followed behind him. He walked to his wardrobe and then opened the double doors. He bent down to reach for a bottle that I could already see at the bottom shelf of the shoe section. "Do you see this bottle?" my father asked as he showed it to me. "Yes, I can see the bottle," I replied. "It is a bottle of acid, and if you were to behave like your siblings, I would drink the acid, and it would kill me," my father continued.

I could understand what my father was trying to tell me. I knew he was not happy that my eldest siblings drank too much and smoked, associated with too many friends that my parents did not approve of, and fight with police officers when stopped because they were driving too fast and under the alcoholic influence. Although my parents would go to bed just before ten o'clock at night, they would wake after midnight to check that we were all indoors and sleeping. Unfortunately, my parents tended to find that a few of my siblings would be missing. A quick examination of the car park in front of the house would reveal a couple of cars would be missing. This remained a significant worry for my parents as they would stay awake until my siblings returned. There had been occasions where it would be the police on the telephone to inform my father that my siblings had been informally detained for either refusing to stop or fighting with the officers. My father would have to drive to the police station, in some cases, at two and three o'clock in the morning to pick them up. I mostly slept in my parents' apartment and therefore was experiencing their anxiety and frustration about my siblings' behaviours.

There was one occasion when my father was woken by a strange noise outside the front of the house. I was sleeping on my father's bed and was woken up as he got out of bed. I watched him reach for his shotgun, snap open the loading chamber and insert two cartridges. I noticed as he closed the chamber and turned off the safety of the shotgun. He was armed and ready to shoot as he entered the living room and calmly approached the windows. I followed him, but I could see my father's hand asking me to stay back as he advanced. I looked at the clock on the wall, and it was ten minutes before eleven at night.

My father gently opened the curtain of the window just enough to peep through. There were the two one-thousand-watt halogen flood lights that made the front area of the house look like daytime. Therefore, making it possible to clearly see what was going on. After a careful examination, my father slid on the safety of the shotgun. "May God forgive me," my father uttered as he stepped back from the window and snapped open the shotgun to remove the cartridges. "What is outside?" I asked with a whispered voice. "Your brother and his friends are up to no good," my father responded. "What are they doing?" I asked as I reached for the window and gently opened the curtain. I saw my brother and his friends pushing one of the cars. It was not clear to me what was their intention. My father was already heading downstairs, which I believe was to confront them. I quickly followed, tiptoeing behind my father as we approached the foyer leading to the outside of the house.

The security guard noticed us coming and turned the lights on. "Good evening, Chief," greeted the security. "Are you watching this, and you are doing nothing?" my father asked, ignoring his greeting. "It happens all the time, sir, and I felt they are teenagers just being mischievous," expressed the security. "What do you mean it happens all the time?" responded my father. "You think it is alright to let teenagers steal cars at night?" continued my father. "No, Chief, they are pushing the car away from the house so that when they start the vehicle, you would not be alerted. They normally return before three am," responded the security. "So, I am to assume that you are in with them on this?" my father uttered. "They are good children that just want to have some fun, so I let them on the condition that they return no later than three am," replied the security.

Our house security guard was nicknamed Edo. As far as I know, he was a family member and trusted security personnel. Edo was about ten years older than my father and had been working for my family since we family moved to Agbor before the end of the civil war. After a brief conversation between my father and Edo, it was agreed to allow William and his friends to take the vehicle for their night outing. We then hid behind the wall and watched them wave at Edo as they pushed the car out of the compound and out of sight. We then stepped outside to watch them start the vehicle, and they drove off. My father then returned inside the house and started to have a conversation again with Edo.

"I worry a lot about my children. I wonder what they are up to, and I care for their safety," my father said. Edo, who seemed as if he knew my elder siblings a lot more than my father, said, "Chief, I understand, and I worry the same about my children, but they will always find a way to do whatever they want no matter how much you try to stop them because you want to protect them." My father thought for a moment and said, "Edo, you are right; good night." My father and I returned upstairs, and I went back to bed.

I noticed that my father had stayed awake till around three am when my brother returned. So, I saw the impact of my siblings' behaviours on my parents and could understand why my father did not want me to act like them.

In the following few days, when my father was not at home, I decided to take a closer look at the bottle of acid. It read Hydrogen Peroxide.

CHAPTER THIRTY-FOUR

Gin on the Rocks

MY MOTHER HAD RETURNED from the United States, and she was surprised to see her brand-new car. She had brought lots of gifts for everyone and had many pictures of their new granddaughter, Grace. She was so beautiful, and I felt that I could not wait to meet her. My father had booked his flight to return to the United States to meet Grace in a few weeks' time. I wondered how my father would react to meeting his first grandchild, given how he behaved to the news of her birth. It was impossible to have witnessed the birth of my eldest sister, Joyce, but I would have liked to experience all the fuss displayed by my parents. Although, my parents were not as rich, confident, and experienced as they were now compared to the time Joyce was born.

I had noticed that since my mother returned from the United States, her relationship with my father had been better, with less quarrelling and fighting. Perhaps my mother was too busy enjoying her brand-new car, as she was the first woman in the region to be driving the new model of the Peugeot 505. All the same, there was a greater level of calm in the house compared to the period before my mother left for the United States.

It was on a Saturday morning, and my father's friends had been invited to breakfast. Ten of my father's close friends had arrived, and it was my duty to usher them to the guest lounge area until breakfast was ready. All my father's friends knew me well, as I was usually with him on most of his visits to them. My mother's creativity in everything she did amazed me, and I knew my father never failed to express his love for everything about her, except for one, she could be feisty sometimes, he would say.

Nevertheless, my mother had planned a five-course meal for breakfast. Although it sounded too unreal to believe, I knew my mother would not fail to deliver. "Mummy, how would it be possible for them to have five different courses for breakfast?" I asked my mother as she got busy in the kitchen. "Do not worry yourself about that; go check the dining room is in order," uttered my mother. There were about five people in the kitchen, including my mother, and they were all busy doing something. They included our two house assistants, my grandmother and my auntie, Tina. Auntie Tina had recently relocated to their new family home not too far from my house.

I left the kitchen to inspect the dining room, and I took a shortcut through the guest lounge, where my father's friends were engaged in conversation amongst themselves. Just as I entered the lounge, one of them called on me and asked, "Where is your father?" I was surprised to hear that question as I thought my father had been out to see them. "Let me go and check," I replied, and turned back and then headed into my parents' apartment to find my father. I walked through my mother's room, and there was no sign of my father. Shockingly, I found my father in his bedroom, sleeping. "Daddy, Daddy, your friends are already here," I shouted at my father as I agitated his leg to wake him up.

"What do you mean they are here?" my father asked as he quickly got himself out of bed. "I asked your mother to wake me as soon as they arrived," my father continued. "Well, they are all here, fifteen of them," I responded. "What is the time?" my father asked. "It is quarter past eight," I replied. "What time is breakfast being served?" asked my father. "I think you should ask Mummy, as I don't know, but soon I believe," I responded. "I am going to have a shower; ask your mother to come talk to me," uttered my father, and he changed into his robe and headed to the shower room. "She cannot talk to you as you are going to be taking a shower, and she is busy in the kitchen," I replied. "Do as I ask, boy!" My father shouted.

I went to the kitchen, and my mother was still busy preparing food. "Daddy wants you to come talk to him in the shower," I said to my mother. "Oh, my goodness, I forgot to wake him as he requested," responded my mother. "Tell him I am busy cooking breakfast," continued my mother. "He insists you come to talk to him in the shower," I responded. "The first course of breakfast will be ready in ten minutes," my mother said as she left the kitchen to go speak to my father. I decided to go inspect the dining room as I was initially instructed by my mother. As I walked through the lounge, I decided to inform our guests that my father would be joining them shortly.

It was about ten minutes later that my father emerged, and the first breakfast course was served. The dining table could take sixteen people around its rectangular shape. The distance between the two ends defeated the purpose of having a quiet conversation with the guests. My father had sat at the head of the table, and his friends made themselves comfortable with a position of their choice. Surprisingly, no one sat at the other end of the table.

The table was decorated with golden cutlery and with white napkins that were being kept folded in a golden holder. There was a large chandelier hanging from the high ceiling and positioned in the middle of the table. The dining room looked exquisite, and my father's friends made pleasing comments about the decoration. My mother had served a small bowl of fresh fish per person for the first course. Hardly was there any significant number of fish in each bowl, but she said it was the taste that mattered as it helped to clean and prepare the palate for the rest of the meal. The second course was akara and akamu, a signature traditional breakfast dish celebrated and enjoyed across all the regions of the country.

The akara is made from ground skinless blackeye beans mixed with some chilli and deep fried in varied sizes as required. The akamu is made from fermented corn and mixed in hot water to give a custard-like texture. In most cases, evaporated milk is added to the akamu, as well as some sugar, to bring out the flavour. The meal is enjoyed by a half-mouth-full bite of the akara, followed by a tablespoonful of akamu to swallow it down. The thought of it is mouth-watering.

The third course was the full English – bacon, eggs, sausages, baked beans, fried slice, mushrooms, and a choice of toast or fresh bread. The fourth course was a combination of various fruits with evaporated milk toppings. The final course, which was much later in the morning, was slices of madeira cake with tea or coffee. The madeira cake was baked fresh that morning. Although there was about ten to fifteen minutes interval between each course, the entire eating time was over three hours. The guests were still at the table having cake and coffee or tea as they chatted to each other by nearly one o'clock in the afternoon. My father's friends appreciated the breakfast and made a conscious effort to thank my mother and her team for delivering a hearty and delicious meal.

My father's friends had left, and the clearing-up had begun. My father was in the kitchen telling my mother how much he had enjoyed the meal and how privileged he was to have her. Again, there was the comment that she was the best cook in the whole world after his mother. "Do you think I would one day surpass your mother with my cooking?" asked my mother. "Although you are the best cook alive, you can never beat my mother, sorry," answered my father. "Fair enough, and may her soul continue to rest in peace," uttered my mother. I was not sure if she was being sarcastic; all the same, they both laughed, and my father gave my mother the best hug I had seen them display.

Saying 'I love you' to each other was something I never heard from them, and I believe it was not done amongst their generation. However, the gestures of love displayed by my father towards my mother was largely obvious. Everyone, including my father's friends and the communities within the society that we lived in, did know that my father loved my mother dearly. This was obvious through my father's behaviour and dedication to my mother. For all my father's wealth and status in society, he had remained married to my mother alone, something of which his friends disapproved.

In the eye of society, it was tradition for a rich man to display his wealth and status by having more than one wife. The greater the man's wealth, the more wives he was expected to marry. However, my father, the richest and the most prominent in the region during his time, had shunned the traditional practice of polygamy. My father would reassure us during the family meetings that marrying more than one wife was something he continued to despise. He would go on to advise us to never take more than one wife.

My mother had only known the love of my father. I believe she was fully sustained by loving my father and could not imagine otherwise. She dedicated her life to my father, and whatever she did daily was in relation to achieving their common goal. My mother had expressed her love for my father in many ways. She was constantly by my father's side, and they would discuss business and family activities together to derive the best possible way forward. Their team spirit was strong, and anyone looking from the outside into their relationship would agree that they had a forever-lasting bond.

My mother never failed to exceed my father's expectations when it came to food and managing the household and family. My father loved his food, and my mother would travel as far as possible to buy the best produce and take time to cook the best quality, delicious meals for my father. Every morning, my mother would ask my father what he would like for dinner, and no order was ever too tall to deliver. I do believe that my father was spoilt, but this was how my mother was showing her love for him. My father had never objected to my mother's tactics in how she disciplined us, and he had always supported her in all her decisions in relation to how we were brought up.

IT WAS JUST AFTER the school summer holiday of 1981, and the rainy season was still with us. It was raining almost every day, and it was becoming annoying to many in the area. Most businesses were affected as sales had dropped due to the reluctance of buyers wanting to shop in the rain. For me and my friends, it was the opportunity to shower and play in the rain after school. My father had only just returned from his trip to the United States to meet my niece. He brought back presents for everyone and one of the favourites of my gifts was my rainboots. "You are only supposed to wear them to places and not to shower in the rain," said my mother. It would be my brother, Matthew, that my mother would ask to carry me out of the rain and into the house when she thought that I have had enough.

I was tall for my age, and no one was big and strong enough to carry me amongst my siblings and cousins living in Nigeria other than my brother, Matthew. At first, he would offer me money and sweets to come out of the rain and inside the house, to which I would normally pay no attention. He would have to chase me first and catch me, and I didn't make it easy for him. Eventually, he did catch me and carry me on his shoulders. "Now I am as wet as you, it's not funny, you know, and I am too old for this," uttered Matthew. "Can I still have the money, please?" I asked. "No, not when I am soaked chasing after you now," he replied. "Now, stay inside and go get a towel and dry yourself before you catch a cold," uttered Matthew. I would be eleven years old in November of that year, and my brother, Matthew, was already nineteen. He was based in Nigeria and was working in my father's construction company. His job required him to travel out of town to coordinate supplies for projects. It was during one of his assignments out of town that his life was changed to the delight of my parents. Matthew knew how to enjoy himself and thought that he was doing a good job hiding his social life from my parents. He was hardly at home and had too many friends to socialise with till late hours, visiting multiple bars and parties. Surely, there were too many different women involved, and that concerned my parents as it contradicted their one-man one-woman policy.

A few weeks later, I had walked back home from my primary school just across from my house. I was greeted by my parents that afternoon as they sat together like a loving couple. I noticed the bottle of Gordon's Dry Gin, a bottle of Martini, and a few bottles of ginger ale. Then I saw my father's shotgun on his left side. First, I wondered why they were home that early, and secondly, why they were so cosy up in the front porch on the sunny afternoon. The answer I received when I asked was, "It's none of your business why we are home early," snapped my mother. "How was school today," my father asked as he dismantled his shotgun and started to clean it. "School was boring, and I am hungry," I answered. "I have made some yam and beans porridge," my mother replied. "Go help yourself with some food and tidy your filthy room," she continued. "Can you not ask someone to bring me something to eat so I can watch Daddy clean his shotgun?" I asked, but I was told that there was no one apart from them in the house. Annoyingly, I headed inside to change from my school uniform. On my way to the kitchen, as I walked past Matthew's apartment, I could hear some movement. I thought my parents had said that they were home alone. Upon detailed investigation, I told my parents that there was someone inside Matthew's apartment and asked how was that possible if he was out of town.

"It must be one of his girlfriends," my mother said. "How many girlfriends is he allowed to have?" I asked. Being ignored as always, my mother proceeded to knock on the door to Matthew's apartment. "We can hear you; please come out to have some food," shouted my mother. I was standing beside my mother, but she had pulled me behind her as the door was being opened. There stood a beautiful young girl. "How old are you," asked my mother. I thought that was not polite and a stupid question to ask such a beautiful girl. "I like this one," I said, but I was quickly asked to shut up by my mother and again pulled behind her. "I am eighteen and studying at the teacher's college," she answered. She was about five feet eight inches tall, with a slim built body. She was fair in complexion like my brother, Matthew. I thought they would make a good matching pair if my brother were to keep her. "My name is Evelyn," she responded to my mother's question.

After so many questions and answers with my mother, Evelyn was at the dining table with me, enjoying the yam and beans porridge. She had now become the official girlfriend of Matthew, whether he liked it or not. Yam and beans porridge remain amongst my favourite meals. Although it could take as long as two hours to cook depending on the beans, however, my mother had a method for reducing the cooking time slightly. She would soak the beans for a few hours before cooking them with chopped onions in enough water that covered the content of the pot. Then she would add blended tomato seeds with more onions and chillies, which were added to the pot and allowed to continue cooking for some time. She would peel the yam, wash, and slice the required portion into small chunks and add to the cooking beans and stir, adding water if needed. She would then add palm oil and salt and stir again. After cooking for a while, the temperature would be lowered to allow it to simmer. The meal would be ready after about twenty minutes of simmering.

I watched Evelyn as she chewed a mouth full of the yam and beans porridge. "Are you one of my brother's girlfriends?" "Do you know how many girlfriends he has?" I asked her. Ignoring my questions, just like the rest, and instead she started to ask me what my name was, age etc, etc. I later left her in the dining room to join my parents, but before they could hear me coming, I heard my mother say, "And I think she is pregnant." I then walked in saying, "No, she is not; I don't see any big belly." I was then asked to shut up and to go tidy my room.

Four months later, the following year in January 1982, we celebrated the birth of my niece. The newborn was fair in complexion, and she became the second grandchild. She was called, Kambi. The moment my father heard that mother and baby were doing fine, he released twelve rounds of gunshots into the air; I still wonder why. Thinking about the fuss that was made when she was born was nothing compared to how my beautiful baby niece, Kambi, was spoilt. She had a gold cot and specially made toys.

My parents bought a new car for Matthew and Evelyn and renovated their apartment, not to mention all the parties. I had never seen my parents so happy. Yes, I was a bit jealous as I lost my spot as the baby of the family at home. All the same, I was so delighted to have a baby in the house that I could play with anytime.

Matthew and Evelyn decided to postpone their wedding for the foreseeable future. I was deeply connected to Kambi; she was more like a sister. She was so lovely and beautiful that she won gold at the regional baby pageant show. My mother took her everywhere she went.

CHAPTER THIRTY-FIVE

They Will Be Fine

W E HAD STARTED TO experience the cold, harsh and dusty Harmattan weather of 1982. It was October, and it was already two months since I started my first term in secondary school. I was attending an all-boys catholic secondary school. It was a completely different learning institution compared to primary school. During my time, secondary school was made up of five-year levels. Again, we would only progress to the next year's level if we passed our exams. There was also the absolute requirement to pass Maths and English subjects. It was not unusual to see students repeating their year up to four times and sometimes drop out of school completely. The school grounds covered a large area with a driveway of over two hundred metres from the entrance gate to the first administrative building that housed the principal's office and the staff rooms. The academic blocks were scattered around the grounds with a short walking distance between them.

The system of secondary school was based on mental control and physical discipline. Although the principal would not hesitate to expel students that had consistently failed to abide by the school rules, the teachers would punish any child by flogging them with a cane if they disobeyed in any way. This included failing to complete homework on time, talking to fellow students in class during teaching, and even getting answers wrong. Other types of punishment include kneeling on the concrete floor with hands raised up in front of the class. Students were also asked to kneel outside under the direct hot sunshine of about thirty-four degrees centigrade. Pupils who arrived on the school grounds later than eight o'clock in the morning after the bell had rung to gather at the assembly were punished either by picking litter and fallen tree leaves or asked to kneel and be flogged. The school days session started at eight am and finished at one forty-five pm.

On Fridays, every student from year one to four was mandatorily required to bring a machete to school to cut the ground lawns. Classes would finish at midday to allow just over an hour to carry out the grass-cutting exercise. Any student failing to comply would be disciplined by flogging and then completing the grass-cutting task during class time the following school day, thereby missing out on learning. I did get some preferential treatment because of my family status, and my brother, William, was a senior, a year five student at the same school.

IT WAS ONE SATURDAY MORNING, and I knew my father was travelling out of town for business. Ben, his driver, had arrived early and was cleaning my father's car. I was awake and had joined my father in his morning prayer as always. "Can you take my briefcase and shotgun to the car?" my father requested. I loved taking the shotgun out as I got the opportunity to play pretend shooting outside. My father would always take his shotgun on long-distance trips. I had to take the cartridge belt too, which meant I must do two journeys to the car. I grabbed the shotgun out of the cabinet and rested it on the floor as I reached for the cartridge belt and tied it around my waist. It was still too big for my waist, even though I had to use the tightest buckle size. I, therefore, needed to support it with my hand to prevent it from rolling down from my waist. Although I was tall, I was very slim, and I did get teased at school for resembling a broomstick. After playing with the shotgun outside, Ben took it from me and placed it in the car. He also collected the cartridge belt. "Go get the briefcase," demanded Ben. I then hurried back upstairs to grab my father's briefcase.

As I approached my parents' apartment, I could hear my mother speaking with a high-pitched and distressed voice. Before I could make out what she was saying, my father had interjected, and I could feel he was really annoyed by the tone of his voice. I arrived in my father's bedroom, and I noticed the briefcase was lying on the bed alongside his short trip suitcase. "Perhaps I should take more of my stuff and stay away as long as possible then," my father said as he was walking into his room from my mother's bedroom. I reached for both cases without saying a word, but my father said, "Wait, I need to put more stuff in the suitcase." I watched him as he unzipped the case and added more clothing. "Take both to the car," my father said as he finished zipping the suitcase closed. I lifted both cases and headed downstairs. I could still hear the quarrelling until I reached outside. I handed the cases to Ben, who then placed the briefcase in the back seat of the car and the suitcase in the boot of the vehicle.

As Ben pushed down the lid of the car boot to close it, I could hear my parents shouting at each other. They had now moved to their private living room, which had windows outside and above where I was standing with Ben. I knew Ben was aware of some of the challenges surrounding my parents' marriage. "Come here," Ben uttered with both of his hands wide open. I moved reluctantly towards him, and as I reached his outstretched hands, he grabbed hold of me and pulled me to his chest and hugged me. "Do not worry; it will be okay," said Ben. I had only just turned twelve years old, and I had no knowledge of how to resolve my parents' occasional flare-up quarrels. I was not sure whether to believe Ben.

A few minutes later, I could hear footsteps coming downstairs, and shortly, my father emerged. He hugged me and said goodbye, and entered the vehicle through the door Ben was holding open for him. He then sat on the right-hand side of the car. Ben closed the door and proceeded to the driver's side of the vehicle. However, before Ben could open the driver's door, my mother had emerged and made her way to the left-hand side of the back seat and sat beside my father. I noticed that Ben was not sure if my mother was joining them on the journey. So, he reluctantly opened the driver's door and lowered his head in to speak with my father. After a very brief conversation with my father, Ben did not enter the vehicle and instead closed the door.

"Come with me," Ben said again, this time stretching out one hand towards me. I went to him, and he guided me into the house, and we headed into the general lounge on the ground floor. "You will have your own life to live, so do not concern yourself with what is going on between your Mum and Dad," said Ben. I really was not sure what he was expecting from me, although I could guess he wanted to protect me from any sad feelings resulting from my parents' quarrels. I sat with Ben for what seemed to be a few hours, and he told me stories about his life. One of the most important learnings I took from our long conversation was that "Sometimes, what seems so beautiful could temporarily turn ugly, but only patience over time can help restore the beauty," said Ben.

My mother later appeared in the lounge and informed Ben that my father was ready for him. Ben gave me a hug, thanked my mother, and said goodbye. I followed Ben outside to say goodbye to my father. Upon seeing me, my father opened his door and walked towards me and said as he hugged me, "You must not worry about me and your mother; we will always find a way in the end." I stood outside as I watched Ben and my father enter the vehicle and drive off the driveway, heading into the street and disappearing into a right turn as I heard the engine of the Mercedes Benz roar to accelerate further. I remained still and focused on the vehicle engine sound until it completely faded away. I wondered if my father would ever return as I walked into the house.

It was not clear what the issue was, and my mother did not discuss with me her reasons for delaying my father from leaving for his business trip that morning. From my further investigations with my siblings, it appeared that no one in the household knew what had caused the quarrel. A few days into my father's absence, I decided to speak to my mother about the situation between her and my father. "Will Daddy be coming back?" I asked my mother. "Yes, he will be coming back before the weekend," she responded. "What is going on between you and Daddy?" I asked again. "You don't need to worry about us, it is the normal husband and wife issue, and it will sort itself out eventually," my mother replied. "Both of you seem to quarrel a lot lately, and surely you don't believe that's alright?" I asked. "I understand what you are saying, but you are too young to be concerning yourself with marital issues," my mother said. She continued, "Focus on your studies and your Dad and I will be fine."

It was a few days later that my father returned from his trip. I noticed he was trying to avoid my mother as much as he could. "Daddy, why don't we go and spend the weekend at the country home?" I asked. "It would do you good and help you relax," I continued. "You are right, my son; I was actually thinking about it," my father replied. "Let your mother know about our plan, and we will leave in the morning," he continued. I was glad that we could leave in the morning as this meant my father would skip going into the office that Saturday morning. Although he was initially working less Saturdays to help him manage his stress and blood pressure, he had been working most of the days, including the weekends, lately.

Spending full weekends with my father alone continued to advance my maturity. My father would speak to me in confidence and would express his strengths and his fears. "I know you cannot understand most of the things I tell you, but never forget them, for when you grow more mature, you will be able to understand them," said my father. "Why are you and Mummy always fighting?" I asked. "Your mother is a lovely person, and I cherish her a lot, but sometimes she does not understand that she needs to calm down," replied my father. He continued, "I need her support in everything I do, as she's all I rely on." I noticed my father's concentration as he spoke about my mother. I could tell he really loved my mother and wished they had gotten along better lately. "Most of the time, we get along fine, but it's only when we quarrel, and I don't seem to understand why it gets so furious," uttered my father. "Do you think it can be resolved, and both of you could get along better as you used to?" I asked my father. "Time will tell, and I am doing my best. Sometimes, I feel I want to run away into the forest and turn into an animal and be free," replied my father. At this time, my father put his arm around me, and we embraced. It was difficult to imagine that my father was unhappy.

We enjoyed the weekend as much as we could. We visited extended family around the village, and we also received guests. One of them was my aunty. My mother did not fail to turn up with our traditional breakfast on Sunday morning and made us lunch in the afternoon before we all left and headed back to the house in the town. My father and I were in his Mercedes Benz while my mother and my sister, Azuka, drove behind us.

IT WAS A FEW DAYS LATER that my father had announced during the family meeting that he was being honoured by the younger generation of men and women from various communities in our area. They were to bestow him with a prestigious title, making him the adopted head and patron of the 'younger generation.' To accept this title and to thank the community of the younger generation, my parents would throw a lavish party, which would be held in our country home in the village.

It was the beginning of the last week of November, and I had just been discharged from the hospital and was recovering from surgery to remove my appendix. Although the operation went well, it was an experience that I would never forget. Administering the general anaesthetic required twelve injections into my back vertebrae until I was not able to move my body and passed out. My mother was behind the theatre doors and could hear me as I cried out loud from my pain and demanded she rescues me from the doctors. "My son, be brave, and it will be over soon," my mother responded to my demands. I had an incision of about four inches wide across my right lower abdomen to remove my appendix. I was in the hospital for a period of seven days, and my mother spent every night with me, with my father coming to stay with me during the day. Their visits overlapped daily, and I could notice again the love they shared for each other. I felt my surgery had brought them closer again, and I was glad it was a small price to pay to see my parents happy again.

They would discuss the party, and I noticed how easily they agreed on things to be done. The party was a privilege for everyone that attended. There was live music and plenty of food and drinks for everyone. My parents received gifts and there were presentations in recognition of my father's achievements to date. We all danced into the night as the musicians sang their hearts out, honouring the love and respect my parents had for each other. Watching my parents do their lone dance was the highlight of the event. It was a slow song and my parents' favourite from a famous musician in the region. Their dance attracted all the dignitaries to the floor to shower my parents with cash. As part of the Nigerian tradition, guests are expected to toss numerous money notes on those being celebrated. This is seen to be a gesture of appreciation, respect, and good luck for the future.

I felt that moment was the time of their life where love conquers everything. It was special to see my parents display their attachment and affection for each other in public. It was then I felt they would be fine.

CHAPTER THIRTY-SIX

Miscalculated Consequence

THE CHRISTMAS CELEBRATION of 1982 was a good one. Our house was full again, with cousins and friends staying with us. There were many activities that went on that kept everyone busy, although there was a little ruffling of feathers here and there amongst everyone, it never materialised to anything significant. My parents got on well, and we also had a nice New Year celebration in our village home. I had turned twelve years old and would be progressing to the second year in secondary school. My brother, William, would be graduating from secondary school at the same time that I would be moving up to my second year. However, I needed to pass my exams, especially Maths and English. My performance at school did concern me a little as I felt I was not really applying myself, and I felt it was because of my parents' issues. However, I had been passing my tests and mid-term exams and had no cause to fail. My other concern was that I was going to lose my brother's protection, and I would do my labouring just like everyone else.

On the other hand, I was looking forward to my independence at school, where I would have to rely on myself for my own protection. Most of my school friends had no elder brothers that protected them, and they were doing alright, so I believed I would be just fine. I was aware of the special bond between my father and I, and showcasing his affection for me was something he continued to display in public. My father would drop in unannounced at my school, and I would be called out of class to the principal's office. My father would embrace me and ask if I was behaving well and listening to my teachers without distractions. The answer would always be a "Yes, Daddy." I would be back in class five minutes later to be teased by my classmates afterwards.

IT WAS ON A SUNDAY, and we were having our usual early morning family meeting. "The Nigerian Television Authority (NTA) have agreed to showcase us as a prominent family in a primetime documentary," uttered my father. "Does this mean we will all be on television?" I asked. My brother, William, looked at me as if I was still a baby and said, "Yes, baby brother, we will be on television, but you are not allowed to say a word as you would spoil it for everyone." The thought of not speaking when I had the opportunity to appear on television was annoying. So, I responded, "It's not up to you whether I speak or not, and I will speak." My mother said, "Enough, you two, listen to your father and let him explain what will happen on the day of the filming." My father carried on talking about the activities of the day and what to expect. We had seen other families appear on the prominent show, and it was exciting. The filming would be the following Saturday, and our country home would be the location.

It was just before nine o'clock in the morning, and the television crew were at our gate. This is really happening; I thought to myself as I shouted, "They are here!" We had travelled to our village home the day before, and we had been preparing for the event. After some hospitality that we had offered the television crew, we progressed to have a serious discussion on what was to be expected, what to say and how to act. My father had appeared on television periodically, and he was a natural. For the rest of us, there was a feeling of nervousness and excitement at the same time. We were able to behave as expected by the crew throughout the filming, and they were happy. Unfortunately, I was not happy as I had not answered one of the questions well. "What would you like to be when you grow up?" I was asked by the interviewer. "I would like to be a doctor," I replied. This was easy, as I got it right. Then I forgot the answer to the follow on question. "Why do you want to become a doctor?" asked the interviewer. "Because...., because..., because....," I responded, as I had forgotten the agreed reason why I wanted to become a doctor. Then, before I could utter the fourth 'because,' I remembered my reason. "I want to help people get well," I said. "That is a good reason, and thank you," the interviewer replied. I thought we would have to do a retake of that, but it was agreed by the production director that it was cute and would make the programme appear more realistic. What everyone failed to realise was the teasing I would receive from my friends and school classmates. My name became 'because, because, because' overnight for the remainder of the school term.

Appearing on national television, on a programme that was watched across the country, helped us to further showcase the love and unity we shared as a family. My parents discussed their affection for each other and their determination to ensure the family remained intact and happy. My father also used the programme to thank my mother for her love and support throughout their journey of accomplishments and to remain successful. As always, my father never forgot to express his belief that anyone can be successful if they have the determination to work hard. "I did not have an easy upbringing and was rejected by my society when I was born with a tooth, and my parents could not afford to send me to school - they didn't even want me there – but look at me today, it's because of my determination and hard work," my father said on television.

However, not everyone was pleased to see us so happy on national television. Some of my father's relatives and friends continued to express their dissatisfaction that my father only had one wife. In every regard, my father continued to ignore them and expressed that he was not interested in living a life of polygamy. "I will never marry more than one wife as long as I live, and I will encourage my children never to embark on such a lifestyle," my father reaffirmed his stand to his relatives and friends.

ONE QUIET DAY, I had finished my homework and was in the living room with my mother watching a film when my father returned late from work. It was about six thirty in the evening, and my father would normally be home from work before five pm. I believed that he had dropped by one of his friends on his way home after work. "Cecilia, one of my friends is asking us to sell to their relative one of our lands in Benin City," said my father. He continued, "We do not have any immediate use for the land in question, and I thought if they needed it for something urgent, we could let them buy the land." Before my mother could give her opinion on my father's request, she demanded who the friend was.

My father provided the name of his friend that was seeking the sale of the land to someone they knew. "No, we will not sell any of our assets, not now, not forever!" replied my mother. "That land is in a prominent and strategic location; we don't need the money, so why sell it?" uttered my mother. "Your friend should never have asked you to sell the land," continued my mother. "I understand your feelings, but there is no need to be annoyed about it, he was only asking if we would sell it," my father said. "Yes, I understand, but this is how it starts – friends demanding favours, and eventually, they are getting it. I will never allow the sale of that land or, indeed, any of our accumulated assets," said my mother.

It was clear that my mother was concerned that my father's friend had made such a request. However, it was not apparent that my father was going to sell the land. Although, my mother knew that out of kindness, my father might sell the land without her permission. "Cecilia, let's leave the matter for now as I am too tired to discuss it," said my father. "Well, there is nothing to discuss; we are not selling the land," my mother responded. My father left the living room and headed into his bedroom. He changed and went into the shower. In a short while, he returned to the living room. His dinner was served and as usual, he invited me to join him, and I ate from his plate. The three of us later watched our favourite programme on television, and there was no mention of the land.

The following day my mother decided to pay my father's friend, that had asked for the sale of the land a visit. The consequence of that visit was something that my mother miscalculated. It was before four o'clock in the afternoon, and my father was already home from work. I had just finished attending a class with my tutor and was playing with a couple of my friends. "Where is your mother?" asked my father. "She is not home yet," I replied. My mother had an office and a restaurant in the same location as my father's business headquarters. Surely, he should know where she is, I thought. "Was she not in her office today?" I asked.

"I was not in the office today as I had a few meetings to attend," my father replied. "Surely, your mother would have been home by now; she normally leaves her office by three pm," uttered my father. "She may have gone to the market," I said and continued, "Are you hungry?" My father was already walking towards the kitchen, and I was following him. He reached for the fridge and then said, "I need a cold beer." He reached for a bottle of beer and anticipating that he would need a glass, so I walked to the cabinet that rested on the west side wall of the kitchen and grabbed a large mug. My father preferred to drink his beer from a mug. "Where is the bottle opener?" my father asked.

I thought he knew of the opener that was attached to the side of the fridge. But then I remembered that he always had his beers brought to him, and there was a bottle opener that rested on the stool beside his sofa. I pointed at the fridge and said, "There is an opener beside the fridge." I was not quick enough for him as he proceeded to use his teeth to open the beer bottle. I thought that was cool and it would be something I would try one day. I reached for the beer bottle so that I could help him pour it into the mug, but he asked me not to worry and did it himself. He placed the mug on the kitchen worktop and then poured the content of the beer into the mug. This meant that there was a lot of the beer's frothy foam, which my father would always avoid by positioning the mug at an angle when pouring the beer.

I could tell there was something wrong as he lifted the mug to his mouth and drank the whole content. He replaced the mug on the worktop and poured the remaining beer content into it. The bottle was now empty, and he carried the mug with him as he left the kitchen heading towards the general living room. I knew he needed space for himself, so I went downstairs to continue playing with my friends.

It was nearly an hour later that my mother returned home. Iyke, my mother's driver, had parked the vehicle with the boot facing the house entrance. I immediately realised that my mother had gone shopping. "Welcome home, Mummy," I said to my mother. "Thank you, my son," she replied. "Go help Iyke and bring in the stuff from the car boot," she requested. My friends had to go home as they noticed I would be busy. So, I helped Iyke and our two home assistants to empty the car boot. It was full of groceries and other associated bushmeats. I know that Iyke hates driving a dirty car, and I noticed as he moved the vehicle and repositioned it to a location where he could clean it. Normally, I would help Iyke to wash the car, and he would give me some cash, but I did not want to miss out on why my father returned home early, asking for my mother. So, I left Iyke to clean the vehicle, and I headed upstairs.

I noticed that my mother had headed straight into the kitchen and started to prepare dinner. "Have you seen Daddy?" I asked. "No, what time did he return home?" I was not sure if my mother was avoiding him, but I needed her to know that my father was not in a good mood and was asking for her. "Daddy was home at four o'clock and was asking after you," I replied. "I don't think he was in a good mood," I continued. "Did he say why he was not in a good mood?" my mother asked. "No, he did not say anything to me," I replied. "So why did you think he was not in a good mood?" my mother asked. "I don't know, I just guessed, and he used his teeth to open the beer bottle," I replied. "Did he not see the opener?" my mother asked again. "Surely there was someone home to attend to him?" she continued. "I was with him, and everyone else was downstairs, and he did not ask for anyone's help," I said.

"Where is your Dad now?" asked my mother. "I think he is watching a programme on the television," I replied. "Alright, let me get dinner started, and I will go and check he's okay," said my mother.

CHAPTER THIRTY-SEVEN

Be The Man You Say You Are

T O SAY THAT MY MOTHER enjoyed cooking is an understatement. Cooking was her passion. It was also obvious to see the creativity that she deployed into her cooking style and the varieties of food she dished out. Her preparation processes could well be the very first ingredient that determined the richness in the taste of her food. As always, the quality of each item that made up the entire components of her meal was never compromised in any way. She was willing to travel hundreds of miles to source the best ingredients for her cooking. My mother's knowledge of complementary foods also helped to provide overall satisfaction in sight and presentation. She operated as if money was never an object that could restrict her passion for creating and delivering the best quality of food possible.

As my mother examined her groceries and the freshly killed meat items, I noticed she was going to prepare egusi soup, and she was going to use assorted components of meat, such as chicken, stock fish, bush meat (bushpig), giant African snails, dried smoked fish, and smoked giant prawns. My father was used to this level of meal as standard and therefore never expected anything less. I knew the meal would be delicious as always, but I wondered if the slight rage I noticed in my father's behaviour earlier could compromise the peace of enjoying the dinner.

After setting aside the ingredients and the meat components for cooking, my mother assigned the responsibility of initiating the preparation to one of our house assistants. She washed her hands in the kitchen sink and reached for the cloth towel to dry her hands, but there were none hanging in the usual place. "Can someone hand me a kitchen towel, please?" my mother shouted. I quickly went to the airing cupboard just in the hallway that leads into the kitchen and picked up a dry towel and quickly presented it to my mother. "Thank you," she uttered. I opened my mouth to say, "You are welcome," but the sudden appearance of my father at the kitchen door rendered me speechless.

"Cecilia, surely you have been informed that I was looking for you?" asked my father. "My apologies, I am aware, but I thought since you are already home, I wanted to get dinner started as I know you would be needing dinner," replied my mother. She continued, "I was just leaving to find you." My father had the same look of unpleasantness that I noticed when he was last in the kitchen, needing a cold beer. "Can we go to the living room to have a discussion, please?" my father asked. "Sure, I am free now, let go," my mother responded. My father turned away from the kitchen door and headed towards their private living room, and my mother was walking behind him.

I was definitely not needed in the kitchen, and I had no other place to be, so I walked quietly behind my mother. As my father approached the door that led into their private apartment, he reached for the handle of the door and turned it; he then pushed it open and walked into the quiet, air-conditioned space. His hand was still holding the door handle as he held it open to allow my mother to enter the living room. I was not surprised that the door was allowed to close behind my mother, almost slamming it on my face as I reached the entrance. I felt it was an indication that my presence was not required.

Out of curiosity, I decided to wait behind the door to listen to their discussion. "How was your day?" I could hear my mother's voice say.

"Thank you for asking, but I was humiliated today by friends because of you, so my day wasn't that great," I could hear my father say. He continued, "Can you explain to me why you saw the need to visit my friend in his home and warned him never to speak to me again about any intention to ask me to sell our land?" Before my mother could answer, my father continued, this time with a raised voice, "Do you realise how disrespectful that was to me?"

There was a brief silence. Then my mother spoke, "There was no intention to be disrespectful towards you; I only wanted to make it clear to him that we do not have land to sell, and he should not have approached you in that regard." My mother sounded calm and seemed to have made her point clear. "He is my friend, and you have no business going to him to speak on my behalf," my father shouted. "Please bring your voice down, as I don't see the reason why you should be this annoyed," uttered my mother. She continued, "He brought it upon himself for trying to manipulate you into selling our land to him.

That land is strategic and in a prominent place. It offers a great asset for our children even if we don't have an immediate plan for it." I could tell my father had become more upset as he said, "All you did by going to see him was display my weakness in controlling my wife." I felt as though my mother had become angry as she responded, "Do I look like I need to be controlled by anyone?" My father did not answer, and my mother continued, "Your friend was out of his place, and I have no regard for him if he thinks we should sell him or his relative a landed asset we have acquired for the future of this family."

The argument between the two of them intensified, and I felt that I needed to go into the living room to try and stop them from completely falling out. So, I reached for the door, opened it, and walked in. "What is wrong with the two of you?" I asked. "Everyone in the house, and indeed the neighbourhood, can hear you quarrelling," I continued. "Can you please stop it?" I added. There was a brief silence, and I noticed my mother reaching for the armchair and sitting down on it. I could see she was in a distraught mood and close to tears. "All I ever wanted is to protect the integrity and progress of this family, and I will stop at nothing to achieve it," said my mother. She continued, "There are many people that are envious of the way we are, they cannot stand the fact that you only have one wife, and they want to destroy us."

I approached my mother; at this time, she had started to cry. "I have worked so hard for this family, you had nothing when you met me, but look at us now, we have risen beyond anyone's imagination, and now, you seek to take their side and destroy us," said my mother. "When will you learn that they don't really like us?" asked my mother. "Who are they?" asked my father. "You mean my friends, my family, or both? Tell me, who do you refer to as our enemies?" my father continued in rage. "I have done all I can to protect you and to keep us out of the reach of those that seek to destroy everything we have built together, but you are just too blind to see it," said my mother. "I know that your relatives and friends continue to pressure you into marrying another wife. Do you think you can handle a polygamous home?" she asked. My father walked closer to my mother and stood in front of her and said, "You do not know what you are talking about." He continued, "I am the man of this household and a Chief of this Kingdom, and I must be respected by my wife and not, as a result, be humiliated by my friends."

I really did not know what was expected of me at that moment, but I felt I needed to telephone my grandfather, my mother's father. "Then be the man you say you are; show your power by not listening to those whose primary interest is to destroy us," said my mother. I felt that my grandfather's presence might calm them down, and he could resolve their issues. As I reached for the telephone, I heard my father say, "That's it, I have heard enough and have taken enough of this disrespect; I am moving to the village." He continued, "Uche, you are coming with me." I was not sure if I was ready to live apart from my mother, but before I could respond one way or another, my mother stepped in and said, "You can run to the village if you want, but you are surely not taking him with you."

The harsh and loud words being exchanged by my parents made it impossible to hear the dialling tone of the telephone. However, I dialled my grandfather's number and waited for the ringing tone. "Hello, who's calling?" I recognised my grandfather's voice immediately, and I said, "Hello, Big-Papa, it's me, and you need to start coming here immediately as my mother and father are quarrelling; please come at once." There was a brief silence, "hello, hello, can you hear me, Big-Papa?" I continued. "Yes, I can hear you; I will leave immediately," my grandfather replied. I then replaced the telephone receiver.

I could still hear the shouting continuing between my parents. I thought I should head outside to await my grandfather's arrival, but before I could reach the living room exit, I noticed the door was being opened. My mother was still sitting on the armchair, while my father was expressing his anger as he paced across the front of the living room, back and forwards across a distance of not more than three metres. He also noticed the door was being opened, so he stood still and stopped speaking as we both watched to see who was coming into the living room.

It was my sister, Azuka. "What are you doing in here?" she asked me. "I have been looking for you," she continued. "I have been here; what do you want?" I uttered. "Come with me at once," she demanded. "No, I am not," I said. She walked towards me, grabbed hold of my hand, and dragged me behind her. "Leave me alone," I shouted, but she seemed determined to achieve her objective and ignored my desire to be left alone. As we approached the exit door, which she did not shut when she entered the living room. She pulled me in front of her and guided me through the open door; without letting go of me, she used her other hand to close the door behind us. "Where are you taking me?" I asked. "To your room," she replied. "It is not good for you to be in there hearing all the quarrelling, so you are to stay in your room and remain there," she continued. "You cannot tell me what to do; you are not Mummy or Daddy," I shouted and tried to free myself from her. Unfortunately, I did not have the strength to free myself, and I ended up in my room, and my sister shut the door behind her. I immediately tried to open the door, but I could tell my sister was still behind it and holding up the handle. I then decided to lay on my bed. I was feeling emotionally exhausted and helpless. I only wished that there was something I could do to stop my parents from fighting.

"Wake up," I heard as someone slapped my feet gently. "Come have your dinner," I heard my mother's voice as I struggled to open my eyes. I took a quick look at my table clock, and it was eight forty-seven pm. I realised I had been asleep for over two hours. "Where is Daddy?" I asked my mother. "You get up and come have your dinner," she replied. "Where is Daddy?" I asked again. "Come have your dinner, and we can discuss that later," she said. "No, I am not having dinner till I know where Daddy is," I responded. "He has left for the village," my mother replied.

Although I expected that would be the case, I felt a strange pain in my stomach and an overwhelming weight of discomfort. I immediately lost the appetite to eat. "I am not hungry; I want to stay in bed," I insisted. "You must follow me and eat now; dinner is already late. Your father will be back in a few days," my mother responded. "No, you do not know he will be back," I uttered. After a brief silence, my mother left the room without saying any more words. I decided to lay my head back on the pillow as I thought about my father. It was not up to ten minutes after my mother had left my room that my grandfather opened my door. "Can I come in?" he asked. "Big Papa, you came," I said as I leaped out of my bed to embrace him. "Of course, I would not ignore your call," he said. My grandfather went on to inform me that my father had left for the house in the village and that he believed he would be back after a few days.

We spoke for over half an hour before he encouraged me to go have my dinner. It was also good to hear from him that he and my grandmother had reconciled, and she had returned home to live with him.

CHAPTER THIRTY-EIGHT

The Shotgun

IT WAS JUST COMING TO the end of the summer holidays of 1983, and my parents had been living apart for over four months. The reality of not having my parents together in one household had a significant negative impact on me. I continued to imagine how my father was surviving being alone in that big house in the village. Apparently, my father would not eat my mother's meals anymore and had been relying on his relatives to cater for his food. Although I could not believe that my father could settle for any other standard of food, knowing that he prides my mother on cooking the best meals in the whole world after his own mother. While my siblings and I continued to visit my father in the village, we never actually stayed overnight. My father had the impression that my mother had instructed us never to stay overnight, which was not the case. However, my father's resentment towards my mother escalated, and his desire for reconciliation continued to deteriorate.

It was one Sunday morning, and we had a siblings' meeting and had agreed to visit my father and encourage him to return home with us. We arrived at the house in the village to meet a multitude of vehicles parked in and outside of the compound. It seemed like there was an event going on indoors, and I wondered why my father never mentioned it to us. We were welcomed by the security staff, but he quickly informed us that we simply could not drive our vehicle in. Matthew, who worked for my father, became annoyed that he was not informed of such an occasion taking place. "How did I not know about this?" he asked the head of security. "I have no knowledge why," he replied. "What is the event about? Who are the owners of these vehicles?" Matthew asked again. "We think they belong to members of the ruling political party," replied the head of security. "Why are they here?" Azuka asked.

The security could not provide any other information. We abandoned our vehicle by the entrance gate and decided to walk into the compound. We had my elder brother's beautiful daughter, Kambi, with us, and we knew that my father would be delighted to see her if not us. We arrived inside the house and headed straight to the general living room, where we heard the noise of people moving and talking. However, the entrance was blocked as a result of individuals standing behind the door and having hardly any space inside to move. We then abandoned the idea of entering through the normal entrance and proceeded to use the back door, which was only accessible from the hallway that links the private bedrooms.

We managed to gain access to the general living room, and it was packed with what I imagined to be one hundred people. I was not sure of the space capacity. Nevertheless, my father noticed us as we continued to force ourselves through the narrow spaces amongst the guests and headed towards my father. Noticing us, my father stood up and asked the person that was making a speech to hold on. "My children are here; excuse me for a minute," my father spoke up loudly. We each embraced my father, and he seemed delighted to see us. "You all came at a bad time, but I am delighted you are here," uttered my father. "You will all need to excuse me as I have to attend to these political party members that are seeking my endorsement," my father continued. "Give me my granddaughter," he demanded, and my niece was equally delighted to go to my father. We left my niece, Kambi, with my father and again squeezed ourselves through the guests and headed upstairs. I headed for the family living room and was followed by my sister, Azuka, and my brother William. Matthew walked on into my father's private living quarters. The living quarters consisted of two bedrooms, a small lounge, and a large bathroom. This was supposed to be both of my parents' living apartments, and it was where I normally stayed with my father whenever we were there for a weekend break. The apartment also had a private staircase that connected to the ground floor. Therefore, there was no need to go through the family living room to access the stairs for going to the lower floor.

While Matthew was in my parents' private living area, we decided to watch television to while away the time until the political conference came to an end, and we could speak to my father about returning home. It was about twenty minutes into the tv programme that we were watching, and we started to hear people struggling and shouting. This noise was coming from the entrance gate area. I reached for the window and slid the curtains apart so I could see what was going on. Surprisingly, it was Matthew carrying my father's shotgun. It appeared that the security staff were not happy with him carrying the shotgun and were trying to overpower him to relieve it from him. "Matthew's got Daddy's gun," I said to my other siblings as I headed through my parent's living quarters to take the stairs to the ground floor.

As I reached the ground floor, I ran outside and headed for the entrance gate. However, the security had relieved the shotgun from Matthew, and I noticed that the political guests had started to come outside to see what was going on. I then saw my father, who was still carrying Kambi, as he walked towards the entrance gate. "What is going on?" asked my father. "It's under control, sir," replied the head of security. My father was later given the details of what had happened. I agreed with the rest of my siblings that it was no longer the right time to speak to my father about moving back home. We waited for the political party to leave, and we had a moment with my father. "I have warned you, time and time again, that shotguns are not toys," my father spoke directly to Matthew. "Start taking life seriously; you are now a father," he continued. We later left the village and headed home without my father.

IT WAS A FEW DAYS later when the chief of police arrived at the front of our family home in town. This was unusual, I thought, as I imagined what could be the reason for the police to visit us. My father no longer resided with us, and we hardly got visits from important people anymore. It was in the afternoon and about an hour after I had returned from school. The police chief was allowed in, and he demanded to see my mother and my elder brother, Matthew. I followed him into our guest living room while Kate went to inform my mother. "You are welcome to have a seat. Shall I get you something to drink?" I asked the police chief. "Thank you, a glass of water would be nice," said the police chief. I then left to get him a glass of cold water.

I met my mother in the kitchen as she was finishing what she was doing to go join the police chief. "I wonder what he needs," my mother asked. "He seems calm, so I think it would be nothing important," I uttered. "It could be that one of your children has fallen out with a traffic officer for the tenth time," I continued sarcastically. I left my mother in the kitchen and returned to hand the police chief the glass of water. "My mother is just finishing up what she is doing and will be with you shortly," I said to the police chief as I placed the glass of water by the side table of the armchair where he was sitting. "Thank you," he said. I then sat on the sofa and started to mentally analyse why he was here.

I had not seen him before, although I had no reason to have met him before. However, I did imagine that he would know my father, given his status in society. The police chief later picked up the glass of water and drank from it. As I scanned him with my eyes from his head to his feet, I noticed that there was something not quite right with his shoes. They were shining and appeared to be in good order. I had not seen many police chiefs, but I knew that most of their shoes did not look this clean. Although his shoes did not look new, I could tell that they were well-maintained. I imagined he did not go about chasing criminals in those nice black shining shoes.

The police chief was about six feet tall and of medium build. He would not be more than fifty years old from my assessment. He had a face marking that suggested he may be from the Yoruba tribe. He may well have been born and grew up in the Agbor area, I thought. I didn't think it was proper to get into a personal conversation with him, so I refrained from asking him about his facial markings and where he was born. I also remembered that my parents had taught me that it was not proper to ask people you have just met where they are from. We remained silent until my mother entered the living room.

"Good afternoon, Mr Humphrey," my mother said as she walked into the guest living room. The police chief then stood up and stretched his hand out to shake my mother's as he responded, "Good afternoon, Madam." He continued, "I am sorry to visit without prior arrangement; I hope you will excuse me?" My mother shook his hand and then walked to the armchair opposite the police chief and sat on it. "You are welcome, Mr Humphrey," said my mother. She continued, "How can I help you; I hope all is well?" The police chief had now sat back down but this time, was not too relaxed and was sitting at the edge of the armchair.

"There is a problem, and I am here to let you know that your husband has claimed that you had instructed your son to visit him at the village house to kill him," said the police chief. "When was this?" I quickly asked as I stood up and headed for the telephone to ring my father. "Sit down!" Said, my mother. My mother then moved to the edge of her seat and looked deeply towards the police chief. I had never seen my mother so focused on looking at someone. "I am sorry. Can you repeat what you have just said as I am not sure I heard you right," uttered my mother. But before the police chief could say another word, my mother continued, "Are you saying that my husband is accusing me of trying to kill him and that I had asked my son to shoot him?" The police officer looked reluctant to answer the question as if he knew it was a baseless accusation. "I am sorry, madam, but it's what your husband has reported to us, and I wanted to come to you directly to inform you that we are opening an investigation, and you and your son are summoned to the police station to give your statements," said the police chief. "We may also have to formally arrest you and your son," continued the police chief.

"When did my husband say this supposed attempt to kill him took place, and to which of my sons is he referring?" asked my mother. "He claimed that the incident happened this past Sunday, and he was referring to your second son, that works in the family business," replied the police chief. "I was there, and nothing of that nature happened and neither was it intended," I interrupted. "Are you sure you were there?" asked the police chief. "Of course, I was there," I replied. I continued, "My mother was not aware that we all went to the village to see my father, and we have not told her what happened." My mother looked at me with a surprised face, "What are you talking about?" she asked. I turned to the police chief, who was at his time expecting me to say something.

"We went to the village to speak to my father to appeal to him to return home," I said. "Then, what happened?" asked the police chief. "Although my brother, Matthew, took my father's shotgun, he was outside wanting to leave the compound when the security men removed the shotgun from him," I said. "My father was holding Matthew's daughter, Kambi, and was inside the ground floor general living area of the house having a political meeting," I continued. I went on to inform the police chief that my father was never in any danger throughout our visit there, and perhaps Matthew was going to look for birds to shoot. "My brother was taking the shotgun outside, and my father was indoors," I uttered. My mother appeared shocked hearing my explanation. I felt it was the first time she was hearing about the incident. All the same, I knew that Matthew was not that stupid to risk throwing his young life away in return for having my father dead. Matthew now had two very young children with his partner, Evelyn, and I didn't think he would like to bring them up from a prison cell.

"Pardon me, Mr Humphrey, I am only just hearing about this incident now," said my mother. "I know you very well, madam, and I know your family well, too," uttered the police chief. "I know you and your husband are good people, and although I am aware of your marital situation, I would not have anticipated such an accusation to be reported," continued the police chief. "I am sorry that this has happened, and I can assure you that I wouldn't imagine the thought of wanting my husband dead and to be killed by my own son," said my mother. "My heart is now broken even further, and I just don't know how this could be happening to me," continued my mother as she started to cry.

"I am very sorry, madam for the trouble, but we would like you and your son to report to the police station sometime soon to give your statements, and we will then carry out our investigation," said the police chief. My mother remained in her seat and continued to cry as the police chief stood up, excused himself and left. I followed him out and watched him enter his vehicle, and drove away.

CHAPTER THIRTY-NINE

It is a Broken Home

MY BROTHER, WILLIAM, HAD finished his further studies after leaving secondary school and was preparing to leave for the United States to attend a university and study criminal law. In the meantime, he had remained at home but occasionally went to the block factory to help. My sister, Azuka, would be entering her final year at secondary school the following September, and she was not boarding anymore. Attending boarding school was never an option for me as my parents always preferred me by their side. I was preparing for my third year at secondary school, but I was finding it difficult given my parent's separation.

My brother, Matthew, had been suspended from the family business following his accusation for attempting to kill my father. So, we were all at home this fateful Wednesday evening, and my mother had called a family meeting. "It is now obvious to us that your father has decided to wage war with us," my mother stated. "It is now his making to destroy his family; he is being manipulated by those that envy our family unity and progress," uttered Matthew. He continued, "To accuse me of the attempted murder of my own father that is baseless is something I will find very hard to forget." I was sitting about ten feet from Matthew, and I could feel his rage. "I would not have guessed that your father was capable of this, given everything that we have built together," said my mother. She continued, "However, I have called this meeting today because I wanted you all to know that I am innocent, as such intent would never be on my mind."

I took turns to examine the faces of everyone, and then I turned my head towards the ceiling. We were sitting in what used to be my parents' private, luxuriously decorated living room. The absence of my father from the house for nearly six months had left a void that no one could fill. I continued to focus on the artistic three-dimensional decorative panel of the living room ceiling as I admired its beauty. I was lost in my thoughts as I allowed my eyes to follow the design pattern of the ceiling. I was no longer present in the family meeting as I wondered why my father would feel the desire to abandon his family. Then I was distracted by the sound of my mother crying.

"Mummy, crying will not solve the problem," I said. "I know; I am just overwhelmed that the only man I know and love for all my life is dealing with us this way," replied my mother as she continued to cry. The family meeting was nothing compared to the ones jointly hosted with my father. The meeting was over in forty-five minutes. For me, the outcome of the meeting was that my mother and brother were innocent of the accusation from my father. It was also uncertain to understand why my father had decided to act in this manner. I thought I knew him, but for the first time, I started to question my father's recent mindset. Was my mother right all along about his weakness to disengage from those that sought to ill advise him and poison his mind about his family?

As we were leaving the living room, the telephone started to ring. My mother was closer to it, and she picked it up. We all delayed our exit as we wanted to know who was on the phone. We stared at my mother as we waited for acknowledgement that it was nothing important so we could continue to leave the living room. "Hang on, everyone, it's your sister and brothers in the United States," uttered my mother as she waved her hand for us to come back in. So, we returned to our seats as we waited, in turn, to speak to Joyce, Michael and Alexander. I was the last to speak with them, and it was a good feeling that they called. The telephone call lasted for about twenty-five minutes, and by the time I replaced the receiver, I noticed that my mother was feeling differently. She was no longer looking as if she would cry again. "That was a good call, and I am happy that your brother, Michael, is coming," uttered my mother. She continued, "Someone needs to get your father to see sense and return home." We all agreed to that as we made our way out of the living room.

A few days later, my mother and Matthew had visited the police station, and they were charged and detained. As a protest, William decided he would remain at the station with my mother and Matthew. I could not believe what was going on. Every attempt Azuka and I made to reach my father was in vain. My family situation quickly became the main headline story in area. The prestigious glamour portrayed in the region by my parents disappeared as everyone, especially in my community, could not believe what they were experiencing. My father did not stop there. He decided to strip my mother of her luxury and convenience. Her vehicles were seized, including all business and assets available to her. My father also seized all contents, including our clothing, books, pots, and pans, in our home in town, where we resided with our mother. He also demanded that my sister, Azuka, and I relocate to live with him in the village. Our refusal further infuriated him, and he decided to cut off our access to any financial support we had.

We managed to live in the house without furniture apart from my bed that my father had left for me. The gesture did not please me in any way. It gave me no pleasure to have a bed while my mother slept in police custody. My father also instructed all my remaining cousins, who happened to be from my mother's side, to leave. Matthew's wife, Evelyn, took their children to her parents as her husband remained in police custody, charged with a crime he never committed. We also lost our chauffeur service to school and had no money to pay for public transport to go anywhere. However, our parents had prepared us for such an eventuality, and we knew nothing must come between us and attaining our education. So, we walked the four and five miles to our respective schools daily.

My mother and Matthew were continuously refused bail, and we knew it was as a result of my father's influence. So, we would stop to visit my mother and brother on our walk to and from school. It was not that bad walking the ten-mile return trip to my school as I had the company of a few classmates, including my best friend, Paul, who previously would get a lift from my chauffeured service.

It was a few days later when my eldest brother, Michael, arrived from the United States. After a meeting with my father, my mother was granted bail and was released. However, Matthew remained in detention. It took several more days before Matthew was released from police custody. Matthew's wife, Evelyn, could not believe what she was experiencing. "I would not have believed that it is the same man that welcomed me into your home that is subjecting us to this pain," said Evelyn. Upon my mother's release, she went to her parent's house to stay.

It was difficult to understand my father's mindset, and every attempt I made to reach him was unsuccessful. I believed he was annoyed at me because I chose to stay with my mother. For me, it was not a choice; he should not have left. A few days later, after an intense discussion between my father and Michael, we learnt that all charges against my mother and Matthew were to be dropped. It was a great relief as it was impossible to wage war with the most powerful person in the region. We were never in any position to win the case, irrespective of the fact that my mother and brother were innocent. Unfortunately, Matthew's position with the construction company was terminated, and he was left penniless. It was impossible for me to understand why my father had taken all these courses of action. We used to be one strong family that loved each other dearly.

I had followed my mother to live with my grandparents. It was joyful to see my mother free even though she had lost everything, including her clothes and her mobility. "Mummy, they can take everything you have worked hard for, but they just cannot take your beauty from you," I told my mother. There were tears in her eyes as she hugged me. "This is also a lesson for you and your siblings. Not everything is always within your control," she said. "I have done nothing to deserve this humiliation, yet I feel no malice towards your father," she continued. We spoke for a while about the situation and how well she was treated during her detention. We spoke about going to church to pray for my father and ask God to show him the way back home and to be the good person he once was.

After a moment, my mother asked me to take a walk with her. We stepped out into the outdoor front opening of my grandparents' house. We followed a walkway that led to the street; we turned left and started to walk, heading south. "I need to ask you for your permission, and I hope you will grant it," said my mother as she changed the subject of our conversation. I quickly became concerned as I knew there was something bothering her. "What is it, Mummy?" I said. "You don't need my permission for anything, and you know that," I continued. "Well, I think I do," she responded. "I feel I need a change of scenery to help me process all that has happened, to set my mind free from it, and to think of a way forward," she continued. "Where would you go?" I asked.

"I need your permission to go live in the United States for a while," she replied. Before I could respond, she continued, "I would have loved you to come with me, but you know your father would never allow me that pleasure." I knew immediately that she should leave the country to help her regain her self-worth again. "Of course, Mummy, I am nearly fourteen, and I can look after myself," I replied. "How long will you stay there?" I asked. "I am not sure, but not a day longer than I need," she responded.

It was a few days later that my mother left for the United States. She had taken my niece, Kambi, with the permission of her parents. My father still had full control of the family remotely, and he must grant the final approval for my mother to take Kambi out of the country, even though her parents had no objections. My mother had brought up Kambi like her own child from the moment she was born. Separating both for a long time would definitely have affected my mother's duration of stay in the United States. So, it was the right decision to allow her to travel with Kambi.

My father, surprisingly, did not hesitate to release the money for the travel costs. Nobody knew how long my mother would remain in the United States, so there was no plan to move to live with my father in the village and neither did he suggest returning home. I believe my father had become used to his life in the village and may struggle to return. Meanwhile, after my mother's departure for the United States, my father had allowed us full access to our family home in town, and my cousins were allowed to return. However, my cousins' parents ignored my father's gesture and regarded it as too little too late. So, none of my cousins returned to live with us.

Matthew's children had returned home earlier, during the same time he was released from police custody. The relationship between Matthew and my father continued to deteriorate. Matthew had lost his job with my father's business, and he was struggling financially to look after his family. However, my father continued to make some money available to Evelyn for the children's upkeep. Eventually, Matthew's relationship with Evelyn suffered, and they were separated. Evelyn took the youngest child and left for her parents' home.

THE PERIOD THAT MY MOTHER remained in the United States and my father was living in the village was the time I felt most vulnerable in every aspect. I felt a sense of hardship and loneliness. I also continued to experience challenges I could not express to anyone. Although most of the challenges were emotional as a result of my broken family, I also experienced some direct and physical encounters that would stay with me for the rest of my life.

My best friend, Paul, lived on the street that was parallel to mine. His house was only five minutes' walk from my home. Paul went to the same primary school as me, and we were attending the same secondary school. We were also in the same class. Our friendship was so strong that Paul got chauffeured to and from school with me daily. He would hang around my house till late and got to enjoy my mother's lovely meals. One of Paul's half-brothers, Richard, was also in the same secondary school as us, and was at that time in his final year, and was also the head prefect of the school.

Paul was a love child born as a result of an affair his father had with his mother. Paul claimed that he was never truly welcomed into his father's family when he was about eight years old when his mother decided to hand him over for his father's care. I also suspected that Paul's half-siblings may have been jealous that he was my best friend, mainly because he benefited from the relationship. So, Richard knew me very well and understood the challenges my family was currently experiencing.

One afternoon, after the final school bell was rung, and as usual, we all made our way to the assembly ground, where our attendance for the end of the day was registered. Any pupil not present was assumed to have left school early and would be punished the following day.

After the registration was taken and other formal school announcements made, the teachers handed over the assembly to the school prefects to conduct their affairs with the students. To my surprise, Richard called out my name and ordered me to appear in front of the assembly. I was not sure why he wanted me in front of the whole school, but I proceeded to join him regardless, and I also did not have a choice anyway. To my surprise, he said to the assembled students, "Uche Oriahi thinks he is untouchable, but I am going to prove to him that he is not." I was not sure why he would assume that and felt the need to care anyway. He continued, "I have decided I will teach him a lesson this afternoon, and he will be flogged with twelve strokes of the cane." He then asked me to turn my back and proceeded to whip me twelve times as the whole school watched.

I did not remember crying as I felt I must put on a brave face even though I was in severe pain. I felt humiliated as everyone at the assembly knew who I was. I felt that Richard was trying to showcase to the entire school that he could exert his position over me and disgrace me regardless of my status. I really did not know why Richard felt I deserved such humiliation. However, I knew that he felt that my family was in so much disarray, and no one would care to confront him. He was right because I never mentioned it to anyone in my family, but only because Paul pleaded with me not to do it, as he would have suffered indirectly the consequences of my family's reaction.

Although this incident continued to affect my mental state, I also did not want to tell my family because I did not want to add to the already distressing issues every one of us was facing. Perhaps, my father or siblings would not have bothered anyway, as they were just too occupied with their own already troubled situation as a result of the family problems.

IT WAS NEARING one year since my mother departed for the United States. I was really missing her, but I was more concerned for my brother, Matthew. It was sad to see him lose his respect and privilege in society. He was regarded as nice and generous. He would help anyone if the solution was within his reach. He had also gone out of his way to help people he hardly knew. Unfortunately, no one would help him, either for the fear of my father or because they just did not have what it took to assist him. It was on a Sunday morning, and I decided I would travel to the village to see my father. My intent was to draw his attention to the consequences of his actions. I took the bus and walked a few miles, and I arrived at our village house. I approached the gate but was informed that my father was not entertaining any guests. "Are you out of your mind?" I shouted at the head of my father's security. "I am definitely not a guest; can't you see that with your eyes closed?" I continued.

I felt I had enough of my father's behaviour, and I was ready to confront him. The security still would not open the gate, so I decided to climb my way into the compound. "Go on, shoot me if you have to," I told the security as I made my way through the driveway towards the main building. I started banging on the doors and windows and calling out to my father.

After a while, he opened the door. "What are you doing here?" he asked. "I have every right to be here, I am your son, and I am tired of the way you are treating us," I responded. "Are you going to let me in, or shall I force myself in through you?" I continued.

CHAPTER FORTY

The Settlement

I HAD NOT HAD THE opportunity of being alone with my father for several years since he had left us. I was maturing into a young adult, and I had gained a lot of life experience, especially from my parents' issues. My father and I had been talking for over an hour, and we were making progress. I wanted to hear from him directly why he had decided to treat us the way he had done. We were in the private living room that is situated on the second floor of the village house. It was quiet, and the only noise I could hear was the sound of the two air conditioning units that were blowing cold air into the very large living room. We were seated on the sofa, but about four metres apart and opposite each other. "You once told the nation on television that your love and affection for your children and your wife are not negotiable and uncompromisable; what really changed?" I asked my father as I looked straight towards him.

"You are asking a good question, but do you think you are mature enough to go into such a discussion?" I decided to move to the armchair closer to my father, and looking into his eyes, I said, "You will be surprised how quickly I have grown in the last few years that you have not bothered to treat me like a son." I was desperate for him to see the hurt I felt because of his actions. "I understand that you may be annoyed, but let me tell you that I am more devasted than I let anyone see," said my father. He continued, "I am hurting from the comments your mother made, and I had no choice but to act in accordance."

This was the first time I heard that there was a comment made by my mother that had hurt my father. "What comment are you referring to?" I asked. "Your mother said that I was not capable of fathering you all," said my father. "This is the first time I am hearing that," I said. "Well, there is no fact to that and just words," I continued. "What do you mean there is no fact to something that serious?" my father responded. "It does not make any sense," I replied. "Why would you say that?" asked my father. "Take a look at each one of your seven children; we all look like you," I said.

My father, who was initially sitting at the edge of his seat, but then decided to push himself in and was now resting his back against the sofa. I noticed he was thinking as he became silent. I, therefore, allowed him the time to contemplate what I had just said about how we all resembled him. After about what seemed to be ten minutes of silence, and he still had not spoken, I decided to get up to stretch my legs. "I am going to get myself a drink. Do you want any?" I asked. "No thanks, but there are soft drinks in the fridge," my father replied.

I could not remember the last time I was inside the house, but it seemed a long time ago. So, I decided to wander around while my father took a moment to consider my statement and perhaps everything that we had talked about for an hour and a half. As I walked into the different areas of the huge house, I noticed some changes to the furniture and the carpets. They looked different and new. I continued into my father's bedroom section, and the first thing that I noticed was an extra-large picture of my mother and father together in a frame that was placed on the floor and resting against the wall. I remembered the occasion when the picture had been taken, but I wondered why my father had to enlarge it, given he was not in a relationship with my mother. I continued into the room and walked into the section that was supposed to be my mother's area which had her bed, dressing table, and her closet. I noticed that my mother's pictures were still hanging on the wall. I walked closer to the closet and opened the door and was surprised to see that my mother's clothes were nicely preserved.

As I closed the door of the closet, I heard footsteps and could only imagine they were my father's. "You all actually have a trait of my unique features," said my father. Without turning my back to acknowledge him, I said, "Have you only just realised that?" I then carried on walking to open the door to the bathroom. I remembered the unique mosaic tiles on the wall and the extra-large bath that I used to play in. "Do you remember when you used to bathe me in this bathtub?" I asked my father. As if he did not hear my question, he said, "Apart from Michael and you, that have my head shape and facial features, the rest of your siblings have my bone deformity."

I thought I should ignore him, too, as I turned the tap for the bath on and said, "I am going to have a bath." I then started to undress. "Are you paying attention to what I am saying?" asked my father. As if I was not interested in what he was trying to figure out, I gently pushed him outside the bathroom; I then closed the door and turned the lock. "I thought you were here to talk?" asked my father. "Yes, but I think I have said enough," I replied as I climbed into the cold water bath, as the tap continued to run. "You children!" My father uttered as I heard his footsteps disappearing into the distance.

A FEW DAYS LATER, Matthew, William, Azuka, and I were attending a meeting called by my father. After a few explanations, my father offered us an apology. I was not surprised as I felt that my father remained one of the most intelligent people in the world even though he could not read and write. I believed he would figure things out eventually and make corrections where possible. Matthew was reemployed and was managing the block factory as my father announced he would be stepping back from the business gradually. We knew that after over five years of living in the village, it would be impossible to expect my father to return to the house in the town. He was turning sixty-two years old but appeared older. His younger sister, Anna, had just passed away after a brief illness at the age of sixty. We continued to spend more time with my father, and it was not long after the reconciliation that my mother returned home from the United States. She had returned with my niece, Kambi, who barely recognised any of us and spoke in an American accent. My mother's first task was to reunite Matthew and his family, reaching out to Evelyn to return home.

My father was determined to reconcile with my mother but was still struggling to overcome his ego. He would rather write to her than go and visit her. It was on a Saturday morning that my father asked me to stop by the village house. "Bring a pen and paper," he said. "I thought that is what you pay your secretaries for," I responded. "Don't be late, and we will go hunting afterwards," uttered my father.

I arrived at the village house as early as I possibly could as I was looking forward to the hunting trip afterwards. "Make yourself comfortable in the dining room, and I will be there shortly," said my father. However, I decided to go to the fridge for a cold drink and returned to the living room and turned the television on to watch a football game. A few moments later, my father was calling me from the dining room. I quickly turned the television off and went to join him.

"I need you to help me write a letter to your mother," said my father. At first, I thought he was joking. "Daddy, pick up the telephone and speak to her; she is at home now," I stated. "No, I want to write to her, so let's do it," my father demanded.

Dear Cecilia,

First, I want to welcome you back from the United States. I hope you have used the time away to rest and reflect on all that has gone on between us for the last several years. I must say that I have missed what we did have, and I wish it was easy to go back and relive that part of our lives. I now believe I would have made a different decision.

However, we are where we are. The most important thing now is, can we repair our relationship? I want to know if you are willing to allow us the opportunity to try and repair the damage done.

I understand that there will be many things to talk about and a lot of questions to be asked and answered. I have reached that stage in life where I want to retire and start to enjoy the fruit of my labour, and I believe you have a place beside me. I know this letter may come as a surprise to you, but I have been doing a lot of reflection, and I have realised that I need to get things right again and pull the family back together. We need to rebuild our trust too. So, I hope that you will join me to start the process. I look forward to hearing from you soon.

Yours sincerely,

Jacob.

Writing the letter for my father allowed me to understand his true feelings about the situation. I could see a completely new approach to his behaviour, and I was happy that he wanted to get my mother back and repair the damage that had been done. I am not sure how my mother would feel when I read the letter to her. I am not even sure if she wanted the relationship anymore. Although my father had released most of her frozen assets, she had not returned to her office, and her restaurant remained shut.

My father and I later left for hunting, but on this occasion, we were not successful and returned empty-handed. It was good to have my father back, and we spoke a lot about the things he would have to change, including relatives he believed he should not allow into his inner circle. We returned to the village house, and I could not wait to head to town to read the letter to my mother.

"Not too fast, boy; I need to seal the letter," said my father as I was about to head out. I handed the letter back to my father. He reached for his briefcase, which was lying by the wall of the dining room and placed it on the table. "I want your mother to know that the letter is truly from me as I doubt she would believe the content," uttered my father. He opened his briefcase and took out sealing wax, and then lit the wick. In a moment, the wax was ready, and my father allowed a few drops on the back of the closed envelope and then depressed his seal on it. He waited a few seconds for the seal to dry, and he handed the letter to me. "Here, deliver it directly to her and make sure she breaks the seal in your presence, and you can read the letter," said my father. He continued, "Ensure it's just the two of you present when you read the letter."

"THANK YOU FOR reading the letter; I will reflect on it and get you to write my response," said my mother. It was a few days later that my mother called me to write a letter from her to my father.

Dear Jacob,

I will go directly to the point. Your behaviour in the last six years has left me with no hope, and my heart remains broken. I could not believe that you were able to treat me and our children the way you did. I still cry myself to sleep most nights. However, I do believe in reconciliation, but it will take some time for us to rebuild the trust.

Yours sincerely,

Cecilia.

My mother did not have any seal, and she managed to sign it, writing her full name. I later delivered the letter to my father and read it to him.

"That is a short and direct letter, isn't it?" he said. I did not respond to his comment. "Alright, I will reflect on it and, in two days, come here after school to write my reply," demanded my father.

For a period of three months, I had written about six rounds of letters to my parents, and I was beginning to get tired of it. I encouraged them to speak on the telephone or meet in person, but I was ignored.

CHAPTER FORTY-ONE

The Faith of a Man

IT WAS EARLY ONE EVENING when I reached the house in the village. I saw my father lying on the sofa in the private living room. "Are you alright?" I asked. "I thought you wanted us to write a letter this evening," I continued. "I am not sure what is wrong with me, but I am not feeling good," my father responded. "Did anyone call the doctor for you?" I asked. "No, but the village herbalist has been treating me," replied my father. "What herbalist?" I asked with frustration. Before he could answer, I continued, "Is this what your relatives are recommending for you?" My father did not answer. I walked closer to him and said, "Daddy, you need a doctor, and I will phone Dr Memeth immediately." Then the thought that my father may not have seen a doctor for over six years that he had been living in the village shocked me.

"No, don't call Dr Memeth; I have not seen him in a while," uttered my father. I could tell he was struggling to speak, and his breathing was not consistent. "Give it a few days, and I will be fine," said my father. He continued, "In case I don't make it, tell your mother that I am sorry for everything I have done; she is a good woman." I was not sure what to make of my father's situation and wondered why he would think that he might not make it. "Daddy, you will be fine in a few days, and you can tell her yourself," I replied with concerned feeling. I decided to stay with my father to keep an eye on him. After a few hours, I realised that the only person that could help my father now was my mother. I told my father I would return shortly, so I left.

I arrived in the family house in the town at about seven o'clock in the evening, and my mother was having dinner. I did not hesitate to interrupt her. "Mummy, I have just returned from the village, and Daddy is not feeling well," I said. "What is wrong with him?" she asked. "I don't know," I replied. "He did say to tell you that in case he did not make it that he was sorry for everything he has done," I continued. My mother paused for a moment and looked into my eyes. "Is he that sick?" Without hesitating, I nodded my head and then went on to speak my response, "Yes, I think he is very ill and needs a doctor or to be taken to the hospital urgently." My mother stood up, and all of a sudden, she started to panic.

"Oh my God! Oh my God! I need to get there now," said my mother. "I drove Daddy's car; I can take you there," I said. "You? Since when did you start to drive?" My father would let me drive his car on the village farm roads, but this was the first time I had driven to town. "I can drive, Mummy; let's go," I said. "No, you are not driving because you can't drive," she said. My mother then called out to Matthew and William, but there was no answer from any of them. "Mummy, I can drive; I drove Daddy's car here by myself," I said. The journey would normally take twenty minutes, but we arrived at the village house after thirty-five minutes as it was dark, and I was not used to driving in the dark. The security was quick to open the gates as they recognised the Mercedes Benz, and I drove through and parked at the usual car porch that is part of the house structure.

I never knew that my mother could run up the stairs, so I could not believe how quickly she made it to the second floor of the house. I was right behind her as we emerged inside the private living room, where my father was still lying on the sofa. I knew this was the first time my mother would have entered the house in over six years. Without taking notice of the appearance of the living room, my mother ran to my father. I was close to tears when I saw my father struggling to raise one of his arms to embrace my mother as he lay on the sofa.

"Cecilia, you came," said my father in a voice I could not recognise. I noticed that his speech was being affected by his illness. My mother started to cry as she cuddled my father. I stood and watched them for a while. It was over six years since I had seen my parents together. I realised that I had missed the love they once shared. I also realised that their love and being together as a couple had an enriching factor towards my own happiness as a person. "Where is the telephone?" asked my mother. "It's over there," as I pointed out the position of the telephone to my mother. "Call your brother, Michael, and tell him your father is sick, and they all may want to come," demanded my mother. I reached for the telephone and called the operator, and requested to be put through to the international number. Unfortunately, I had to leave a message on the answering machine.

"I am going to take you to the hospital now," my mother told my father. She then turned to me and said, "Ask one of the security men to help us take him into the car." About fifteen minutes later, I was driving the car with my parents in the back seat. We arrived at a newly established private hospital about forty minutes later. My father was rushed into the emergency room as if he needed an operation. My mother had followed him, and I was asked to remain in the hospital lobby. While I waited, I decided to use the hospital telephone to call my sister, Azuka, and update her on my father's situation. "If Michael or Joyce, or Alexander call, please inform them of the situation," I said. "Will Daddy be alright?" she asked. "He is in the right place now, so let's hope for the best," I replied. I replaced the telephone receiver and went back to the designated waiting area. After about an hour and a half, since we arrived, my mother emerged. I quickly stood up and walked towards her. "What did the doctors say?" I asked her.

My mother put her arm around me and said, "Let's go catch some fresh air." I was not too happy with the idea of going outside, as I felt she was going to give me bad news. However, I had no choice but to follow my mother outside. It was very late into the night, and the sky was pitch black. Although the hospital grounds were well-lit, we were able to walk around as we talked. "It was good to see your father in the flesh after over six years; I have missed him," said my mother. "I can tell he was delighted to see me, too," she continued. "Alright, all that aside, what did the doctors say? What is wrong with him?" I asked.

My mother stopped walking and turned to me. She placed both of her hands on my head, each slightly covering my ears. She then pulled me closer to her and said, "Your father is suffering from a stroke." I do not understand what that meant for my father. "What does that mean?" I asked. "The doctors said it's as a result of a heart condition and could be linked to poor control of his high blood pressure," my mother replied. "So, will he be alright after treatment?" I asked. "It depends on so many factors, and the doctors do not know," replied my mother. "The doctors say we will have to move him to a government specialist hospital where they have the right knowledge and equipment to treat him," continued my mother. "I need to sit down," I said to my mother. There was a bench not too far from us and we decided to walk towards it. As we sat down on the bench, I started to imagine the worst-case scenario. "Will he die?" I asked my mother. "I am not contemplating that option, as we will fly him to the United States if he cannot get the best treatment here," replied my mother.

I felt as though I was not getting any assurance that my father would be alright. I had just turned seventeen years old, and I was not in any situation to contemplate losing my father. My father had told me that I would travel the world and would attend the best university to gain my education. He had reassured me of this promise after the reconciliation. So, I felt this could not be the end. I felt surely; he would need to see me achieve the ambition he had set for me. After some time sitting on the bench with my mother, we decided to go back into the hospital to ask if I could see him.

We were informed that he had been taken into a private room and we could go and stay with him. We entered the room, and I approached my father. My mother followed me, and we stopped beside his bed as he lay on his back. "Daddy, can you hear me?" I asked him. I noticed that he tried to move his head, but it seemed to be too much effort for him. I then reached for his hand. I could feel his grip, and while I looked at his face, I noticed he was trying to speak. "Cecilia," my father called out.

My mother took his hand from me and said, "Yes, I am here. Can you not see me?" I then noticed tears building up in my father's eyes. "Forgive me," said my father as the tears started to roll down sideways, heading for his ears. I quickly grabbed some tissues from the bedside table and soaked up the tears on both sides. "I am here, and I have forgiven you," uttered my mother. My mother decided she would stay with my father while I drove home.

My siblings in the United States had made contact, and Michael was on the plane heading home. We waited for Michael to arrive and then headed straight to the hospital to see my father. After seeing my father, Michael spoke with the hospital doctors, and my father was to be transferred immediately to the government university teaching hospital. It was believed that my father was not stable enough to make the journey to an international hospital.

Upon arriving at the new hospital, my father was stabilised, but his condition was not improving. We later informed his friends and relatives, and they were able to visit him at the hospital. It was about two weeks after Michael had arrived, and it became obvious that there was nothing more that he could do, so the family decided that it was better he headed back to the United States to be with his wife and children.

IT WAS NOW OVER two months since my father had been in the hospital. Again, he remained stable without any signs of improvement. I continued to visit my father almost daily in his private hospital room. On one particular visit, perhaps he was waiting for me to arrive, I approached him as he lay motionless on his bed.

As usual, I reached for his hand, and I asked him, "Daddy if you can hear me press tight on my hand," which he would normally do, but on this occasion, I felt the pressure he applied was weak. I would look into his eyes as we continued to communicate using hand pressure. After spending a few hours with him, I left the hospital to return home. I arrived home to find out that shortly after I left the hospital, my father had died.

I remember my mother crying uncontrollably after hearing the news. I could not cry, and the following morning, I got ready to go to school. I know my mother had not managed to sleep, and we had family and friends that had stayed overnight at the house. "Where do you think you are going?" my mother asked. "I have exams at school today, and I cannot afford to not do them," I replied. My mother then told me that it was not proper for me to attend school for a few weeks because my father had died. She said your school will understand and you will sit for the exams at a later date. "It is time to grieve," she said.

Sadly, I felt as if I did not know how to grieve for my father. We had unfinished business, and it was not yet time for him to die. Unfortunately, my father's time ran out at the age of sixty-two, and I know my time will one day run out too. When I was just ten years old, my father told me, "Life is an ultimate gift; how long the gift last varies, some very short, some in the middle, and some lasting very long, but what matters is what you do with your gift."

I CONTINUE TO REMEMBER my father as the man, who was not meant to live, yet was saved by a King. He could not read or write, yet he built a community and improved lives.

The End.

Author's Reflection

Author's Reflection

It was fascinating to me when I first heard that my father was born with a tooth and his village wanted him killed, but he was saved by the King. I thought it was amazing that he managed to leave his village alive and then became successful. I think my father believed that he had made good decisions that led him through his challenging upbringing and saw him become a successful man, although with limited abilities. Therefore, he believed that since he was able to achieve success by making decisions and sticking with them and eventually, they did yield the dividends he expected, he thought that this approach would also work well in his relationship with my mother.

I think he was wrong, and for the first time in his life, something did not quite work out as he anticipated. I believe, though, that his approach would eventually have brought my mother and him to a better place, as he envisaged. A place where their love for each other was renewed, and they would have been happy again forever more. I surely believe that they loved each other very much, and happiness forever for them was possible. The problem was that my father failed to realise that achieving success in business and managing a loving relationship are two different things, which each require a different mindset.

My father should not have moved out and stayed out for as long as he did. He should not have listened to others that advised him against his own feelings and intentions. I believe that it was the support he received from them that helped him to stay away from my mother and us for so long. He also failed to realise that the very people providing the support he was receiving were biased towards his own feelings and intentions. Well, maybe he knew he should not be listening to others, but why did he? He became bitter and was determined to deliver what he believed was right without considering the consequences.

Perhaps he felt he was not happy with my mother and needed to get her to change her ways, but wanted to make her feel she could lose him if she did not. So, he decided to teach my mother a lesson. A lesson just enough to get her to change. Unfortunately, it backfired on him. He did not adequately evaluate the consequences of his actions as to how they impacted him and our family. My mother, on the other hand, was too stubborn to accept conditions she believed were against her own convictions. Why would my father not be happy with my mother? My father often complained of my mother's attitude towards him, which he believed was aggressive. However, I believe he could have been interpreting assertiveness, which she had always displayed, for aggression.

In the end, I believe that my father's pride destroyed that one love he cherished more than anything, his love for my mother. His heart was broken, and he could not imagine living life without her. I feel that some of the decisions my father made regarding our family in his later life were not right. Eventually, though, he realised, and was trying to reconcile. Unfortunately, his health was failing, and it was too late, and sadly he died heartbroken.

Take A Step!

Take A Step!

I feel that I am brave to write this book. Most importantly I want to use my story to change people's lives. We need to believe that success in life is always within our reach. We just have to trust our instincts, believe in ourselves, and not be afraid to dream big. Being brave is about having the courage and confidence to reject the status quo and the poor situation we find ourselves. Instead of accepting what we have inherited from birth, let us believe that we have the determination to pursue positive change that leads to the path of self-actualisation, a change that starts with one step at a time. We can always redirect our next step once we are on the move. We do not need to have all that is required before we embark on the journey of accomplishment. All we need is the ability to dream for a better world for ourselves and the determination to take the first step.

There is a realisation that with success comes great responsibility, as well as the opportunity to continue to improve and grow. It is a continuous journey that requires us to keep going no matter what. However, we must be responsible for our actions, and the impact of the consequences to us and others must then become a new focus once we find success, regardless of what that success means to us. We must continuously and consistently challenge our actions to ensure that we are fair to ourselves and others.

There is always a choice; get up and go for it, or just sit and wait. Writing this book is me getting up and going for it. I choose that option over doing nothing. Am I worried that perhaps readers will laugh at it and say it is not good enough? Yes, I am. However, I decide to reject that feeling from keeping me back from expressing myself in showcasing my father's life journey to the world. I feel I have to do my part, which is to write this book to the best of my abilities. The rest is out of my control.

So, if you are like me that worries about your abilities and doubts your confidence, remember that you owe it to yourself to challenge your fears and prove your thoughts wrong. If my father and mother that could not read and write were able to accomplish so much, what is to stop you and I from doing better? We just need to be brave and challenge that anxiety, and take a step.

The Ultimate Gift

"Life is an ultimate gift; how long the gift last varies, some very short, some in the middle, and some lasting very long, but what matters is what you do with your gift."

Late Chief Jacob Okwueze Oriahi